d items

IND(
GH COU

FURIES AND FIREFLIES OVER KOREA

Furies and Fireflies over Korea

The Story of the Men of the Fleet Air Arm,
RAF and Commonwealth
who Defended South Korea, 1950-1953

Graham Thomas

GRUB STREET · LONDON

Published by
Grub Street
4 Rainham Close
London
SW11 6SS

Copyright © 2004 Grub Street, London
Text copyright © 2004 Graham Thomas

British Library Cataloguing in Publication Data
Thomas, Graham
  Furies and Fireflies over Korea : the story of the men of the
  Fleet Air Arm, RAF and Commonwealth who defended South Korea, 1950-1953
  1. Great Britain. Royal Navy. Fleet Air Arm – History
  2. Korean War, 1950-1953 – Aerial operations, British
  I. Title
  951.9′04248

ISBN 1 904010 04 0

Typeset by Pearl Graphics, Hemel Hempstead

Printed and bound in Great Britain by Biddles Ltd, Kings Lynn

DEDICATION

This book is dedicated to all the Fleet Air Arm pilots who flew with such
distinction during the Korean War. It is especially dedicated to the men who
lost their lives flying over enemy territory in the line of duty.

CONTENTS

FOREWORD

"In going where you have to go, and doing what you have to do . . . you dull and blunt the instrument you write with. But I would rather have it bent and dulled . . . and know that I had something to write about, than to have it bright and shining and nothing to say, or smooth and well-oiled in the closet, unused."
                    Ernest Hemingway, from the Preface to *The First Forty-Nine Stories*

This is a story about men, about courage, about belief in one's friends and an unshakeable passion for adventure. The Korean War – not unlike the Second World War – was about doing the right thing.

War is an atrocity that the human race has a seemingly unquenchable desire for, but occasionally – as brutal as it is – it is justified, because the carnage leads to peace, liberation and a better future.

Despite this, the men and women who play a part in war, have their emotional scars to carry. Some can talk about it, some can't; others die before they get the chance. What I particularly like about this book is Graham Thomas's unceasing desire to document the words of the men who flew in the Korean War. He met the survivors; he read the logbooks of the deceased and constructed a narrative that showcases young lives under terror. And he did this because he has an uncanny emotional attachment to the lives of the pilots of the Armed Forces. As a fellow reporter, I witnessed this obsession first-hand. Graham would be close to tears when discussing a recent interview with a veteran and this emotional attachment came through in his resulting features.

Unlike many military histories, this book has the human factor, so rare to pull off successfully. However, I believe Graham does it well and, more importantly, I know the surviving veterans who fought in Korea think the same way too.

This is a book not just for the academic to learn from, but also the pupil in primary school. Because although Graham's book is an exciting adventure story, it also shows fear, doubt, and the horror of war.

Let us hope we one day learn from the horrors of our history books.

Craig Cabell
Focus – the house journal of the Ministry of Defence
London, January 2004

AUTHOR'S NOTE & ACKNOWLEDGEMENTS

John Lansdown's excellent and comprehensive *With the Carriers in Korea* has already recorded the history of the role of the Fleet Air Arm during the Korean War, and my intention in this book has therefore been to provide its counterpart in recording the feelings and impressions of some of its surviving pilots. They are representative of the men of the Royal Navy who flew and fought in the war, which was waged by the United Nations with the forces of sixteen countries.

Their stories give the reader a glimpse of what it was like for these men as they flew, fought and lived during those turbulent times, describing everything from the missions to the heat below decks on the Royal Navy's aircraft carriers. I have also tried to convey through their words what it was like to fly the majestic Firefly or the mighty Sea Fury, recording their impressions, feelings and the rush of adrenaline as they rolled into a dive to hammer the enemy with bombs and rockets.

War is bloody, emotional, painful and rarely as controlled as the powers-that-be might wish us to believe, and the Korean War was no exception. As in all wars to some degree, the men in Korea did not know exactly why they were there. Their goal was to cripple Communist North Korea's ability to wage war. They had a job to do, and whether they did it well or whether it should have been done at all are issues we can explore with the beauty of hindsight. Although the men were playing their part in helping the South Koreans retain their independence from the North, which had attacked their country unprovoked, it is probable that few of them knew how this war had begun, and as a result there are few references to the political or strategic background in their stories. These pages convey their perception of the war as they experienced it.

The enormous role of the United States Air Force in the Korean War has been amply covered elsewhere, but the contribution of the Fleet Air Arm described in this book is less well known. I have also included other aspects of the air war in Korea, such as the RAF pilots who flew on exchange with the US Air Force, including John Nicholls (later Air Marshal Sir John Nicholls) who shot down a Mig and Lieutenant J. Joe MacBrien, the Canadian pilot who flew with the US Navy. As regards the aircraft carriers, I have concentrated on the Royal Navy carriers, since the Australian carrier HMAS *Sydney*'s story has been amply covered in Brian Cull and Dennis Newton's excellent *With the Yanks in Korea*. She was on station in Korea between HMS *Glory* and HMS *Ocean* between the autumn of 1951 and the spring of 1952.

The cost of the war in Korea was high. By the time the ceasefire was signed the civilian and military death toll is estimated to have been almost two million, and yet the border between North and South was at almost the same point as it had been when the war began.

So did the fighting by the Fleet Air Arm over the western coast of Korea achieve anything? I believe it did. It helped to demonstrate that the West would not stand by in the face of naked aggression. However debatable its successes seemed at the time, the war achieved its objective of keeping South Korea independent of the North. It was a war in which the Fleet Air Arm pilots flew with courage, determination and pride. This book is not only for them, but for their colleagues who fought and died in a frustrating war they could scarcely understand.

Acknowledgements
I would like to thank several people for their help in making this book possible. Chiefly, I would like to thank the veterans I interviewed who freely gave me their time and their memories. Nick Cook, Paddy McKeown, Tommy Leece, John Treacher, Alan Leahy, Pug Mather, Arthur Skinner, Ted Anson and Harry Hawksworth are the foundations upon which this book is built. Help from the Fleet Air Arm researchers who provided me with squadron histories and other bits of information was invaluable. The Fleet Air Arm Officer's Association put me in touch with the pilots in the first place and without them there would be no book. I would also like to thank Craig Cabell for his inspiration and Amy Myers and Grub Street for their persistence.

NB: Where a chapter features the reminiscences of a particular pilot, his name appears under the title on the first page of that chapter, and also on the contents page.

Chapter One

OVERVIEW

On Sunday, 25 June 1950, at 4 a.m. Far Eastern time, the communist armies of North Korea attacked along the 200-mile border between the North and the South, known as the 38th Parallel. They attacked without warning, and North Korean troops rolled across the border in a fierce assault that left the South Koreans, who were inferior in numbers and equipment, reeling. The war that followed lasted over three blood-soaked years.

The communist attack caught the West by surprise too, despite the fact that intelligence reports had been coming in to Washington for some months and border incidents initiated by both sides had been common. The news reached Washington late on the Saturday night, local time, and after urgent discussions the matter was laid before the United Nations.

Since it was currently boycotting the United Nations, the Soviet Union was unable to veto the resolution that was immediately passed, calling for North Korea to withdraw its troops to the 38th Parallel. When the resolution was ignored by North Korea, a second one called for forces to be sent to aid South Korea, who had urgently requested help. Of the sixteen nations who responded, the US played by far the greatest role, and the other fifteen agreed to accept a US commander-in-chief of the United Nations force. President Truman's choice fell to the obvious: General Douglas MacArthur, hero of the Pacific War. It was a decision that was to have dramatic results.

In Britain, despite reservations about the motivations of the US in going to war, there was immediate popular approval for its limited contribution. Its first step, on 29 June, was to send its Far East Fleet of one light carrier, two cruisers and escorts to support the US Navy. HMS *Triumph* was the carrier, and she would be followed during the course of the war by HMS *Theseus*, HMS *Glory*, HMAS *Sydney* and HMS *Ocean*, each carrying out separate tours.

Flying from their decks, piston-engined Sea Fury fighters and Fairey Firefly fighter-bombers would play a key part in the war, attacking North Korean positions. Although the pilots were flying obsolete aircraft, it didn't stop them from being effective fighters, and making a valuable contribution to the war effort.

Run-Up to War

What motivated the North to launch this unprovoked vicious attack on the unprepared South? There is no clear-cut answer save that its communist leader, Kim Il Sung, was determined to unify the country by joining the independent republic of South Korea to his 'Democratic People's Republic of Korea', as it had been termed since 1948. Watching his every move with intense interest were his big brothers, the Soviet Union and China, both of whose territories might be affected by the invasion's outcome through their proximity to Korea.

Until 1905 Korea had in theory been an independent state, although in the preceding decades a power struggle had been waged between first China and Japan, then Russia and Japan. After the war between China and Japan in 1894, the highly desirable prize of the ice-free ports of Port Arthur and Dairen in Manchuria, which bordered Korea, were ceded by China to Japan, but pressure from Europe demanded their return to China.

A few years later Russia leased the ports and railway concessions from China, and Japanese fear that Russia intended to use them as a base to invade Korea, which they regarded as 'theirs', led to war between the two countries in 1904. The outcome, being a Japanese victory, resulted in Russia losing the ports, leaving Manchuria and recognising Korea as a protectorate of Japan. This Korea remained until the end of the Second World War.

Two days after the atom bomb was dropped on Hiroshima in August 1945, Stalin declared war on Japan to ensure that the Soviet Union's sphere of influence expanded, and the Red Army promptly moved into Manchuria and towards its border with Korea. At this point the United States woke up to the fact that unless emergency action was taken the Red Army could quickly take over the whole of Korea. Washington acted swiftly, and somewhat to its surprise the Soviet Union agreed its own sphere of influence should end at the 38th Parallel, dividing the country approximately in two. Japanese forces in the North surrendered to the Russians, and those in the South to the Americans.

Korea's warm-water ports, rich mineral deposits and hydroelectric power were an inviting prize for the Soviet Union, not to mention that North Korea's north-eastern tip was not that far from its port of Vladivostok. The Soviet Union installed the communist Kim Il Sung as head of North Korea, supporting him with weapons and military armaments. In the South, the US set up a free-style economy under Syngman Rhee, who had spent years in exile in the US. The country became rife with corruption, however, and in 1947 the US requested the United Nations to step in. Free elections were set up, but Rhee was still elected leader in the South. The North declared itself Democratic People's Republic of Korea a year later, and by 1949 the Red Army had withdrawn from North Korea and likewise had US troops from the South.

There seemed no urgent threat to South Korea. Nevertheless both North and South dreamed of unifying Korea, and minor border incidents were continually taking place. Kim Il Sung made overtures to rebellious factions in the South, and badgered Stalin to support an invasion. His requests were turned down until 1950, when Stalin saw that with Manchuria now under Chinese control again, a unified Korea could have great advantages for him, if only to embarrass the West. With the US apparently no longer interested in Korea, the opportunity had arrived. Once the war began, the Soviet Union remained in the background however, supplying equipment and materials but not troops. There was also still the other big brother closely watching the scene: China, under the communist rule of Mao Tse Tung, and at loggerheads with its former ally, the US.

Three Years of War

The first available UN ground forces to arrive in South Korea after the invasion, one US infantry battalion, reached it on 1 July, and a few days later came face to face with the North Koreans who had now taken Seoul, the South Korean capital, and were sweeping south. The battalion, hopelessly outnumbered and out of its depth in unfamiliar terrain, was forced back into retreat. The next UN ground troops would not arrive for some days, but in the meantime American aircraft had thrown themselves into the fray by dropping vast numbers of bombs, in the vain hope of disrupting the enemy.

As the weeks passed, the UN forces were pushed back until it looked as if they would be outflanked as the North Koreans reached the vital supply port of Pusan, in the south-west of Korea. The Battle of the Pusan Perimeter was hard-won by the UN forces, and an initiation into the bitter war that was to follow.

MacArthur's counterplan was to land troops at Inchon, on the western coast of Korea, not far from Seoul. The success of this landing on 15 September enabled MacArthur to push the North Koreans back to the 38th Parallel, where he impatiently awaited permission from the UN to take his forces into North Korea, with the aim of unifying Korea and ousting the communist regime.

There remained the major problem of China. Despite Washington insisting that the Manchurian border with China would be respected, China watched warily, envisaging UN and South Korean troops, masterminded by the US, sweeping up through North Korea towards its own territory. Chinese troops massed on Manchuria's border with Korea, the Yalu River, having warned Washington that if the 38th Parallel were crossed, China would actively enter the war. Washington underestimated the threat, and on 7 October the UN officially sanctioned its forces to cross the 38th Parallel in pursuit of the unification of Korea.

The advance towards the Yalu River began with preparations for amphibious landings on the east coast of North Korea. A week later, over 300,000 Chinese forces began to cross the river to establish themselves on the Korean side, probably for defensive rather than offensive reasons, and clashes with the first troops to arrive, who were South Korean, followed. With no immediate major Chinese attack, Washington's fears subsided, but by 1 November the UN troops were in battle with the Chinese forces. Later in November, as MacArthur raced for the Yalu River, the Chinese launched their offensive in earnest. The scene was set for disaster, with the humiliation of UN forces forced to retreat back across the 38th Parallel twelve miles into South Korea. Seoul fell for the second time, and all the gains made by the UN forces after the Inchon landings were lost as they reeled under the Chinese onslaught. It was not until early January 1951 that UN forces were able to hold their ground. By early February they had recaptured Inchon, and General Matthew Ridgway, the new commander of the UN ground forces, succeeded in holding a line just south of the 38th Parallel.

At the same time a major political battle was in progress. General MacArthur firmly maintained that the Chinese would be incapable of waging a modern war and was publicly insistent that the fight should be taken to the

Chinese homeland by launching attacks on Chinese bases and coastal ports to bring about China's military collapse. Relations with President Truman in Washington, who disagreed, were already poor and they worsened. MacArthur's outspoken views and Truman's exasperation finally met head-on when a letter from MacArthur was read to the House of Representatives in Washington on 5 April 1951, in which he aired his impatience with Washington's restraint over China, thus giving Truman little choice but to put in motion what he had long wished to do. MacArthur was relieved of his duties, and his place was taken by General Ridgway.

On the ground, offensive and counter-offensive now alternated as the war see-sawed on. Late in April the UN forces held firm at the Imjin River, south of Seoul, and here the British 29th Brigade played a prominent role, when the Chinese forces moved against positions held by the brigade, and a battalion of the Gloucesters took the brunt of the assault, losing most of their number to death or captivity.

The Soviet Union, alarmed by the now advancing UN forces, called for both sides to hold armistice talks, but they collapsed in August, while the bitter fighting continued around Seoul.

The talks resumed on 25 October, and during them General Ridgway ordered offensive ground operations to cease in the hope that it might be jointly agreed that all outstanding issues could then be settled within thirty days, with the current line just short of the 38th Parallel being taken as the agreed border. It was so jointly agreed, but the thirty days expired without solution and offensive operations began again in the New Year of 1952.

As the land war continued, the two forces battled it out in static lines with very little movement. In June 1952 General Mark W. Clark succeeded General Ridgway as UN Supreme Commander and obtained approval to bomb North Korean power stations to prevent their industry, and that over the Manchurian border, from continuing to operate.

Several plants were chosen for these attacks, which took place over a 48-hour period. It included four power stations in North Korea at Chosin, Fusen, Suiho and Kyosen. By the time the dust cleared and the raids were over nine-tenths of North Korea's hydroelectric power system had been destroyed.

Over the next three months UN forces concentrated on attacking and destroying North Korea's heavy industry. A lead and zinc mill was hit, a light metals plant and tungsten mine were bombed and a chemical plant destroyed. On 1 September 1952 a massive naval strike of American aircraft wiped out the oil refinery at Aoji.

A stalemate war continued as the armistice talks dragged on, with armies now dug into underground tunnel complexes, and air power being a major tool for bringing pressure to bear on the communists. The main conditions of a ceasefire had been settled long since. All that remained outstanding was the issue of whether repatriation of prisoners of war should be voluntary or not. However, an end to the war still seemed a long way off as the UN continued to attack and destroy North Korea's industry.

In November 1952 General Eisenhower was elected President, replacing Truman, and made good his promise to visit Korea. He returned from his three-day visit determined to finish the war. By April 1953 the negotiations had begun in earnest again.

Nevertheless the UN Far East Air Force got the go-ahead to knock out twenty dams. Destroying them would wipe out the whole of North Korea's rice crop and heavily damage railway lines and roads by flooding. The UN High Command decided to destroy the dams on a gradual basis so the people of North Korea could lay the blame for loss of food on the doorstep of the communists for prolonging the war.

On 13 May 1953 US aircraft lifted off into the morning sky heading for the Toksan dam on the Potong River north of Pyongyang. During the raid the dam was breached and destroyed and the resulting flood of water laid waste five square miles of rice fields and more than 700 buildings. Five miles of railway line and two miles of road were swept away by the flowing water. The airfield at Sunan was deluged under the tonnes of water that poured out of the breached dam. In one raid more damage had been done than in weeks of the frustrating attacks on a variety of targets.

The Chinese and North Koreans finally abandoned the sticking point of repatriation of PoWs, paving the way for a ceasefire. Some say it was the devastation caused by attacking and destroying the dams that made the communists back down. Others have suggested that the communists backed down because of a grim warning from the US that unless the deadlock at the talks was broken and the communists abandoned their demand about the PoWs, they (the USA) would widen the war and possibly use nuclear weapons. The dam-busting was seen as the first ruthless step towards massive devastation born from years of deadlock, frustration and obfuscation. The armistice was at last signed on 27 July.

The Air War
From the beginning of the conflict UN aircraft hammered the North Korean communications and logistics support networks in support of ground troops. It was a risky business and saw expensive aircraft and highly trained pilots attacking at high speed and low altitude to bomb a culvert or strafe a truck. This type of flying was called interdiction and was repetitive. UN aircraft could attack the same railway one day, the enemy repair it that night and the aircraft go back to destroy it the following day. This might seem a gigantic waste of effort and resources but this kind of warfare could be crucial in stopping the communists from mounting offensives and building up supplies.

For the US Air Force, the F80 Shooting Stars, Mustangs and Thunderjet fighter-bombers took the brunt of this work while US Marine Corsairs and US Navy F9F Panther jets and Skyraiders along with the Royal Navy's Fireflies and Sea Furies did the same task.

For the UN the most worrying development in the air during the war was the appearance of the Russian-built Mig 15 jet fighter which outclassed all the aircraft in Korea when it was first encountered in the skies over the Yalu River flying from its Manchurian bases.

Based on a German swept wing concept and powered by a derivative of the Rolls-Royce Nene engine the Mig was 100mph faster than the F80 Shooting

Star and the F9F Panther. It could out-turn, out-climb and out-dive the American jets and it was only the poor training of the Chinese pilots that enabled the Americans to hold their own against such an advanced machine. The first examples of the Sabre were far better able to cope with the Mig than the Shooting Star or the Panther, but it was not until the F version of the Sabre which arrived late in the war that the Mig was finally outclassed.

Many histories point to intensive air battles between the Mig 15 and the American F86 Sabre. There are wild claims of massive kills by the Americans, eighty per cent of the Mig jet fighters, which on close inspection seem to be exaggerated. If Chinese losses of Migs had been as bad as has been claimed their inventory could not have increased from 400 jets at the beginning of the war to 3000 by its end. The first jet-to-jet victory in history came on 8 November 1950 when Lieutenant Russell Brown in his F80 Shooting Star shot down a Mig 15.

In November 1950, as the North Koreans reeled under the UN counter-offensive and were pushed right back up to the Yalu River at the Manchurian border, General MacArthur ordered that the bridges across the river be destroyed by air. Although this would cut off the North Korean route of escape and force them to surrender there were problems. Manchurian air space could not be violated, which imposed severe restrictions on what the UN air forces could do. They could not attack the flak batteries on the Manchurian (Chinese) side of the Yalu and they could not pursue enemy aircraft or attack enemy troops fleeing into China.

Attacking a bridge is a difficult job at the best of times. The standard practice of attack was to follow the road leading to the bridge and drop the bombs just over the bridge so they walked or rolled along the road and caused maximum damage. But to do that would mean UN aircraft pulling out of their dives in Manchurian air space. They had to attack from the side.

On 9 November aircraft from the USS *Valley Forge* and the USS *Philippine Sea* flew 225 miles to Sinuiju where they attacked four bridges. Three were damaged but the Sinuiju railway bridge remained intact. By the end of the month the river had frozen, however, and the Chinese could cross from anywhere over the thick ice.

Because of North Korea's mountainous geography, road and railway transport was largely in the narrow plains of the east coast or the broad plains of the west coast. There were no paved roads, only gravel or dirt and they ran parallel with the single-track railway lines. Most bridges in the North were over shallow creeks and rivers, which could be bridged easily and quickly with timbers if the bridges were destroyed.

The most frustrating aspect of the UN air interdiction campaign to attack targets well behind North Korean lines centred on the repair gangs used by the enemy. They were made up of peasant labour, who could quickly restore road surfaces, move rubble, repair track, fill craters and construct bypasses. Nor did the peasants stick only to the roads; they were able to move large quantities of supplies along trails and other paths. Carrying an 'A' frame on his back the North Korean peasant could haul, albeit slowly, mortar rounds, artillery shells, ammunition, food and small arms to the front line. Mules and horses transported larger quantities of military supplies over these paths and trails.

Despite the UN's efforts, by June 1951 the communists were still getting half their supplies by rail and road. The eastern railway system ran along the coast and was in easy range of naval bombardment but the west coast system was by far the larger. In the west, trucks and other vehicles moved exclusively by night and the communist overnight repair of roads and railway lines equalled the rate of destruction during the day.

At the end of May 1951 the UN launched Operation Strangle. This was an attempt to destroy first the North Korean road network in a band across the width of the peninsula just north of the 38th Parallel, in order to cut their supply routes, and second their railway network. Intensive air attacks on roads and constricted passes where detours would be hard to build, on bridges, railway lines, shunting yards, round houses and engine sheds were designed to bring the communists closer to agreeing a peace. The USAF attacked targets throughout the west while the 1st Marine Air Group had responsibility for the east. They flew dawn to dusk raids, strafing and bombing anything that moved. Night attacks with flares sometimes caught the enemy unawares and some targets were destroyed.

In the static war, however, this was not enough and Operation Strangle failed to cripple the communist machine. Peasant labour repaired breaks within twenty-four hours, and pontoon bridges that the communist forces had hidden during the day were brought out at night and set up. In addition, some bridges were laid below the waterline so that UN aircraft couldn't detect them and they could be used under the cover of darkness.

Operation Strangle was wound down and as winter closed in Operation Moonlight Sonata was launched. The bright moonlit sky over North Korea provided improved visibility for the American air forces, making railway lines and roads stand out from the landscape. Each flight would be of five aircraft, comprising Douglas Skyraiders or Corsairs that had been launched around 0300hrs. Like Operation Strangle, however, Operation Moonlight Sonata was not a success as it relied too heavily on good weather.

In its place, UN forces launched Operation Insomnia in May 1952 that saw two strikes of six aircraft attacking railway lines to trap locomotives and their wagons. These strikes would destroy the track before and after the train, leaving it stranded when daylight came; the train would then be destroyed by UN air forces. It, too, proved to be ineffective.

In October 1951, however, the UN had had a dramatic success that proved just how important air superiority could be. Guerrillas reported that a meeting of high-ranking North Korean and Chinese Communist Party members was taking place at Kapsan. Similar to the daring raid by RAF Mosquito fighter-bombers on Gestapo headquarters in the Second World War, a raid was organised to hit the compound where the meeting was taking place.

On the morning of 29 October 1951, eight US Douglas Skyraiders roared into the air carrying an impressive array of weaponry. Each carried two 1,000lb bombs, one with a proximity fuse and the other a contact fuse. They also carried one napalm bomb and eight 250lb bombs. In addition, each Skyraider had four

20mm cannon that carried half incendiary rounds and half high explosive. They hit the compound without warning and all but one of the bombs found their mark inside the target boundary. Only part of one wall was left standing. The rest had been obliterated. The guerrillas reported 509 Communist Party members had been killed and the party records destroyed.

Despite successes such as this the campaign of interdiction did not achieve the objective of isolating the battlefield. The enemy, no matter how much he was hit from the air, still managed to get supplies to the front line troops. One of the reasons for this was the willingness of the communists to take casualties in order to hold their positions. The communists used deception and ingenuity to keep their lines open and their transportation and communications capabilities working. They would create flak traps by hanging an open parachute from a tree and luring an aircraft down to investigate to see if the parachute belonged to a downed UN pilot. By the time the pilot came down to lower level he was within range of the well-concealed gun positions and usually flew into a storm of anti-aircraft fire. They built dummy trains; trucks, tanks and troops out of cardboard and straw that from the air looked like the real thing. When UN aircraft dove down to attack the enemy's flak gunner would open up.

Part of the problem with the UN air war was that the source of the North Korean supply lines was in Manchuria. UN forces could not cross the border from North Korea into Manchuria and so only the routes themselves could be attacked. Moreover, the UN air forces had limited numbers of aircraft and could not keep 956 bridges and 231 tunnels out of action for the whole length of the war. So their only answer was to attack all the communication lines in a belt right across the Korean peninsula. Within this belt every bridge, tunnel and road was attacked and bombed, but still it did not cripple the communist supply route, mainly because the communists had unlimited manpower at their disposal to repair roads and bridges and they could take heavy punishment. In addition, UN aircraft lacked the sophisticated night fighting capability that is common in most military aircraft today and so night flying was extremely difficult.

Meantime, while the air war raged all across North Korea, the airmen of the Royal Navy flying off their aircraft carriers in the Yellow Sea off the western coast of Korea did their bit to bring the communist aggressors to the point where they would agree to a truce.

Chapter Two

OPENING SHOTS

Lieutenant John Treacher, HMS *Triumph*

When the North Koreans poured across the 38th Parallel on 25 June 1950, HMS *Triumph* was anchored two miles off Ominato in northern Japan on her way back to Hong Kong. She heard about the invasion late that Sunday evening. "My cabin mate came in," Lieutenant John Treacher recalled, "and said, 'Have you heard the news?'"

The Royal Navy's Far East Fleet, under Admiral Sir Patrick Brind, KCB, CBE, was ordered to Okinawa on 29 June to join the US Seventh Fleet under United Nations' command to mount strikes on enemy targets. HMS *Triumph*, together with two cruisers and escort, was about to enter the war. Commanded by Captain A.D. Torlesse, *Triumph* carried the 13th Carrier Air Group (CAG), which consisted of two squadrons, 800 Squadron with twelve Seafire 47s, and 827 Squadron with twelve Firefly Mk1s. The US Seventh Fleet comprised the aircraft carrier USS *Valley Forge* (flagship of Admiral Hoskins, USN, in overall tactical command), with one cruiser, nine destroyers and three submarines. The aircraft onboard *Valley Forge* were a mixture of Grumman F9F Panther jets, the superb Douglas Skyraider piston-engined fighter-bombers, and the latest version of the veteran Chance Vought Corsair naval fighter (of Second World War vintage).

A week before the North Koreans had invaded, the Seafire pilots onboard *Triumph* were going about their business as usual, conducting patrols, practising deck landings and take-offs, which were not without anxiety. "Seafires were the last of the Spitfire breed," Lieutenant Treacher told me. "It was never a great deck aircraft because of its narrow track undercarriage but it was a good performer. We lost two or three on our early sorties, but we only lost one pilot who was killed in an accident back on the deck trying to land." Accidents happen, especially in wartime, and unlike the Fireflies, whose wide undercarriage could absorb the hard deck landings on a moving aircraft carrier, the Seafire's narrow undercarriage was much more delicate and needed to be landed with care. A single-seat fighter, the Seafire was harder for novice pilots to manoeuvre. Within the first week four Seafires were written off through bad landings. During this time the Fireflies were carrying out flight drills and testing the catapult that would sling them into the air on each sortie. It hadn't been tested since April 1949!

The British ships arrived on station in the Yellow Sea off south-west Korea on 2 July. As the sun began its slow climb into the summer sky, at 0545hrs, nine Fireflies and twelve Seafires catapulted off the deck of HMS *Triumph* on the first naval sorties of the Korean War. Their objective was the Haeju airfield north west of Seoul, and the aircraft swept out of the morning sky, swarming over the airfield, firing their rockets and damaging buildings and hangars. No aircraft were parked on the airfield, in fact none were seen. All of the Fireflies and Seafires returned to *Triumph* with only a few suffering minimal damage from small arms fire.

"Two aircraft suffered damage from their own rockets," wrote 827 Squadron's diarist, continuing with, "while the CO's aircraft returned with a hole in his fuselage from light flak."

The first marques of the Firefly had a limited range of between 120 and 130 nautical miles, which forced the carrier and her escort to steam further north so her aircraft would be in reach of new targets.

At 1100hrs on 4 July 1950, twelve Fireflies escorted by seven Seafires attacked a railway bridge in the Yosan Haeju area, close to the 38th Parallel. Flying in formation towards the target, they split into line astern formation as they closed in, diving on the bridge from 5,000 feet. Rocket after rocket pounded the area covering the target in smoke, dust and debris. Turning away the Royal Navy fighters pressed on, searching out targets of opportunity. Spying a column of troops a handful of Seafires and Fireflies broke formation, rolling into a steep dive, strafing and rocketing the enemy before returning back to *Triumph*. Only one aircraft suffered flak damage.

During the first few weeks of operations aircraft recognition, particularly by US forces, was proving difficult. Many had problems distinguishing the Seafire F47 from a Yak 9 and often shot at the Royal Navy aircraft. To remedy this, British machines were painted with white stripes similar to the black and white stripes of Allied aircraft during the Normandy landings in the Second World War. The 827 Squadron diarist wrote: "We have been told to paint the old D-Day black and white stripes on our wings as an aid to recognition. But somebody got the painting itch and we now have a large Union Jack right across the flight deck just forward of the after lift. Another aid to recognition!"

American aircraft such as the Corsair and Skyraider had a much better range than the early Fireflies and they also had versatility in their firepower. They could be catapulted off the deck with any combination of rockets, bombs and drop tanks. Unfortunately, Fireflies and Seafires did not have that kind of versatility. "We had long range tanks fitted to the Seafires and flew till they went dry," Lieutenant Treacher recalled. "The engine would cough and the aircraft drop back a bit when you switched tanks."

A crucial problem facing HMS *Triumph* was replenishment[1]. To maximize the time on station, the Air Repair Department of HMS *Simbang*, the Fleet Air Arm shore base at Singapore, was disembarked onto the supply carrier HMS *Unicorn*. That became the Royal Navy's supply and replenishment carrier for the whole of the conflict.

---

[1] See Chapter 1 of *With the Carriers in Korea* by John Lansdown.

During the next two weeks after the first strikes aircraft from HMS *Triumph* provided Combat Air Patrols (CAP) and Anti-Submarine Patrols (ASP) while aircraft from USS *Valley Forge* struck at North Korean targets. A few days later, the British carrier headed back to Sasebo in Japan on 22 July 1950 for repairs to her stern gland. One of the RAF's huge Sunderland flying boats was tied up alongside her in the harbour. "A very welcome sight indeed," wrote 827 Squadron's (unknown) historian. "She arrived with our mail."

In port, twelve new aircraft were embarked from HMS *Unicorn* and by 24 July *Triumph* was underway, heading back into the conflict. Again, her aircraft provided solid CAP and ASP cover flying a total of 84 hours over four days while *Valley Forge* attacked land-based targets. "They hit an island so hard I thought it would roll over and sink," said Treacher.

At one point, a Seafire from 800 Squadron was shot down by friendly fire from a crew of an USAF B29, which probably mistook the sleek fighter for a NKAF Yak 9. An American destroyer picked up the Seafire pilot and returned him to *Triumph* the next day. "I was saying good morning to a B29," Treacher told me, recalling the incident. "I woke him up and the top gunner hit my wingman, Commissioned Pilot White, in the fuel tank behind his head and he had a nice fire! He parachuted out, and was blind, but was picked up by a USS destroyer."

By 30 July 1950, HMS *Triumph* and its escort of ships said au revoir to Korea as they sailed for Kure in Japan for repairs. From Kure *Triumph* continued to Sasebo, where Rear Admiral Andrewes hoisted his flag and returned to the war. Throughout August and September she carried out a series of strikes and air searches to tighten the blockade on North Korea's western shores. This stretch of coastline had several islands, inland waterways and an unnavigable area for large ships, so armed aerial reconnaissance was essential to see what the enemy was up to.

Seafires raced low over the coast on 13 August 1950, taking photos of Mokpo and Kunsan which were both deserted. Mokpo was considered by the British to be an important port for the enemy to ship supplies eastwards towards the front, so bombs and naval offshore bombardment had routinely hammered it. Now it lay in ruins as the Seafires roared over it. The fighters caught sight of a few small junks in the vicinity as well as a couple of coastal ferries, which they immediately strafed with cannon fire.

The next day, *Triumph*'s aircraft concentrated their efforts further north on Chinnampo, the main North Korean naval base. Although early morning photographic reconnaissance showed virtually no movement, the aircraft ran into persistent flak over the town and returned to the ship as soon as possible.

Roaring off the deck, six Seafires and six Fireflies headed for the Taedong estuary, near Chinnampo, that afternoon. Slung under their wings were 60lb high explosive rockets that ripped into three ships moored in the estuary. The twelve aircraft saw several hits on a freighter, a coaster and a camouflaged minesweeper. As tracer shells from light anti-aircraft fire stretched up towards the aircraft, the flight turned quickly away and headed back to the ship.

Treacher notes one incident: "We had the Mark Two Fireflies and a Walrus amphibian on HMS *Triumph*. A chap called Peter Canin piloted the Walrus. On one occasion one of our guys went down out of range of the helicopter so Peter landed on the water and picked him up. Corsairs were watching over him to make sure the Koreans didn't pick him up and he was escorted back at 95 knots with the Corsairs weaving alongside."

Other operations included some by coasters who attacked and sunk some junks at Kunsan while Fireflies and Seafires swarmed over railway lines in the Mokpo area heavily damaging several wagons. "We rocketed and strafed trains and ammunitions dumps as well," Treacher said during our interview.

Roaring off the deck on 19 August, Treacher's section led by Lieutenant Lamb rose into the sky and wheeled away heading inland. Concentrating, Treacher kept the aircraft in formation, behind and to the side of the No. 2 aircraft. Reaching their height, the aircraft moved into line astern formation as they headed for the target: a 150-ton motor junk.

"This vessel was camouflaged and carried a deck cargo," wrote 800 Squadron's official diarist. "After a few strafing runs it caught fire and was seen by a later sortie to be completely burnt out."

The next day the squadron ran into heavy flak for the first time. In the morning, four Seafires of 71 Flight led by Lt Handley formed up on the port side of HMS *Triumph* for an armed photographic mission, headed towards Chinnampo. "They flew up the river as far as the capital Pyongyang," notes the squadron diary. "All the factories seemed to be working full blast even though there was very little movement on the river. As the flight approached the capital they were engaged by heavy and accurate flak!" As soon as the mission was complete the aircraft headed back to the ship as fast as they could.

The entry on 27 August 1950 in 800 Squadron's diary had an amusing note to it, which was also a little worrying for the aircrews: "Albert, our dummy 'man overboard' was dropped over the side and despite the signals the attendant destroyer HMCS *Sioux* took absolutely no action for about five minutes. An excellent way of making yourself popular with the Admiral and gaining the confidence of the aircrews."

August ended on a sad note for the ship and especially for 800 Squadron. Landing on the deck after a long sortie on 29 August, a Firefly failed to catch the arresting wire and rocketed into the barrier. One of the propeller blades ripped away from its root, slicing through the window of the operations room, shattering the glass and fatally wounding the commanding officer of 800 Squadron, Lieutenant Commander MacLachlen. "We suffered the loss of the CO of 800 Squadron today," records 827 Squadron's diary. "While in the operations room he was hit by a piece of propeller from a Firefly that entered the barrier. He died later without regaining consciousness and was buried at sea that same evening. Requiescat in Peace."

The next day the ship sailed back to Sasebo, ending another patrol. "In the first three months of the war we were just beginning to get into our stride," Lieutenant Treacher told me. "We had no air to air combat although we heard about the air battles going on elsewhere."

The war was at a dangerous point for the allies. The United Nations forces held a small 60-mile square area on the south-east corner of Korea known as the Pusan Perimeter. It was the only port they had, a vital one since it had reasonable facilities for bringing in troops and supplies. Aircraft from the US Seventh Fleet carriers USS *Valley Forge* and USS *Philippine Sea* attacked North Korean troops, guns and supplies on the front line, desperate to slow down the advance and give the soldiers on the ground holding the Perimeter some support. The enemy advance slowed dramatically owing to the mastery of the air and the sea that the United Nations forces enjoyed at this point.

More pilots were embarked aboard HMS *Triumph* while she was in harbour. In 800 Squadron's diary there is an entry concerning the crowded conditions on the ship. "Two more pilots arrived tonight, Mr Fieldhouse and Mr Darlington. Soon there will be no more room in the ship with so many new pilots and the funny part about it is that there are only nine [Seafires] aircraft left to fly. One trip per operation will be the way now."

Triumph's next patrol began on 3 September 1950, when she sailed back into Korean waters to the west coast. Seafires and Fireflies flew mostly CAP and reconnaissance patrols managing to shoot up a couple of 50-ton junks. A few days later the ship sailed for the east coast to relieve the American carriers supporting the defence of the Pusan Perimeter. 100 miles north of the 38th Parallel and fifty miles off the port of Wonsan on the eastern side of Korea, six Seafires and six Fireflies catapulted off *Triumph*'s deck, climbed to height and formed up just off the port bow of the ship and headed inland.

"It was an armed recce of the town of Wonsan and the road and railway communications to the south," wrote 800 Squadron's diarist. "The town of Wonsan was completely covered by low cloud so the strike proceeded south along the main railway line. They found nothing until they headed back towards the coast when a train was spotted." Seafires from Lieutenant Abraham's section, (73 Flight) along with two Fireflies, dropped into their diving runs spraying the train with cannon fire and rockets. "Several hits were seen and the engine received a direct hit," continues the entry. The locomotive exploded into clouds of steam and flames while boxcars were riddled with 20mm shells. The rest of the day's strikes hammered three tunnels damaging both ends on each one in ferocious attacks by *Triumph*'s Fireflies and Seafires.

As operations mounted, more Seafires became unserviceable through the wrinkling of their metal skin caused by hard deck landings. As 800 Squadron's diary noted: "The engineers dropped a bolt from the blue this afternoon when they wrote off four more of our aircraft they considered unsafe."

Now the squadron was down to five serviceable Seafires. "I think it's fair to say that it's not a case of the pilots breaking the aircraft but the aircraft breaking themselves," continues the diary. "These four were new aircraft and they haven't been subjected to anything out of the ordinary. Either this must have been a particularly old and weak batch or they were strained somewhere before coming to us!"

With most of southern Korea under North Korean control in early September 1950 and the Pusan Perimeter under threat, General MacArthur regained the initiative by ordering the amphibious landing of American forces at Inchon on the western coast of Korea.

Because of tidal problems the landings had to take place on 15 September, so the entire US 1st Marine division including air was brought to strength and set sail from San Diego in mid-August. Inchon had a well-protected harbour that was ice-free and was only twenty-five miles from Seoul. It was also only sixteen miles from Korea's best airport, Kimpo, which was controlled by the enemy. In every other respect, however, Inchon was probably the worst possible site for an amphibious landing. Besides its high tidal range with large mud flats at low water, there was very little sea room for manoeuvring, the island of Wolmi-do dominated the entrance to the port and several other islands looked over the waters. Perfect positions for gun batteries.

The operation was codenamed Chromite, and it was for the most part an American Marine operation. For several days before the landing, attacks were made up and down the western coast to keep the North Koreans guessing. American naval jets attacked Chinnampo, Ongjin, Inchon and Kunsan. Operating from escort carriers USS *Sicily* and USS *Badoeng Strait*, Marine Corsairs pounded Wolmi-do with napalm on 10 September, virtually destroying everything on the island.

Heading back to the west coast of Korea, HMS *Triumph*'s role during the Inchon landings was to carry out reconnaissance and fly covering combat air patrols. Her aircraft were also to provide cover to ships en route to the landings, fly interdiction missions over the landing zone, and air-spot for the British cruisers HMS *Jamaica* and HMS *Kenya* sailing with *Triumph*. Not least of *Triumph*'s objectives was to keep the door shut tight for communist forces in a blockade up and down Korea's western coast.

As she steamed back into western waters, *Triumph*'s aircraft provided air cover for the attack force as it moved towards Inchon. By 13 September, Fireflies were flying armed reconnaissance sorties along the coast. At this point, *Triumph* could get less than a dozen aircraft in all into the air at any one time, from the Firefly and Seafire squadrons, so the importance of each sortie had to be weighed up before the engines even coughed into life.

The assault fleet at Inchon was led by seven US destroyers followed by three LSMRs (Landing Ship Medium Rocket) equipped with 5-inch rockets. Behind that was the amphibious force headquarters ship, USS *Mount McKinley* with several other ships including the two cruisers HMS *Kenya* and HMS *Jamaica* at the rear.

Before the sun rose on 15 September, two Fireflies each fitted with two 45-gallon drop tanks climbed away from *Triumph* heading towards the landing area. They were to air-spot for *Jamaica* and *Kenya*. The addition of the tanks would give the two-seat fighters two hours over the target area while the ships blasted away at enemy coastal positions. Circling above flak pouring from enemy guns below, the Fireflies directed the fire, watching while several white puffs of smoke rose up into the air from the ships pounding the ground around the landing area. Suddenly, there was a blinding flash of flame and thick black smoke as the top of a hill literally blew off when some of HMS *Jamaica*'s shells landed on what was probably a hidden store of explosives and sent debris thousands of feet into the air.

That afternoon, Treacher's flight, 72 Flight, led by Lieutenant Lamb rolled into its dives, attacking a coaster and several flak positions. The coaster loomed in Treacher's sights as he dived on the enemy, and the two lead Seafires climbed swiftly away after releasing their rockets. Quickly, Treacher checked his instruments and kept the aircraft steady. His eyes rapidly sweeping over the dials, he thumbed the firing button and his rockets were away. Pulling the control column into his stomach, he climbed quickly away and formed up with his flight high above the enemy, as the Fireflies went in to keep the pressure on the North Koreans.

As the landings took place, Seafires and Fireflies flew standing patrols, bombardment-spotting for ships to pound enemy positions, clearing the way for the advancing UN forces. By the end of the day, 13,000 troops and their equipment had landed at Inchon. Only twenty-one people died and 174 were wounded. The landings were a great success. "We flew a lot of top cover for the Inchon landings," Treacher said. "We did a lot of joint ops with the Marines and we were incredibly impressed by them." For five days after the landings, aircrew from *Triumph* flew bombardment-spotting sorties for the cruisers as well as armed reconnaissance missions north and south of Inchon.

On 16 September, HMS *Triumph* was still stationed off the west coast of Korea supporting the landings. Treacher tucked his Seafire loosely behind the lead aircraft as the section headed for gun positions on an island near Haeju. They flew in a staggered line of four aircraft, behind and beside the one in front. Treacher could see the target area below. Tracer shells poured up towards the diving fighters. He flicked the master switch, then fired. The rockets under the Seafire's wings shot away from the aircraft smashing into the enemy positions below. Levelling out Treacher fired several bursts of cannon fire at the gun positions. The Seafires quickly formed up with the rest of the squadron, wheeled away and headed back to the ship.

The same day, another Seafire attacked two junks, destroying one and damaging another. Treacher recalled: "It was a good atmosphere on the ship. The parachute boys were always on edge to make sure the equipment worked whenever anybody bailed out. When you get into serious ops everything else falls into place."

Throughout this time there had been virtually no sign of the North Korean Air Force. Several ships were anchored in the approach channel to Inchon, when on 17 September 1950 the situation changed. Two North Korean aircraft came in low over the water flying from north to south. The sun was just peering over the horizon when a piston-engined Yak 3 fighter and a Stormovik bomber roared over the line of ships, and pushing into a gentle dive they dropped their bombs near USS *Rochester*. One bomb hit the aircraft crane but failed to detonate.

Both enemy machines continued their descent, boring in on HMS *Jamaica* anchored 550 yards away. Cannon and machine-gun fire erupted from the aircrafts' guns raking the bridge and upper deck of the cruiser with shells. Crews on *Jamaica* reacted quickly, bringing their guns to bear, shooting down the Stormovik while the Yak turned away, dropping low and heading for home. The 800 Squadron diarist recorded: "The Americans didn't reply to the enemy fire, but HMS *Jamaica* shot down one (Stormovik)." This action by the enemy forced *Triumph* to scramble her Combat Air Patrols twice that day only to find them to be false alarms.

Still jittery from the day's previous attacks by enemy aircraft, *Triumph*'s pilots carried out their normal duties of bombardment-spotting and armed reconnaissance, always keeping one eye open for enemy aircraft. Near Chinnampo, Seafires damaged a 500-ton ship; another was set on fire on the slipway while flak positions were hit. By 19 September there were only four Seafires and eight Fireflies left. Only one armed reconnaissance was flown by the Seafires that day where a patrol craft was damaged again in the Chinnampo estuary.

In the evening three Seafires were scrambled to deal with some rice-carrying junks in the Haeju area. "After a long search two medium sized junks were sighted, both fairly innocent looking," wrote 800 Squadron's diarist. "Rocket hits were attained and a final strafing run made sure that no more rice would be carried."

At the end of her tour in Korea, HMS *Triumph* steamed away from the conflict forever on 21 September 1950, heading to Sasebo in Japan with her aircraft at the end of their operational life. Four days later, she set sail for the UK to be replaced by HMS *Theseus* carrying new aircraft and fresh pilots to fight a different kind of war.

"The buzz on the ship is correct. We sail tonight," wrote 800 Squadron's diarist. "The Admiral came aboard and addressed the ship's company, expressing his gratitude for the splendid work done and wishing us all a happy homecoming."

By the end of the month, Kimpo airfield had been recaptured by the Marines and became a working tactical airfield. Seoul was again in South Korean hands and the North Korean Army was in retreat. Inchon had overturned what could have been a military disaster in days. It was a stroke of imagination and intuition that should go down in history as one of the greatest of all military victories. All four objectives had been realized: the capture of Wolmi-do island, the recapture of Seoul itself, rapid seizure of Kimpo airfield and the restoration of the South Korean government to power.

It was MacArthur's overpowering sense of the objective, his self-confidence, his personality and ability to bring together all the necessary forces as quickly as possible that won the day. Without him could Inchon have occurred? If it hadn't happened what would have been the outcome for the marines clinging to their toehold on the Pusan Perimeter? The entire peninsula of Korea would have become communist controlled.

Airpower and mastery of the seas had allowed Inchon to take place. But, as General MacArthur was authorized to start attacks inside the 38th Parallel in early October a new enemy changed the course of the war as China perceived a threat to its border with Korea. HMS *Theseus* was on its way towards the onslaught that was to follow.

Chapter Three

FIRST PATROLS FOR HMS *THESEUS*

Lieutenant Tommy Leece

The autumn and winter of 1950-1 was a period of dramatic successes and reversals for the United Nations' forces. The Inchon landing enabled MacArthur first to force the North Koreans back over the 38th Parallel, and then to obtain permission to follow them into North Korea. However, that action led to China's intervention in the war. In November 1950 China launched its first offensive and forced the UN troops to retreat back into South Korea. On 1 January 1951 the Chinese launched another offensive and the outlook started to look bleak for the United Nations' defence of South Korea.

HMS *Theseus* arrived in Sasebo to replace *Triumph* on 4 October 1950. Under the command of Captain A.S. Bolt, the ship carried twenty-one new Hawker Sea Fury FBIIs of 807 Squadron and twelve Firefly AS Mark Vs of 810 Squadron. These squadrons and their equipment made up the 17th Carrier Air Group commanded by Commander F. Stovin-Bradford. Not only were the aircraft brand new, so were the pilots. They had been carrying out extensive training en route to Korea, but were still relative virgins of the air.

An entry in the official 810 Squadron diary dated 2 October provides a glimpse of what life was like as *Theseus* set sail from Hong Kong towards war. Again the diarist is an unknown pilot: "The six Fireflies and eleven Furies took off from Kai Tak to carry out practice strikes on the ship." RAF Spitfires also took part in this exercise. "Needless to say," continues the diarist, "on this occasion the Firefly group did not get through to the ship, we were all shot down without a doubt!" It was a good thing this was just an exercise. Once all the aircraft had landed onboard the aircraft carrier they were lashed down securely as the weather closed in.

In the aftermath of the Inchon landings the outlook was good for the UN forces. MacArthur's daring assault had snatched victory from what looked like certain defeat, completely turning the tables on the North Koreans in the space of three weeks. By 1 October the UN's first objective of pushing the North Koreans back behind the 38th Parallel had been realized but the second objective to bring peace to the area had yet to be achieved. To complete the success, MacArthur wanted to pursue and destroy what was left of the North Korean People's Army across the border. The go-ahead came in the form of a UN resolution on 7 October 1950, which allowed MacArthur, backed by President Truman, to cross the 38th Parallel if he deemed it necessary.

On 9 October, American and Commonwealth troops swept across the frontier, behind South Korean troops who had already crossed the border some days before in hot pursuit of the North Korean People's Army (NKPA). MacArthur's strategy was twofold. The first part was for UN forces to move fast up the north-east stretch of North Korea to cut off the NKPA retreating towards Manchuria. The second was for American amphibious forces to repeat the success of Inchon and land at North Korea's major eastern port, Wonsan.

South Korean troops (ROK) attacked quickly up the east coast towards Wonsan with strong air and naval support facing limited opposition. To get the Wonsan landings under way, British, Australian and Philippine troops replaced the American 10th Marine Corps in the Inchon area so the Americans could prepare for the landings at Wonsan. What should have taken five days of minesweeping to clear the approaches took fifteen. Nevertheless, ROK troops rolled into Wonsan on 10 October, while the 1st Marine Division finally came ashore fifteen days later after many of the mines had been cleared.

On the west coast of Korea in the Yellow Sea, HMS *Theseus* began its first patrol on 8 October. She was joined by HMS *Kenya*, HMS *Constance*, HMCS *Sioux* and HMCS *Cayuga*. Rear Admiral Andrewes transferred his flag to *Theseus* that same day. His small fleet represented a host of nationalities, including Australian, British, Canadian, Dutch, French, Japanese, South Korean and American. The tasks facing them were to maintain the blockade in the Yellow Sea, and fly strikes on selected targets in the Chinnampo to Haeju area, thus keeping the enemy off-balance. A piece of cake? Not really. The fleet was a hotchpotch of different ships and the best had to be made from their incompatibilities. Throughout the war every Royal Navy aircraft carrier would travel with a small fleet of destroyers or frigates escorting her.

In November 2002 I interviewed Tommy Leece, who as a young Royal Navy Fleet Air Arm lieutenant flew Sea Furies with 807 Squadron from HMS *Theseus*. He told me: "The ship's tour of duty started in October 1950. The whole of that month was operations and I joined the ship in November." Before arriving, Leece already had several hours of vital flying time on a Fury: "We did a lot of general work-up [training] for the war. I had about twelve hours of Army co-operation work. HMS *Theseus* carried the first squadron of Sea Furies to take part in the Korean War. They replaced the Seafire 47s, which weighed twice as much as the old Seafires. Oddly enough, the Seafire was faster than the Sea Fury. I had a race once at level flight between my Seafire and a Sea Fury. Well the Sea Fury pulled ahead but the Seafire slowly overtook the Fury in level flight."[1]

By day there appeared to be no movement from the North Koreans. From the air UN pilots saw very little activity. Their road traffic was cleverly camouflaged. It was only the experience and understanding of the lay of the land the pilots gained with time that enabled them to spot enemy movements during the day. Flying low, however, made them fair game to light machine-gun and rifle fire, so over the countryside most aircraft kept above 1,500 feet while over towns the safe height was 5,000 feet plus[2].

---

[1] Several books have claimed the Sea Fury to be the fastest piston-engined fighter. One wonders how true that statement is in the light of Tommy Leece's race.

[2] This information is from John Lansdown's *With the Carriers in Korea* as well as squadron histories.

During the night North Koreans could move rapidly and quickly under the veil of darkness. Throughout the conflict they became very adept at repairing damage caused by daylight bombardments to targets such as bridges, which were crucial objectives for British aircraft. Time after time, Fireflies and Sea Furies would bomb the same bridge after the North Koreans had repaired it. As road and railway communications throughout Korea depended on large numbers of bridges owing to the mountainous terrain, Fleet Air Arm pilots hampered their repair by dropping bombs with 6 to 8 hour delayed fuses during the last daylight raid.

Whilst British fighter-bombers swept over the countryside, strafing and rocketing targets where they could, Mosquito controllers (low flying two-seat observation aircraft) would often direct them. Fireflies and Sea Furies could not see enemy troops lying in wait in the side of a hill or even perched on a ridge, they were well hidden and deadly at close quarters, but so were the Royal Navy fighters, who would often spray the suspected area with bombs and rockets (even though they may not have seen the enemy), causing hundreds of casualties.

The weather was always a problem for aircrew in Korea. Much of the country is rocky with peaks between 5,000 and 6,000 feet high and pilots had to use great skill to steer their aircraft through the low clouds that shrouded many a geographical death-trap.

Flying in these conditions proved how capable British aircrews were. Even the most experienced pilots did not have much flying time behind them before joining the war, and there were casualties. "In the mountainous areas it was difficult to know just how high you were but you just got on with it," Leece told me. Lives were lost, although not many, considering the inexperience of the pilots and the difficulties they faced.

The Fireflies carried 55-gallon nacelle fuel tanks while the Sea Furies carried 45-gallon drop tanks. A nacelle tank was part of the wing of the Firefly whereas the drop tanks were carried under the wing on the Furies and could be easily jettisoned.

In general, each sortie was planned to last approximately two and a half hours with fifty sorties flown per day.[3] On one day sixty sorties were flown.[4] Servicing, aircraft handling, and re-arming were done with precision through good drill even when the temperature was below freezing on deck. In fact, the interval between sorties was roughly two to three hours.[5] In emergency situations this refuelling and re-arming routine was thrown out of kilter as parked aircraft had to be moved forward fast enough to allow emergency landings.

"Because of the stores each aircraft carried, from bombs to rocket projectiles, the catapult was used for every flight," Leece told me. "However, once, when the catapult went down, Rocket Assisted Take Off Gear (RATOG) was used to get the aircraft off the deck. That was hairy. If you fired the button

---

[3] John Lansdown's *With the Carriers in Korea* goes into more detail about sorties.
[4] The original record during the conflict was set by HMS *Triumph,* then pilots from HMS *Theseus* topped that record at sixty sorties a day, according to John Lansdown's book.
[5] This was entirely dependent on the weather.

too early the whole thing would fizzle out and not accelerate properly. So you had to wait for the right time. You opened up the throttle and went belting along with a rocket on either side of the cockpit. They'd fire at the same time and you'd leap into the air."

Sometimes only one rocket fired and that's when the take-off became very hairy indeed. "If you fired the rockets too late on the deck of the ship you wouldn't get the full benefit so you had to do it in exactly the right spot," Leece continued. "It was only used on occasions because it was dicey. You bit your nails and hoped everything would work out OK."

With an average ship's maximum speed being approximately 22 knots, it was impracticable to launch Furies with two 500lb bombs and drop tanks as they demanded 28 knots speed for catapulting, however, Fireflies needed only 21 knots. The logical result of this was that the Fireflies carried bombs on operations and the Furies the rockets. This configuration, however, would later reverse as the war progressed and pilots and ship crews gained more experience in take-offs with heavy loads. The aircrews also found that the Sea Fury was much more stable than the Firefly and had better visibility so the change back to Furies with bombs and Fireflies carrying rockets made sense. But Leece and his fellow Fury pilot flew mostly with rockets.

On the morning of Sunday 8 October HMS *Theseus*'s first patrol started with a flight of eight Sea Furies flying CAP and practice interceptions on a group of four Fireflies. During the landing, one Firefly missed the hook, jumped both barriers and crashed into two other Fireflies on the deck parked beyond the barriers. Initially, the wheels were torn off when they struck the first barrier then the aircraft went straight through the second, swinging hard, and the Firefly smashed into the tails of the other two aircraft, "breaking both their backs," wrote 810 Firefly Squadron's anonymous diarist. "The aircraft was eventually dropped over the side while the other two, which are write-offs, are to be reduced to spares."

Though a terrible start for the first patrol it was the last serious landing accident while the ship was in the operational area. The destruction of the three aircraft reduced 810 Squadron's capability by twenty-five per cent but the remaining nine Fireflies regularly flew off on sorties. A real credit to the aircraft handlers.

For Lieutenant Leece flying was frustrating in the early days. Most of the sorties he flew were CAP cover over *Theseus*. When he wasn't flying the CAP details he was doing dummy dives on the ship or practising flight drills and attacks. He wondered when he would see action. He also recalled how crowded the ship was: "Really and truly we had all the extra people on board for war time conditions. The ship had been originally designed to be expendable for the invasion of Japan that never materialised." Cramped and hot, sleep was difficult for the pilots. "We had bunks but it was bloody crowded on board," Leece recalled.

On 10 October 1950 a daring and courageous rescue of a downed Sea Fury pilot took place. In the afternoon, a flight of four Furies, led by Lieutenant Commander Stovin-Bradford, attacked several huts and vehicles with tremendous ferocity. As Stovin-Bradford pulled away from the burning buildings, he saw Lieutenant Leonard's Sea Fury beside him shudder from enemy fire, then career and lose height. Thin wisps of smoke and vapour trailed from the aircraft as Leonard fought to keep his Fury airborne. Ahead lay a paddy field and Leonard deployed all his skill to steer the stricken aircraft straight for it. With his engine running rough and the temperature climbing, Leonard had no time to think about bailing out and in any case he was too low. Instead, he made an emergency landing in the paddy field not five miles from the target. As the Sea Fury hit the field it broke up, severely injuring Leonard. Two Sea Furies from the same flight stayed behind, circling over their comrade and keeping watch while their friend lay prostrate in enemy territory.

Flying one of the remaining two Furies circling over Leonard, Lieutenant Ford radioed back to the ship for a helicopter. Almost immediately one was dispatched from Kimpo. Ford's aircraft was nearly out of fuel but he continued to circle, keeping out of range of any ground fire but also keeping the Royal Navy pilot in sight. From the corner of his eye, Ford saw a large twin-engined aircraft coming in fast. He grinned as the big American Grumman F7F Tiger Cat fighter formed up on him briefly, then took over the role of watcher. Ford banked into a turn, heading back to the ship, his Sea Fury almost on fumes by this time.

The big American fighter circled above the downed Sea Fury as a rescue helicopter came in low, hovered near the wreckage then quickly touched down to rescue Leonard. The only cargo the chopper came with was a doctor, and between him and the pilot they managed to drag the injured man away from the wreckage. Suddenly machine-gun fire ripped the earth all around them and enemy soldiers poured out from an abandoned farmhouse to execute the rescue party. Thankfully, they were terrible shots. The doctor dragged Leonard towards the helicopter several yards away and as soon as they were on board they took off. In the air, the doctor gave Leonard a blood transfusion.

"First of all we had a Sea Otter on board for search and rescue," Leece recalled. "But then we got choppers and in fact some of the pilots shot down were the first Brits to be rescued by helicopters." As the helicopter climbed away from the scene, the Tiger Cat dropped into a shallow dive and raked the wrecked Sea Fury with cannon fire, completely destroying it.

"We would fly with four aircraft on a patrol," Leece remembered. "If one was hit and went down he'd come up on the radio and the other three would set up a rescue CAP and go round and round him. You'd keep that up as long as you could before you ran out of fuel and would have to head back, or until the chopper came out."

On 13 October, Fireflies and Sea Furies took off from HMS *Theseus* and climbed to 5,000 feet, heading inland towards the port of Chinnampo on the west coast of Korea. The targets were buildings and stores in the port itself. Slung under the wings of the Fireflies were 500lb bombs, while the Furies acted as escort. Just before reaching the target, the Fireflies peeled off into steep dives, dropping their bombs with great precision. Dust and debris shot into the sky as each bomb found its mark. Moments later, tongues of flame began licking the structures as the last Firefly climbed steeply away. By this time the gunners had woken up and were peppering the sky with light anti-aircraft fire, but the raiders had gone.

On the way back, the Fireflies pulled away from formation as the Furies dropped down low over the Chinnampo estuary. Flying in pairs, the Furies roared over the water, their cannon belching shells as they strafed two mine-laying junks in the mouth of the estuary. The Furies didn't hang around to see their results but climbed quickly away and headed back for the ship.

By now, the United Nations forces and South Koreans were well across the 38th Parallel. Lieutenant Leece said, "There was a shifting line every day as the allied forces gradually worked their way up into North Korea. Attacking troops on hills and supporting the Army was great practice for us."

At this time of the year the weather was beginning to play a major part in operations, sometimes making visibility very difficult. "As winter set in the sea used to freeze over and it would get bloody cold," Leece continued. "We used to fly over pack ice!"

The following day, fog over Sariwon made bombing a bridge by Fireflies impossible so they switched their attention to Chinnampo again. They rolled into their dives, bombs whistling through the air, pounding into buildings and depots throughout the port. As the Fireflies pulled away, the pilots could see the devastation. Several buildings had been completely destroyed and those that remained standing were currently under rocket attack from the Furies. Smoke rose high into the cold October morning sky as the port of Chinnampo burned. The Furies wheeled away, strafing North Korean troops in trenches and coastal positions on the way back to *Theseus*.

These missions sound clinical, almost inhuman sometimes, but most of the men I interviewed said that was how it was. They were told to do a job and to do it well. They were not involved in the political process, and probably knew nothing of it, and most believed the war was just because of North Korea's aggression. They were given fixed targets and most of the time the Koreans shot back with anything they could. Many UN aircraft were brought down not by large AA fire but by small arms fire (light machine guns or rifles) as they pulled out of their dives.

With each bomb dropped, and each rocket that howled into buildings, the pilots never knew if they were incurring civilian or military casualties. They kept on flying and fighting to the best of their ability. This was war; them or us. As painful, bloody, messy and horrific the losses were, the pilots couldn't lose sight of their objective: to cripple the enemy and personally survive.

There is a fascination about war and regimental history, but there is another side to it besides the spit-and-polished shoes: the lives of the innocent and the good. War has a costly price whatever its humanitarian reason, and one must always keep sober council when discussing its intricacies. Dennis 'Hurricane' David asked Craig Cabell (MOD *Focus* magazine) in June 2001, when discussing a photograph of his younger self: "Do you see the sadness in my eyes? That is a young man who had witnessed too much death for his age."[6]

Even though the Fury pilots didn't always see the pain of their sorties, they

---

[6] Interview for *Focus* with one of the Battle of Britain Hurricane aces.

witnessed the loss of comrades, the stress and intense heat of battle. As Field Marshal Montgomery told his troops in a signal (instructing the Eighth Army to move from Alamein to Tunis): "The enemy will try to stop us. But if each one of us, whether front line soldier, or officer or man whose duty is performed in some other sphere, puts his whole heart and soul into this next contest – then nothing can stop us."[7] It is the courage of the common soldier that impresses future generations, and the courage – and determination – of the pilots during the Korean War has been bitterly underplayed over the years.

Bad weather kept the aircraft silent until 0900hrs on 15 October. Only then could a flight of Furies catapult into the air and head up the coast. Dropping down to 1,500 feet, the Fury pilots poured rockets into a group of trucks desperately trying to get under cover. But they were too late. Several trucks were destroyed and one exploded, erupting into brilliant flame, literally jumping off the road from the explosion. The Furies headed away, hunting for other targets, and attacked a bridge near Sariwon but failed to destroy it. They would try anything that could slow down or inconvenience the enemy. Flying just below the clouds they dropped onto a pair of mine-laying junks severely damaging them with cannon fire. Turning for Chinnampo, they destroyed several warehouses with rockets, then they finally headed back to the ship. No other flying took place that day, because HMS *Theseus* had to steam away for refuelling.

"We would do airfield recces or fly up a road and if you saw anything then you'd have a go at it," Leece said.[8] "By January 1951 we were flying close army support, strafing troops east of Suwon. I remember rocketing and strafing a factory during one of our close Army support strikes." The factory was destroyed and the US Eighth Army took the town on the 17th.

At dawn on 18 October 1950, Furies and Fireflies catapulted off the ship's deck, heading inland. Lieutenant Leece tucked his aircraft in beside the leader as the Furies climbed rapidly. They banked away and Leece had a quick look at the Fireflies continuing north in support of the advancing UN troops. Turning his attention to the mission in hand he checked his instruments quickly, staying in line astern formation with the other Furies. The back of his throat was dry with anticipation. While the Fireflies headed north, the flight of Furies flew over Chinnampo and the coastal areas, running into some accurate anti-aircraft fire from the North Koreans.

"We had set targets, of course," Leece told me. "But if you were just going along the road and somebody sighted something, your leader might decide to attack. So you'd pull up to operating height, check your sights were in line, then suddenly, the adrenalin would start to pump. But then you would start weaving a bit before dropping into your dive, and once you're in a dive you don't have time to be afraid. You are just trying to make sure your dive is as accurate as possible because you don't want to fly into the ground."

---

[7] From the memoirs of Field Marshal Montgomery published by Collins in 1958.
[8] He is talking about attacking moving targets, which were targets of opportunity. The pilots I interviewed when asked said that people shouldn't have been out if they were innocent.

However, one of the Furies did dive-bomb into trouble. Shells ripped into Lieutenant Bevans'[9] Sea Fury and the steady roar of the great Centaurus engine became a clatter as it began cutting and coughing. Fighting the controls, Bevans reported his predicament to his leader and to the ship controllers. Would he have to 'ditch' the aircraft or could he make an emergency landing?

Centring the controls on a glide position, he worked the trim wheels quickly, trying to keep the nose up as the engine continued to cough. Below him was the cold water of the Yellow Sea as he put the Sea Fury in a gentle glide towards *Theseus*. He decided to try for an emergency deck landing.

On the ship, aircraft handlers moved quickly, driving the parked aircraft as far forward as possible, giving extra inches of precious space for Bevans' landing. The Sea Fury's wheels banged heavily on the metal deck and the batsman gave Bevans a frantic 'cut' signal. The arrester hook grabbed the wire and the aircraft jerked to a heart-stopping halt.

On 19 October, Pyongyang, the North Korean capital, fell to the US Eighth Army and ROK forces were firmly established in Wonsan. On the 26th units of the ROK forces reached the Yalu River where they were attacked and decimated by the Chinese. On the 29th, the US Seventh Division landed at Iwon and by the end of the month UN forces were looking across the border between North Korea and Manchuria near Chosan on the Yalu River. The next day they were fighting the Chinese.

The 20th October saw HMS *Theseus* in the far north-west corner of Korea, dangerously close to China. In the Sinanju, Chongju, and Sonchon areas, Furies rocketed engine sheds and warehouses. Plumes of flame and smoke erupted from the projectiles pounding into the buildings. Further east the Fireflies dive-bombed several buildings before ending the day's flying.

The next day the Furies headed towards the Changnyou area. Following a railway line that disappeared into a short tunnel, the Furies split up. Leece peeled away with his leader, heading for the rear of the tunnel while the other group poured their rockets into its mouth before climbing steeply away.

Climbing hard to gain height, the flight wheeled around and the lead Fury rolled into a dive onto the rear of the tunnel. Seconds later, Leece pushed his Fury into a dive, his thumb lightly resting above the firing button. The mouth of the tunnel grew closer in his gun sight. Ahead he could see the leader's Fury just pulling out of its dive, its rockets hammering the rock around the tunnel. Leece waited, then at the last moment unleashed his rockets, pulling the stick instantly back to climb steeply out and avoid the debris and smoke thrown up by his assault. Heading for home, the pilots were well pleased with themselves, sure they'd destroyed a train in the tunnel.[10] "The Sea Fury could pull 4gs maybe 5 in a dive," Leece recalled. "There were recommended power settings but we didn't worry too much about that as long as we had enough speed to keep going. But you just had to concentrate on the dive. Check your altimeter, kick the rudder, nose down, quick check of the target in your sights, let

---

[9] Later he became Lieutenant Commander Bevans, temporary CO of 807 Squadron.
[10] This action is detailed in 810 Squadron's official diary written by an unknown diarist.

the speed build up, wait, then fire off your rockets."

According to Leece, however, using the Fury's cannon in a dive was a different matter. "That's when it got tricky because you had to get closer," he explained. Once, while diving on troop positions on a hillside, with his cannon spitting shells, Leece pulled out far too low. "I thought, Christ! I didn't think I was going to make it out that time – I went skimming over the grass."

But the first patrol ended on a sour note. Steaming away from the Yellow Sea the crews onboard *Theseus* discovered that the catapult was unusable. If it didn't get fixed during their rest period flying would be very limited indeed on their next patrol. Their ten days of rest in Japan, away from the war, never seemed enough and before they knew it, they were back in the thick of it, their catapult still unserviceable.

With the catapult out of action, six Fireflies, including their servicing crew, had had to be left behind at Iwakuni to reduce the number of aircraft parked on the deck and provide more room for take-offs. The remaining aircraft were now flying off the deck with no stores, no bombs, no rockets and no drop tanks. This severely limited the range of operations that could be mounted, and virtually every sortie was combat air patrol over British and American ships.

This second patrol for *Theseus* was entirely uneventful because of the disabled catapult and when it was over she steamed into Hong Kong for repairs. It took the whole of November for the catapult to be repaired and tested. But before long, with a full complement of pilots and planes once again, she sailed back to the Yellow Sea off the western coast of Korea for her third patrol.

On 26 November, the situation in the war had changed dramatically for the worse. What had seemed a sure victory for the UN forces was now a quick retreat as 200,000 Chinese forces swept over the Manchurian border in a fierce offensive. UN forces fell back first to the Chongchon River and then to near Pyongyang, which would fall on 5 December. Many Marines had to be evacuated from Wonsan and more from Chinnampo.

Into this mêlée came HMS *Theseus*, her aircraft providing air support for the retreating UN forces. Flying began on 5 December when five Furies attacked several boxcars with rockets. Three were blown off the rails while three more were severely damaged. The weather hampered operations as snow showers limited visibility.

The next day the weather was worse, forcing a flight of Furies to rocket a coastal village rather than their main targets further inland. As the big fighters headed away they left the village burning. That same day, more Furies flew an armed recce over Chinnampo in support of the evacuation from the port. The day after, Furies and Fireflies attacked troops, transport, warehouses, dumps, and junks with rockets and cannon fire, causing great damage to these targets in the Chinnampo to Pyongyang area.

The next day (8 December), the Furies were again successfully pounding similar targets with rockets. At the same time the Fireflies flew armed reconnaissance patrols further north, dive-bombing three bridges and causing damage though not destroying them. Troops were strafed in a village and more buildings were hit in the Chinnampo area. In all, 115 flying hours were achieved on this day.

Then the weather closed in again and the next day four Sea Furies could not get back to the ship because of snow showers and low visibility. Snow and sleet swept across the decks of *Theseus* and men held onto whatever they could find to avoid being blown into the sea. The four Furies diverted to Kimpo airfield and came back to the ship on 10 December, when the weather had marginally improved. The conditions overall were appalling.

The following day saw a change in the weather, thankfully for the better, allowing Furies to catapult off the deck in the early morning and head back again to the Chinnampo/Pyongyang corridor. Leece's flight followed the main railway line towards North Korea's capital. "We used to get up early in the morning on the milk run and everywhere was red lights on the ship because you didn't want to bugger up your night vision," he said. "When we got up onto the flight deck it was freezing."

The flight was vectored onto a fast-moving train north of the city by Mosquito controllers. The Furies climbed quickly gaining much needed height before rolling into their dives. Leece searched the sky for familiar puffs of flak but saw none.

"Echelon, break," came the cry in his headphones and Leece saw the lead Fury roll into a steep dive. Seconds later, he was following his leader down, watching his rockets hit the ground and the remains of the locomotive. Great plumes of dust, smoke and steam obliterated the target as the Furies quickly climbed away.

On the same day, an entry in 810's Squadron diary described an unusual and sad event. "During the return of the last strike they saw four American F80 (Shooting Stars) one of which they believe to have been shot down by a Mig 15 – and then there were three!! Not a happy sight to witness."

The Fireflies returned again to the Pyongyang area the next day to pound bridges with 500lb bombs. On 13 December the Fireflies dive-bombed Chinnampo, leaving several stores and buildings blazing and then went on to attack more bridges in the area.

The Sea Furies were just as busy. Despite the poor visibility a flight of Furies created mayhem for the enemy. In a low dive, Lieutenant Leece fired his rockets at several warehouses already hit by the other Furies. Pulling out of his dive, he quickly joined up with the rest of the flight; splitting into pairs and dropping low they strafed troops, a floating crane and a staff car, leaving the area filled with debris and confusion. Their efforts were providing much needed help to the retreating UN forces.

The last exciting event of the patrol was when North Korean Mig jet fighters attacked the ship's helicopter when the Furies flying the Combat Air Patrol were relieved. The helicopter suffered only minor damage. "Later the same day," recorded 810 Squadron's diarist, "the AGC[11] reported that he saw a Mig

---

[11] Air Group Commander.

15 ahead of him – which was lost behind a puff of black smoke as it opened up and flew away!"

The fourth patrol for HMS *Theseus* began on 16 December when she left Sasebo and sailed into the teeth of dreadful weather. Steaming north, gale force winds ripped across the decks for two days.[12] All flying cancelled, the ship heaved and plunged in the large swells that ran under her. Rain, sleet and snow, pushed by winds of 55 knots and sometimes gusting to 60 knots, made staying in the open almost impossible. The handlers were bent double against the wind, working tirelessly to keep the aircraft serviceable for when the weather broke.

A thick layer of ice and snow covered the deck, but the aircraft were lashed down against the gale force winds as *Theseus* slowly made her way towards Korea. But by 18 December, the weather had eased enough to begin flying. Crews worked feverishly, desperate to clear the snowbound flight deck and de-ice the aircraft. Finally, three Furies managed to climb away from the ship heading for the coast. The bleak frozen land looked desolate, devoid of movement to the pilots as they thundered inland. But on closer inspection, tracks, footprints and tyre tracks could be seen in the snow that blanketed North Korea as the Furies swept on.

That afternoon, the weather improved slightly to allow another flight of Furies to get airborne. Lieutenant Leece's Fury quickly gained height as it catapulted off the deck. Under full power he climbed away from the aircraft carrier, formed up with the rest of the flight and then they all turned inland. Below, the pristine white landscape seemed surreal, a vast fairy-tale land. The rockets slung under Leece's wings would make sure the fairy tale would turn into a nightmare. Vectored onto their targets, they found two Chinese tanks out in the open and immediately rolled in to attack. Rocket after rocket crashed into the armour plating and the ground around the enemy vehicles. With each explosion, dirt, snow and ice flew into the air as the Furies attacked.

With UN forces now back south of the 38th Parallel, the Chinese were building up for what the UN forces believed would be another offensive on Christmas Day. Evidence of enemy activity was abundant on 19 December, one of the Sea Furies' most successful days. In a morning raid, the Sea Furies, including Leece's flight, roared inland destroying seventeen trucks and three tanks with rockets and cannon fire before a low cloud base rolled in making flying difficult. They flew three strikes during the day, smashing a moving freight train with eight rockets. At the end of Leece's last sortie of the day while on the way back to the ship, his flight dropped low over a snow-covered road strafing two trucks caught in the ice while trying to cross a river. Cannon shells ripped into the vehicles that erupted into flames as the Furies swept over them and out to sea.

The Fireflies were equally busy that day. Climbing slowly and buffeted by turbulence, they sought clear air above the low cloud. Several minutes later, the fighter-bombers emerged into a bright blue sky. Unable to see the ground below

---

[12] John Lansdown details the dreadful Korean winters with some colour.

the pilots carried on, hoping to find a hole that would show them the ground and a target. The search didn't last long. A few minutes later they discovered the Pyongyang/Sariwon road through a hole in the cloud cover. One by one the Fireflies peeled off, dropped through the hole, heading straight for a large bridge. Bombs rained down on the structure, exploding on all sides, sending great plumes of water into the air. Though not quite destroyed, they severely damaged the bridge.

Bad weather hampered flying for the rest of the patrol limiting the number of sorties each aircraft could fly. Despite this, Furies and Fireflies were able to smash a pontoon bridge, strafe several trucks, and destroy five boxcars and a barracks over the last few days of the patrol.

One Sea Fury had to ditch on Christmas Eve because of engine failure. The aircraft went down four miles ahead of *Theseus* and, although the pilot was in the water for thirteen minutes, he was picked up unhurt by an American destroyer.

On Christmas Day, water was discovered in one of the Fireflies' fuel tanks forcing the rest of the flights to be cancelled while further checks were done. "Was on the whole a fairly busy Christmas with the odd spot of panic thrown in for good measure," wrote 810 Squadron's diarist. "Not by the aircrew as much as maintenance!! This was not the Christmas many had hoped for – and most had thoughts for those keeping the home fires burning."

UN forces had been forced to withdraw under heavy fire from Chinese and Korean forces, although Christmas Day passed without the expected new Chinese offensive. Virtually all the territory the UN had taken during the heady month of November was nothing but a memory. The Royal Marines 41st Commando and US Marines had fought a running battle for four days as they retreated from Koto-ri. Eventually, they had arrived tired and hungry at Hungnam beachhead where they were evacuated on Christmas Eve. All of this fighting was in the face of bitter cold and vicious snowstorms.

Enjoying air and sea superiority the UN forces had been able to withdraw in an orderly fashion while under heavy fire. Pounding the enemy from the air kept them from turning the withdrawal into a complete disaster. In fact, the withdrawal of UN forces went so well that many described it as an Inchon in reverse.[13] More than 105,000 military personnel, 17,500 vehicles, over 350,000 tons of cargo and 91,000 refugees between 11 and 24 December were evacuated from the North and transported down to Pusan, making the withdrawal a complete success from that point of view.[14]

By the end of December UN forces held a line roughly along the 38th Parallel. Tentative moves towards a ceasefire had been mooted by the UN but were rejected by the Chinese who attacked again on 31 December swarming across the border. Three days later, Seoul was abandoned, the government fled to Pusan and UN troops withdrew forty miles to the south to regroup. Then the Chinese push began to slow down and by the 25th UN forces were able to

---

[13] The retreat of UN forces can be found in Robert Jackson's *Air War Over Korea*.
[14] These figures came from John Lansdown's book and *Air War Over Korea*.

launch a counter-offensive. It wasn't until February, however, that they managed to regain Inchon and Kimpo, and Seoul itself was not retaken until March.

HMS *Theseus* returned from Kure into Korean waters on 7 January 1951 to start her next patrol. She was involved from the outset in the bitter see-saw struggle that finally saw the line hold at the 38th Parallel. Blizzards swept across her decks pushing snow almost horizontally like a million tiny pins into the parked aircraft.

As the wind howled and moaned around the ship's island (the giant superstructure sitting on the side of the flight deck of every aircraft carrier) and across her decks, sending icy particles flying in all directions, aircrew and handlers huddled in whatever shelter they could find, many remaining below decks. All they could do now was wait.

On 10 January, the weather had calmed enough for strikes to continue and Leece flew close support for ROK troops strafing and rocketing targets of opportunity near Yongmae-do. 810 Squadron's Fireflies were also on the scene attacking buildings, lorries and junks. Originally, they had been detailed to fly to the front but the weather was so bad they, like the Furies, were detailed north. "Found the cloud base on the deck when we were going to the front and that was not good!" 810 Squadron's diarist wrote. "The alternative target of Yongmae-do was the outcome of ROK cries for help. It had been occupied by North Korea/Communist Chinese forces and certainly today felt the weight of our attention! During the day some 7,000 rounds of 20mm were fired by both squadrons – more records [broken] someone cried!"

On 13 January the stirrings of peace began with the UN overwhelmingly voting for an armistice, but four days later the Chinese rejected the five principles on which it was based. The war raged on.

On *Theseus*, the terrible conditions of early January eased enough for regular flying to start again, but on 14 January the catapult's main reeving failed in the afternoon after 880 shots. The cloud base dropped from 3,000 to around 800 feet. A flight of Sea Furies had roared off the deck that morning, loaded with rockets before the catapult failed. Heading inland they flew just under the cloud, keeping a wary eye on any flak that might come reaching up for them.

An American Mosquito spotter directed the Furies towards engine sheds. Thanking their controller, the flight leader flipped his fighter over and dropped into a shallow dive, the other Furies followed suit. Rockets shot from the Furies into the engine sheds. Wheeling round, the fighters strafed sidings, railway trucks and enemy troops.

Flying now at 600 feet, in hazy conditions with mountains on all sides, the Furies strafed and rocketed store dumps and several buildings in the Suwon area. Later that day, after the catapult failed, the Furies were flying with only cannon ammunition. A flight of six swept over the Suwon to Inchon road spitting cannon shells at any troop concentrations they saw. Fireflies dropped several 500lb bombs on villages in the area, inflicting casualties on Chinese forces.

When the catapult failed that day, the rest of the flights switched to RATOG as the diarist of 810 Squadron described: "No trouble getting airborne – only trouble seemed to be with jettisoning the expended equipment which 'delighted' in making holes and large indentations in the fuselage!"

On 16 January, the Furies were strafing and rocketing troops in the Suwon area as well as flying a recce north of Seoul. Later that day, when all the aircraft had been recovered, HMS *Theseus* turned away from Korean waters and sailed back to Sasebo for rest and maintenance.

Chapter Four

LAST PATROLS FOR HMS *THESEUS*

Lieutenant Tommy Leece

In late January 1951, the United Nations' forces began their counter-offensive and by March had reached the 38th Parallel once more. To push them back the Chinese mounted a counter-offensive in late April and the Battle of the Imjin River took place with units of the British 29th Brigade taking the brunt of the fighting. The UN forces retreated but the Chinese offensive petered out. Meanwhile, in April, President Truman relieved General MacArthur of his duty and replaced him as Commander-in-Chief UN Command with General Matthew Ridgway.

Before sailing, HMS *Theseus* had been relieved by USS *Bataan*, an American aircraft carrier now operating off the west coast. Both ships could operate in an eighteen-day cycle, keeping the enemy under air attack almost every day. Seoul and the area surrounding it to the east, west and north was still in communist hands when *Theseus* returned to Korean waters on 25 January and *Bataan* sailed back to Sasebo for a rest.

The 25th was the day that Operation Thunderbolt, the UN counter-offensive was launched, and the Fireflies and Furies were quickly in the action. The first flights of the sixth patrol began in earnest with Fireflies catapulting off the deck. The weather had now improved dramatically. Carrying 60lb high explosive rockets and two 500lb bombs, the two-seaters were heavier than ever.

They climbed steadily in fine skies above the cloud up to their cruising height above the range of North Korean flak. Directed by airborne controllers, the Fireflies bored in on their targets. Splitting into pairs, the aircraft attacked several villages suspected of hiding Chinese forces. Their rockets pounded some huts and gun emplacements around the villages.

For the Fury pilots it was the milk run. "We'd start with pre-dawn take-offs," Leece said. "We were sixty miles off the coast and it was shallow water. When the ship was travelling at speed you could see where it had been because the mud had been stirred up."

That same day, Leece's flight, led by Lieutenant Lavender, was directed onto several troop positions, buildings, and some boats in the Kanchawan area. The Fury's huge radial engine purred smoothly as the flight headed into the target zone. Below, Leece could see a small cluster of boats just as the first Fury peeled off into a dive. He tapped his rudder bar, pulled the stick over and the world suddenly started screaming up at him. Far below the leader's rockets were already saturating the area. He watched the other Furies unload their rockets and cannon fire on the enemy, then he pressed the firing button. As usual, the Furies didn't hang about to see the results of their anger, but quickly climbed away.

Unfortunately, they didn't escape unscathed. Flying over Sariwon, after attacking several buildings in the area, Lieutenant Commander Bevans felt his aircraft shudder harshly and the stick jerked in his hands. He'd been hit by enemy flak as he pulled out of his dive.

"We did get flak," recalled Leece. "When you go down low you stand a good chance of being knocked down by rifle fire. We went down near the Chinese border one day and came down right over Pyongyang airfield, which was loaded with flak."

To avoid being hit again, Bevans pulled into a tight climbing turn, leaving the target area and heading back to the ship. He pushed hard on the rudder pedals, getting very little response as his Fury drifted this way and that. The hit he'd sustained had damaged the rudder and control was almost gone. Calling up the ship, he warned her of his situation, while above him Leece and the rest of the flight watched in shock.

Pushing the rudder pedals almost to the floor, Bevans worked the controls quickly as he brought the aircraft in on a slow turn towards the deck. Lining up the nose with the ship's tower, he pushed the canopy back and peered out, keeping the batsman in view. Sweat rolled down his back as he stepped hard on the pedals, trying to keep the aircraft as straight as he could. A gentle pull back on the stick and the nose came up slightly as he pulled back on the throttle to lower his speed. He retracted the main wheels, feeling them bump as they left their housings in the wings.

Suddenly, he was over the deck. The batsman gave him the 'cut' sign and Bevans yanked the throttle back, stalling the aircraft so it landed heavily onto the metal plating. Rolling forward, he leaned back in his seat, glad to be down. When the Fury had been pushed forward beyond the barrier[1] Bevans and the aircraft handlers inspected the aircraft's rudder. It had been hit by a 40mm shell that had ripped a hole in it nearly a foot in diameter. It was a narrow escape for Bevans.

Sadly, on a routine combat air patrol over the ship, another pilot's Sea Fury flicked into a tight turn and a spin, which continued until the aircraft hit the sea. No parachute floated out from the cockpit. Fifteen minutes later HMS *Comus* arrived where the aircraft had gone in but found only wreckage. There was no sign of the pilot.[2]

Fireflies mounted several attacks the next day, the 27th, in the Suwon area, bombing and rocketing factories, troop emplacements and villages. The Furies didn't miss out on the excitement and Leece's flight was up early,

---

[1] There were two barriers on each of the Royal Navy aircraft carriers which were both a kind of wire netting. Beyond the barrier was the deck part where the rest of the aircraft were parked.

[2] There is no indication in any of the source materials I studied as to why this aircraft went down. It was a routine patrol ahead of HMS *Theseus*. The only reasonable explanation could be some sort of mechanical failure.

bombardment-spotting for the USS *St Paul*. In the same sortie Leece went on to rocket and strafe buildings, railway yards, oil drums and other targets of opportunity.

Later the same day, on his second sortie, he climbed away from the ship after leaving the catapult. Throttling back to cruising speed he formed up quickly on the rest of the flight and they headed inland on an armed reconnaissance along the Kaesong–Seoul–Tokchang area where he unloaded his rockets into several warehouses (used by the enemy for stores) almost obliterating the buildings into dust and smoke. "We couldn't see if our rockets had destroyed the buildings or damaged them," he told me.

The next day, the 28th, another Sea Fury went down, to anti-aircraft fire. Lieutenant Keighley-Peach was flying a reconnaissance mission of roads northeast of Seoul when several shells slammed into his aircraft from very accurate ground fire. Rapidly losing power, Keighley-Peach turned his aircraft towards a narrow valley near Tongduchon-ni. In his hands the Fury's light controls were heavy from damage. He could see the altimeter needle rapidly dropping as he fought to stay airborne long enough to crash-land. Grabbing the canopy jettison release handle he pulled it quickly. Smoke poured out from under the aircraft as he worked the pedals, trying to line the aircraft up on the smooth piece of ground ahead of him.

The Fury hit the ground hard with the spinning prop stopping suddenly as the blades hacked the ground. He jettisoned the cockpit hood, which flew back, but the Fury was sliding. Peering through the smoke (which was now pouring into the cockpit) he craved clear sight and mind. Suddenly, he flew forward against the seat harness as the Fury hit a copse. It came to a dead stop. A wrenching crash followed, as the tail ripped away from the fuselage. Quickly unstrapping his harness, he climbed out of the cockpit, jumped onto the ground and ran as fast as he could for a ditch not far away. Knowing he was in enemy-held territory, he hid as best he could.

Lying in the mud and dirt, he looked up at the rest of his flight, maintaining a cover above him. Ninety minutes later, the familiar sound of a helicopter grew closer and closer and elated, he watched the American helicopter come in close and touch down. Climbing quickly into the chopper, relief flooded through him. He was now safe and moving away from danger. "Most of our casualties," Leece recalled, "were nearly all due to operating at low level. A lot of our guys got shot down."

Over the next couple of days, the Combat Air Support missions continued with the Furies and Fireflies flying Mosquito-directed[3] strikes on villages, gun emplacements and trenches. "We worked bloody hard at this time," Leece told me. "It was incredible and when you were operating so far away from home you built up a huge team spirit. While HMS *Triumph* had the Seafire 47, we had the Fury and we could go off for two or three hours on sorties whereas the Seafire was good for little more than an hour."

[3] These were the airborne controllers who flew Harvard trainers if they were American, or Astors or other light utility aircraft if they were RAF or British Army Air Corps.

During a dawn armed recce flight (on the morning of 27 January 1951), Leece's flight had strafed and rocketed a boat near Haeju. It was the only flight he made that day: "One day we went up to Chinnampo on a morning run looking for signs of sampans or junks. We'd jump them as soon as we saw them and caught them on the hop a lot that way."

His last flight of January was on the 29th, where he flew a morning recce north-west of Seoul, rocketing and strafing several targets before landing back on the deck 2 hours and 35 minutes later.

Bombardment-spotting for the USS *St Paul*, Furies directed the ship's guns onto the Nippon factory at Inchon. As the aircraft flew above the flak they watched shell after shell pound the factory area. Great balls of fire leapt into the air as the 8-inch projectiles from the American ship rained down destroying several factory buildings.

On 30 January 1951, the Furies twice flew bombardment-spotting for the Canadian destroyer HMCS *Cayuga* over Inchon while Fireflies attacked several troop emplacements further north. On the first day of the new month the weather was fine. Leece's flight of Furies was only able to get airborne for one sortie, each Fury flying close support, strafing troops and dock installations and rocketing an enemy headquarters at Angyang.

The Fireflies were also very active that day as the entry in the squadron's diary describes: "During the forenoon the cloud gradually dispersed over the front and so the third detail headed for targets near Suwon attacking villages and a factory. Under the control of a Mosquito aircraft and Army support units they bombed enemy positions on hillsides and in the woods. This was followed by rocket and strafing runs apparently with great success according to the controllers!"

The next day, flying in his usual No. 3 position in a flight of four Leece flew two sorties. The first was in the morning, bombardment-spotting for HMCS *Cayuga* and HMS *Ceylon* whose guns were pounding enemy positions in the Inchon area. One Mosquito controller vectored the flight of four Sea Furies onto an oil container, gun positions and troop emplacements, who were rocketed and strafed by the fighters. Climbing away from the target area, Leece craned his neck around just as a huge explosion from the oil container lit up the sky. In the afternoon, the flight practised dummy rocket attacks on some friendly destroyers. That same day, one Fury managed a heavy landing on the heaving deck during very high gusting winds, bursting a tyre. This accident brought to an end the lucky streak of 1,463 accident-free deck landings.

"We flew 3,446 sorties and that's a hell of a lot for one ship in 86 flying days," Leece told me. "We won the Boyd Trophy because we went over 1,000 deck landings without an accident." Indeed, a signal from the Fifth Sea Lord extended the Admiralty's congratulations to HMS *Theseus*.[4]

Another Fury was shot down by small arms fire but crashed not far from the *St Paul*, which soon plucked the pilot from the water with her helicopter.

---

[4] The signal is reprinted in its entirety in *With the Carriers in Korea*.

HMS *Theseus* flew sixty-six sorties on 3 February; however four Sea Furies were lost. "They went flat out to get the aircraft into the air," wrote 810 Squadron's diarist. 810 was the Firefly squadron onboard *Theseus*. "We had nineteen Fireflies in Combat Air Support alone!" Fireflies had attacked several enemy troop positions that day, also foxholes, mortar positions and a village. The entry in 810 Squadron's diary continues with this note: "The area was filled with UN aircraft – all queuing to unload their bombs, napalm and rockets. As many as fifty aircraft were counted at one point!" As dusk drew in and the last aircraft detail had been brought aboard, *Theseus* turned away from Korea and set sail for Kure in Japan.

By 10 February, UN forces had Inchon and Kimpo airfield back in their control and were pushing forward to the Han River near Seoul, which they finally crossed on 7 March. On 15 February, Leece flew an armed photo recce flight over Chinnampo. The flight of Sea Furies rocketed a bridge, damaging it but not destroying it. The next day, Leece was on close support detail strafing and rocketing barracks along the Han River. Over the next couple of days he flew support missions and a combat air patrol over the carrier.

After a morning of poor weather on 18 February 1951, a detail of four Fireflies climbed away from the carrier to attack two bridges near Kaesong. The 810 Squadron diary records: "We noticed that efforts have been made to repair all road and railway bridges in the area. There were no hits on the bridges."

March was a much busier month, and on the 6th Leece was bombardment-spotting for HMS *Kenya* whose shells landed south of Chinnampo. That same day the Fireflies attacked a large building in Haeju which ROK intelligence claimed was an ammunition dump. "There was one direct hit and many near misses," runs the entry in 810 Squadron's diary. "Although causing damage it did not bring about any explosion associated with ammo dumps!"

Another entry by the squadron diarist for the following day described the write-off of three Fireflies. "We finished the day [7 March 1951] having three aircraft less than we started with. Mr Young came in low and ended up in the barrier loaded with his depth charges. A young midshipman in the rear seat, there only for a pleasure trip, had a little more fun than he bargained for!" The evening saw both Lieutenant Nunn and Lieutenant Tobey hit the Number One barrier causing damage to their engines. "Bouncing hooks yet again," the diarist wrote.

The following day there was another accident. A Firefly bounced over the first barrier and slammed into the second and caused havoc amongst parked aircraft. "It was then a case of making the deck ready for the rest of the a/c to land on," notes the 810 Squadron diary. "Not a record to be published in *The Times* – four aircraft out of commission in two days."

On the afternoon of 11 March 1951, Leece's flight of Furies strafed and rocketed several trucks near Haeju. The next day, the Furies were up again, this time flying close support, rocketing enemy hill positions on a ridge near Maehwa-San. Despite their depleted numbers, the Fireflies managed to get four details into the air that day, attacking a variety of targets with bombs and rockets. The highlight was a double bridge on which the fighter-bombers dropped six 1,000lb bombs. Subsequent hits saw one span of each bridge collapse under the hail of bombs.[5]

On 13 March, the Furies strafed trucks and railway sheds near Haeju, then Leece continued flying a photo recce over Changyong where the flak was particularly heavy. The following short entry in 810's squadron diary describes a Firefly raid that same afternoon: "A flight of four Fireflies (a detail) attacked a bridge near Haeju with 1,000lb bombs. There were four hits and four near misses and the bridge was destroyed."

The last Firefly detail of the day with the help of a Mosquito control attacked the village of Hongch'on with bombs, rockets and cannon fire. "The village was reported to contain a battalion of enemy troops. Approximately sixty-two buildings hit and destroyed," recorded the diary.

On the morning of 24 March, Leece was back in the thick of it, flying close support. His flight of Furies strafed a village near Haeju with cannon fire and rocketed several enemy trucks in the area before heading back to the ship. Two days later the Furies crossed the coast heading inland to the area north of Seoul where they strafed several villages. They were directed onto enemy trenches in the same area and the Furies raced towards these positions. Dropping low, they fired their rockets, sending great plumes of dust and smoke into the air. After a break of two days, Leece took to the air again (29 March) flying north-west of Pyongyang. After dive-bombing some troops in a wooded area, his flight flew on to strafe villages near the capital.

Ahead of him, Leece could see his leader's (Lieutenant Lavender) aircraft shake from a hit by flak. Almost at once Lavender's engine started running rough. Lavender quickly glanced over his instruments. Temperature and oil pressure readings were off the scale. The mighty radial engine coughed and choked as he tried to remain airborne. He knew he wouldn't make the ship, so he needed to find the closest friendly airfield. It was Suwon. Radioing the controllers he told them his predicament and they immediately directed him to the airfield where he just managed to land before the engine cut completely. Leece and the rest of the flight circled overhead to make sure their leader landed safely before returning to the ship. Lavender arrived back on the aircraft carrier the next day.

That same day, Fireflies bombed a double railway bridge near Sariwon with great success. One span collapsed on to the second bridge, which caused a span to be damaged on that one as well. Only four bombs were dropped by the British fighter-bombers. The last Firefly detail of the day hit enemy barracks with 1,000lb bombs, destroying most of the buildings and making the rest uninhabitable.

HMS *Theseus* steamed to the east coast in the early part of April 1951. The morning flight on 9 April saw Leece tucked in behind the leader, as the flight of Furies headed towards the Wonsan area where they strafed lorries, oil drums and assaulted enemy barracks with their rockets.

That same day, Fireflies attacked a warehouse and a mine-laying base to great success. "Two large buildings were attacked with rockets and strafed," wrote 810 Squadron's diarist. "The rockets and bombs caused large fires at both

---

[5] A detail, according to 810's diary, is a flight of 4 aircraft.

targets." By afternoon, the Furies were back over the same area, strafing boats and rocketing enemy warehouses.

The next morning, while flying an armed recce, American Corsairs bounced Leece's flight, mistaking the sleek Furies for Russian La9s[6]. The Furies took evasive action and dived away.

"Whilst I was flying as No. 2 to Lieutenant Lavender," Leece explained, "the flight was observing enemy activity in the valley and caught sight of two US Marine Corsair fighters. We turned to starboard, climbing to 4,000 feet when the two Corsairs dived into the valley, dropping one bomb each. Recovering, they started to climb in our direction. We continued a gentle turn to starboard until the Corsairs were closing when my leader ordered break. I opened the throttle fully and commenced a steep-climbing starboard turn when there was a loud bang from the engine, so I throttled back thinking it was the engine but it wasn't. I didn't know I'd been fired at.

"The leading Corsair was dead astern of me and he opened fire and I saw many tracers flashing over my port wing and turned violently starboard and away. The Corsairs did not attempt to follow me. They thought they'd shot me down because my wing was on fire. They were American Marine pilots. The only reason the fire went out was because it burnt out the bottom of the wing tank. The top of the wing was glowing red. I was very lucky.

"I can only conclude that they hadn't been paying attention to their aircraft recognition bulletins. They were used to seeing American aircraft in the area. We were on the east coast where the Corsairs claimed they'd shot down two La9s. They couldn't have been properly briefed. We had bloody great black and white stripes painted over the wings and fuselage."

A footnote to Leece's encounter with the Corsair was added by an unidentified Firefly pilot in 810 Squadron's diary. "Everything had to be rushed forward because Lieutenant Leece was returning after being shot up by an American land-based Corsair. He was a very lucky man for his starboard wing tank had caught fire. He made a good landing."

On 12 April, the Fireflies were very active attacking bridges and a stores dump in the Hungnam area with mixed success. On the first detail they hit one of three bridges in the area. "Two spans were knocked out and another damaged," runs an entry in 810 Squadron's diary. "The detail then rocketed stores dumps and strafed an engine and some trucks."

On the next three details the damage to the remaining bridges and stores dumps was minimal, but the squadron lost one Firefly as the following entry explains: "Mr Bailey made a very good job of ditching when his engine finally packed up – lacking oil pressure due to either being hit by flak or just one of those things. Excellent work by all concerned made the stay of Mr Bailey and Aircraftsman Loveys[7] in their dinghy fairly short – fifty minutes all told. Two helicopters (essentials of which we lack) shepherded by Sea Furies made the pick-up and returned them on board chilly but all in one piece."

---

[6] La9s were radial-engined single-seat fighters originally seen towards the end of the Second World War. Their appearance made people mistake them for Sea Furies.
[7] Loveys was the observer in Bailey's Firefly.

On 14 April, Leece joined up with his flight, led by Lieutenant Lavender, and the Furies headed inland towards Puhang on an armed recce where they sent rockets blasting into the mouth of a tunnel before turning back towards the ship. On the way home, the pilots strafed several boats.

The next day *Theseus* steamed away from eastern waters heading back to the Yellow Sea. The ship arrived with its escort of destroyers two days later. That day (17 April) it was Leece's turn to fly the standing combat air patrol over the ship, but the next day he was flying over enemy territory again. North-west of Pyongyang his flight rocketed and strafed several motorboats and a command post.

Two days later he flew an armed recce over Chinnampo and was directed to attack several troop concentrations in the area. Each Fury raked the hapless soldiers with cannon fire before rocketing a shed and several boats. That patrol was the last one for HMS *Theseus* in Korean waters and she set sail for the UK. HMS *Glory* would be her replacement. Lieutenant Leece's tour was over.

Chapter Five

HMS *GLORY* ENTERS THE CONFLICT

Lieutenant Michael Darlington

During May and June 1951, the United Nations forces regained the initiative and drove the North Koreans back across the border. In July, armistice negotiations began at Kaesong but collapsed the following month when the North Korean delegation walked out. In August, fighting around Seoul intensified. Operation Strangle, the air war targeting enemy front line supplies, was widened to include railways and roads.

HMS *Glory* arrived in Japan on 22 April 1951 for her first patrol carrying the 14th Carrier Air Group (CAG) under the command of Lieutenant Commander S. J. Hall. This CAG had twenty-one Sea Furies of 804 Squadron and twelve Firefly 5s of 812 Squadron. The ship also carried a single Dragonfly helicopter for rescue purposes.

It had long been expected that the Chinese would mount a spring offensive and information from prisoners, captured documents and other sources pointed to an all-out attempt by the communist forces to push the UN out of Korea entirely.

It began on the day of *Glory*'s arrival in Japan when Chinese forces attacked the US Eighth Army positions along a line south of Kaesong to Chorwon and Kumwha[1]. Many of the communist troops were fresh from Manchuria. British and American forces contained the first penetration by the enemy but the Chinese managed to create a bridgehead across the Imjin River west of Kaesong. Facing them on a ridge of high hills was the British 29th Infantry Brigade, whose 1st Battalion from the Gloucestershire Regiment, at Solma-ri, took the brunt of the assault by the Chinese. For three days the gallant British soldiers held their positions against the overwhelming odds of the Chinese forces, while the other battalions were withdrawn. Attack after attack left the regiment with barely one hundred men and completely surrounded, over forty of them managed to escape to safety. But their stand had stalled the enemy's offensive, preventing them from rapidly breaking through and giving the UN forces precious time to regroup.

Elsewhere, the communist forces continued to attack, forcing the US Eighth Army to fall back to defensive positions on the Kimpo peninsula north of Seoul, which was once again threatened with capture. A series of rapid counter-

---

[1] HMS *Glory* arrived in company with the cruiser HMS *Belfast*. The destroyer HMS *Concord* and other ships were in the vicinity providing bombardment in support of the army. See *With the Carriers in Korea*.

attacks by American and UN forces kept the enemy from fully exploiting their gains and by 3 May the attacks were slowing down as the Chinese withdrew out of range of the UN's artillery to regroup and reorganize. On the 16th they attacked again against the US Eighth Army in a bid to wipe the Americans out.

After days of hard fighting the Chinese had taken enormous casualties and gained nothing. Their offensive was stopped by UN forces who counter-attacked on the 23rd, pushing the Chinese completely out of South Korea by the end of May. The Chinese had suffered approximately 100,000 casualties and 12,000 troops taken into captivity as well as a huge amount of equipment either destroyed or captured. By mid-June UN forces were back across the 38th Parallel some fifteen miles in the west and central regions and nearly thirty-five miles north in the east. The spring offensive for the Chinese had turned out to be a complete disaster.

Although HMS *Glory* arrived in Korean waters on 26 April 1951, with the usual escort of destroyers and frigates, continuous rain, low cloud and very poor visibility kept the aircraft lashed to her decks for two days before the weather improved.

Regular flying began as the weather cleared and the Furies swept inland over the Haeju area in support of the ground forces under attack from the Chinese, and attacked factories, vehicles and boats with rockets and cannon fire. Visibility was still very poor, however, with low, thick cloud covering most of the area around the ship and the coast.

Lieutenant Stephenson, flying a Sea Fury on combat air patrol duties, must have become quite disorientated after straying into the thick cloud cover for the aircraft was never seen again nor was there any sign of wreckage.

Commissioned pilot Michael Darlington of 14 Flight flew his first Korean armed reconnaissance flight on 29 April. Led by Lieutenant Campbell, the Sea Furies roared up the coast, strafing and rocketing junks and railway installations. Other Furies struck inland, hitting troops north-east of Seoul who had been marked by American Mosquito spotters.

Darlington found himself on combat air patrol the next day flying in hazy weather over the ship. The rest of his flight headed up the coast, targeting a Bofors gun installation and some junks.

Flying done for the day, Darlington stood on the deck of *Glory*, watching the aircraft handlers pushing the Furies and Fireflies away from the barriers as the last of the aircraft landed. He could feel the ship beginning to pick up speed as she changed direction, heading further out to sea for replenishment, as was routine after a few days. Tomorrow they would take on supplies from HMS *Unicorn*. There would be no flying and most of the pilots would take the opportunity for physical fitness or have a couple of beers in the ship's bar.

Back off the western coast on 2 May, *Glory*'s crew saw USS *Bataan* steaming towards them.[2] The two carrier forces joined up and began flying joint offensive armed reconnaissance flights. The four Furies of 14 Flight

---

[2] The Chinese spring offensive is detailed extensively in Max Hastings' *The Korean War*.

catapulted off the ship that day, one after the other, climbing quickly away. Darlington, flying in No. 4 position, was the last off the ship. The sound of the huge radial engines filled his ears as he joined up with the rest of the flight. They turned, flying up the coast again. He later wrote in his diary: "We were flying an armed recce." In his headphones Darlington could hear the directions coming across from a Mosquito controller flying low, obviously spotting for targets. Gently touching the controls, Darlington kept the Fury steady behind his leader, the flight's No. 3 Lieutenant Campbell acknowledged the controller's directions and quite suddenly, Darlington watched the leader peel off, diving onto some junks. All four Furies rocketed the boats, strafing them as they pulled out of their dives. Climbing away the fighters headed for the next target, some boxcars near Haeju, which they plastered with rockets and cannon shells.

The Fireflies were directed onto a large building in Haeju that they successfully bombed. In another action, Furies of 15 Flight attacked a large building that had been identified by guerrillas as a key target. Pulling out of his dive, however, Lieutenant Barlow's engine spluttered. Instead of a smoothly purring engine it now ran rough. Working the controls quickly, he tried desperately to get more power from the dying engine with no success. Radioing his plight to the rest of his flight he realized he had no choice but to ditch. To soften the blow he came down unharmed in a river in enemy territory and was picked up by an American helicopter, which took him to Seoul. The rest of his flight strafed the wreckage, setting it on fire.

The next day, a flight of Furies flew a coastal armed reconnaissance mission. The last position in any flight of four usually gets the worst of the flak because enemy gunners are by then fully awake and the element of surprise is gone. In the No. 4 position, Darlington managed to avoid flak this time as they rocketed junks, gun emplacements and stores. On the same flight, the Furies bombardment-spotted for HMS *Kenya*.

This day, 3 May, the Furies flew twenty-nine sorties over North Korea, as 804 Squadron's diarist recorded: "On most occasions today the flak was found to be a bit above average in intensity especially the areas around Pyongyang. We flew twenty-nine sorties today over North Korea."

The next day the weather socked them in, as the diary relates: "On 4 May the weather was useless for flying with low cloud and fog over the land. No sorties were flown, although USS *Bataan*, US light carrier in company with us, now made an attempt in the rain." Wind-driven rain swept across the decks of the two carriers hampering any attempts to get aircraft in the air. Late that afternoon, one flight of Furies got away during a break in the weather and headed inland where they rocketed several warehouses and enemy gun positions.

During the morning of 6 May, a flight of Sea Furies rocketed and strafed several junks caught in the mud up and down the west coast. That afternoon Darlington piloted one of the last Furies to land. The batsman gave him the necessary sign and he quickly cut his engine, the Fury landing hard on the metal deck. As he shut down his engine with the five-blade propeller slowly grinding to a halt and the aircraft handlers quickly pushing the Fury forward to clear the way for the next aircraft, he realized his first patrol was over. The next day the ship headed back towards Japan.

The stay in Sasebo was short and by 11 May HMS *Glory* was back in Korean waters off the west coast. There was a lull in the ground war as the communist forces were preparing for the second stage of their spring offensive to drive the UN out of Korea[3]. That day, Michael Darlington's flight was up for one sortie, flying close support. In formation, the Sea Furies headed up the coast. Spying some fishing sampans and junks, they dropped into close line astern formation then rolled into their dives strafing and rocketing the vessels. Continuing the raid, the Furies climbed rapidly away, then latched onto roads and valleys in the Haeju area seeking to destroy enemy trucks, troops and stores but they came home to *Glory* without seeing anything more.

The following day, Darlington flew close air support in the No. 4 position. That morning they attacked sampan and junk vessels near Chinnampo. "The first four Furies reported that most of the bridges in their area showed signs of being repaired," wrote 804 Squadron's diarist. "A tribute to the Chinese bridge repair gangs, which are apparently conscripted villagers who work all through the night. Later a mortar team practising on the beach was spotted and attacked by the last armed recce flight of Furies inflicting four casualties and ensuring the practice was definitely abandoned."

The diarist for 804 Squadron – presumably a pilot himself – wrote a brief account of a false alarm the following day: "HMCS *Nootka*, one of our Canadian tribal class escorts, nearly caused alarm and despondency by asking for a CAP at dawn because she was very far north chasing junks when daylight arrived. However, she managed to complete her job and steam south at high speed!"

14 Flight's second sortie of the day was attacking railway tunnels. The flight dropped into a shallow dive from 5,000 feet, each aircraft following the other down. Under their wings, the Furies carried rockets and their drop tanks. Just as Furies from HMS *Theseus* a few months before had attacked tunnels at both ends, so did 14 Flight for the first time.

Splitting into two, they swooped down on either end of the tunnel in the hope of catching rolling stock. Great plumes of smoke shot from the rockets as they launched from their moorings when the Furies attacked. Darlington held the Fury in the dive, watching his leader's rockets hit the mark, then it was his turn. Firing, he felt the Fury buck slightly from the turbulence and quickly pulled the stick back into his stomach, climbing rapidly away and hoping the enemy below hadn't got their sights on him.

With all aircraft back on deck, *Glory* turned away from the coast for replenishment at sea. The weather turned again, low cloud and heavy drizzle forcing the flying to a minimum. "We were flying combat air patrol again on 15 May 1951," Darlington wrote in his logbook. Normal CAP duties up until then consisted of two Furies but on this flight the number was increased to four despite the poor visibility. The UN forces had decided to simulate an assault from the sea near Chodo Island to pull troops and supplies away from the front

[3] For more information see Max Hasting's *The Korean War*.

and relieve the pressure on allied forces now coming under the heavy attack from the second part of the Chinese spring offensive. Heavy air opposition was expected which is why CAP was increased to four aircraft that day.

On 16 May in variable weather conditions, Furies escorted Fireflies that bombed and rocketed villages, bridges, strafed oxcarts and bombardment-spotted as well. The following day Darlington was in the thick of the action, attacking enemy coastal positions. Buildings and junks were rocketed and strafed. Over the last three days of the patrol, Furies and Fireflies flew more than 155 sorties often in poor visibility, rocketing and strafing villages, buildings, junks, sampans, troop and gun positions. One Firefly was shot down and the crew was picked up by *Glory*'s helicopter.

The last day of the patrol, 19 May, the Furies were bombardment-spotting when USS *Bataan* arrived to relieve *Glory*.[4] "One section of Furies spotted for HMS *Ceylon*," wrote 804 Squadron's diarist. "The target area was straddled with no direct hits. In the early afternoon two Furies again spotted for HMS *Ceylon* on a village with stores in it and this time it was a direct hit!"

However, hitting the target even with bombardment-spotting was difficult, as the diarist continues: "It was found that if the target was fairly long and narrow and lay across the line of fire it made it possible to straddle continuously without hitting."

As the last aircraft landed back on *Glory*'s decks, engines were shut down, aircraft parked and lashed to the deck as the wind swept across the ship. Turning away from the coast, *Glory* steamed back towards Japan, ending her second patrol in Korean waters. This time the stay in Sasebo would be more than two weeks because of repairs to the ship.

By the end of the month, the Chinese offensive petered out and UN forces were pushing forward. Some military thinkers believe a series of amphibious landings by UN forces moving rapidly up the east coast of North Korea could have won the war at this time. But since the Chinese had entered the war, conflict was held entirely within the Korean peninsula[5].

Towards the end of June, both sides were beginning to make gestures towards peace. Although the negotiations tentatively began the bitter fighting continued. The talks would last two years because the communists could not agree on one point – the repatriation of communist prisoners of war. Many did not want to return to North Korea but the Chinese and North Koreans wanted all of them repatriated.

HMS *Glory* began its third patrol, setting sail from Sasebo on 3 June 1951. Flying started the next day and Darlington was on an armed recce in the No. 4 position. The Furies climbed away from the ship under thick cloud. Junks were attacked in the Kumsan areas. Near Kaeson away from the front, Furies and Fireflies strafed troops and rocketed railway lines, heavily damaging boxcars.

"The first flight of the following day was a combat air patrol," wrote Darlington in his logbook, "lasting three hours." The Fireflies bombed

---

[4] The two carrier forces had only been working together during the height of the land fighting for a few days. USS *Bataan* was the normal replacement for HMS *Glory*.
[5] The UN Supreme Command did not want to widen the war.

buildings near Kamsan, also destroying them. One Firefly was lost after it was hit by light flak and ditched in the sea.

The Furies flew thirty sorties that day, with one detail being particularly hairy. "The last trip of the day went after a camouflaged stores dump," wrote 804 Squadron's diarist. "That was hit with rockets and exploded. Bits of the stores dump were seen to go past one aircraft flying at 2,000 feet!"

On the way back from the sortie, one Fury ran into engine trouble and ditched successfully in the sea and was picked up unharmed. "Any suggestion that the Fury is a bad ditcher seems to have been disproved pretty accurately since we've been out here," wrote 804 Squadron's historian.

On 6 June, 14 Flight was operating in the Chinnampo area, and again in the No. 4 position, Darlington watched the three Furies staggered ahead of him peel off, rolling into their dives. Moments later, he flicked the stick sideways, pushed his throttles forward and the Fury rolled into a dive, following the others down. Rocket projectiles shot from their rails under the wings, smashing into a barge and a building, which both exploded spectacularly. Flames shot into the air as the ammunition inside erupted. After this successful raid, the Furies headed back to the ship, while the Fireflies bombed Songhya-dong in the Chinnampo estuary and damaged a bridge in the same area before turning out to sea for home.

That day an entry in 804 Squadron's diary mentioned the dangers of low level flying especially when pulling out of a dive. "A lot of aircraft are coming back with holes in them mostly caused by .303 but sometimes with bits of earth and parts of their own rockets!"

Michael Darlington flew armed reconnaissance for the next two days against targets of oxcarts, a jetty and two junks. One Firefly was hit by flak in the nacelle fuel tank but the pilot reached the coast before ditching near the island of Paengyong-do. Both he and his observer were safely rescued and returned to HMS *Glory* the same day.

On 8 June, Furies swept inland searching for more of the enemy's ammunition strongholds. Intelligence reported targets which included railway boxcars and a stores dump that the Furies subsequently obliterated with rocket and cannon fire. They rolled into steep dives as the low cloud made target spotting difficult.

That night, with all her aircraft lashed down on the deck, *Glory* headed away for replenishment. While the tanker lay alongside *Glory* on 9 June, pilots and handlers got a breather from the heavy flying routine.

While the fuel flowed from one ship to the other, the hands on *Glory* discovered that the thousands of gallons being pumped into the carrier's tanks were contaminated with corrosion. An old pipe supply that had corroded and hadn't been used in a long time was the culprit. With less fuel than usual the patrol would be cut short. Nevertheless, HMS *Glory* headed back to start attacking North Korean positions the next day.

Aircraft poured off the deck early in the morning for a combined strike at Osan-ni. The Furies carried their rockets and the Fireflies 500lb bombs. All around the village were flak emplacements that opened up as soon as the aircraft arrived. Each aircraft dropped into their dives, bombing and rocketing the centre of the town. The air was filled with the smoke from the projectiles. Climbing away from the target area, the Fury leader radioed back to the ship that they could see the centre of the village burning. Bright orange flames licked the buildings.

The Furies had a successful day. After the first combined strike, the big radial-engined fighters were back in the air, destroying several buildings on the Chinnampo waterfront before plastering nine oxcarts with rockets and cannon shells. Four of the nine blew themselves to bits, clearly being used to transport ammunition.

The enemy would use any means in his power to transport ammunition and supplies. UN intelligence sources confirmed they were using oxcarts for that purpose. So the slow, vulnerable oxcarts became fair targets for UN aircraft.

The first strike on the same day was another combined effort where both Fireflies and Furies hammered several troop installations and buildings at Osan. They ran into flak and climbed quickly to 7,000 feet.

The next day Darlington and the rest of his flight attacked several transformers and damaged three. Later, a detail of four Furies rocketed several buildings near Chinnampo, which exploded while the Fireflies dive-bombed a railway bridge causing some damage.

After all the flying was finished HMS *Glory* set sail for Sasebo. Over the next few days the bad fuel (which had been taken aboard on 9 June) was transferred over to RFC *Green Ranger*, with new fuel coming onboard *Glory*. The tanks were then flushed out and the fuel dumped overboard. On 15 June *Glory* left Sasebo and arrived in Kure.

The fourth patrol began with a reorganization of 804 Squadron. Darlington's flight, No. 14, received a new leader, Lieutenant Kilburn. The ship arrived in Korean waters on 22 June, but this time Captain Colquhoun (commander of the *Glory*) shifted the ship's area of operations north by thirty miles. The ship was without its helicopter and he wanted to be sure they were as close to a helicopter base[6] as they could be, which was the reason for moving northwards in the first place.

Rear Admiral Scott Moncrieff came aboard from HMS *Cardigan Bay* that day, as the history of 804 Squadron related. He confirmed a rumour that had been going round: "While in the wardroom he said that he was doing his best to get us a refit in Sydney, Australia. So our latest buzz around the ship seems to have good support."

On 23 June, flying began in earnest, and while the first two flights couldn't find a Mosquito aircraft to vector them onto enemy positions, 14 Flight had more luck. Catapulting off the ship's deck, the four fighters formed up and headed inland with Darlington flying No. 4 as usual. Contacting the Mosquito controlling aircraft, they were directed onto several airfields in the western area. "An ancient biplane has been dropping bombs on Suwon," wrote the Squadron diarist. "They thought it was operating from airfields in our area, but

---

[6] This base was at Chodo Island.

nothing was seen though." The fighters looked for the Suwon bomber, but came up empty-handed.

The next day, Darlington's flight was flying close air support near Chinnampo, attacking several gun positions in the estuary (and houses containing troops in the same area). 15 Flight, led by Lieutenant Commander Birrell, had a close shave. Dropping low, Birrell could see several boxcars as he tore along over railways and roads from Haeju to Chinnampo on a fast reconnaissance run and these were very juicy targets. Ready to pour rockets into them he realized something was wrong. The boxcars had no wheels. Flak trap! "He was hit by a 20mm shell that exploded inside his ammunition tank," says the entry in 804's diary. "Luckily it was empty and he got back safely." Peeling away as fast as they could, Birrell led his flight quickly back out to sea and the safety of HMS *Glory*.

Fireflies were also very busy. Rolling into their dives, the two-seat fighter-bombers fell on some factory buildings, accurately dropping their bombs and sending great clouds of dust and debris into the air. As they pulled out, several explosions ripped through the factory as the buildings began smoking. Climbing quickly away the Fireflies strafed and bombed several buildings on an island in the Chinnampo estuary. Three of the two-seaters carried 1,000lb bombs and these they dropped on a bridge at Hwasan-ni, causing damage.

The next day, 25 June, the Furies flew a total of thirty-two sorties. But the first flight started out badly when they were not able to raise the Mosquito controller. "There seems to be plenty of finger trouble at JOC[7] on this score as the same thing has happened before," recorded 804 Squadron's diary.

It was a busy day for 14 Flight. Though Darlington's first sortie was a routine combat air patrol over the ship, his second was the most surprising one. Still searching for the Suwon bomber, Kilburn led 14 Flight towards Hanchon. Suddenly bursts of tracer and cannon fire shot by the Furies as four straight-winged silver jets made a quick pass. "Break, break," Kilburn cried over the radio. Immediately, the Furies split up as the jets came back again. Winks of flame from guns in the nose could be seen as they attacked the Furies. Darlington kicked the rudder and pulled the stick into a quick roll, then into a dive.

Suddenly the four jets were gone. They'd been American F80 Shooting Stars, which had mistaken the Furies for North Korean aircraft and attacked. No one was hit during the scrum but it was unnerving nonetheless. "It is almost inconceivable that anyone could mistake a Fury with its huge black and white stripes on it," wrote 804 Squadron's diarist. It seems friendly fire incidents are something every pilot has to live with.

The Furies were very busy the next day, bombardment-spotting for both HMS *Morecambe Bay* and HMS *Cardigan Bay*[8]. As each pilot in Darlington's flight took turns spotting for the ships, Darlington watched the shells smash into several villages far below. Flames belched from huts and buildings, erupting like the morning sunrise.

[7] Joint Operations Centre.
[8] John Lansdown states these ships were frigates.

Over the R/T he could hear the other pilots directing the fire from the ships off the coast as they pounded the villages. Gently putting the Fury into a turn, he kept an eye out for enemy aircraft as the flight circled, watching the destruction below.

After the bombardment, the Furies peeled away, and Kilburn led the flight away from the coast, spotting five enemy tanks alongside a road. Dropping into a dive, the four Furies fired their rockets at the vehicles, raking them with cannon fire at the bottom of their dives. One by one the Furies attacked, rockets blasting from under their wings, shooting into the tanks. Some were direct hits while others blew craters in the ground. Rockets expended, 14 Flight climbed quickly away, heading back to the ship, while other Furies continued to rocket the tanks. The diary is blunt: "The area was well and truly plastered."

At Toktong-ni Fireflies bombed railway sidings and sheds, then went on to Anak where they were directed onto a building reported to have been a headquarters for the enemy. Drenching that with bombs, they also attacked a factory near Pyongyang.

The next day, *Glory* steamed away from the coast for replenishment at sea, and intelligence reports shed some light on the tanks of the day before. "They seemed to think they were dummies though for what reason they were there, no one seems to know. There was no flak trap and they were certainly very convincing."

By 28 June, *Glory* was back on station, and Furies and Fireflies stormed off the deck, one after the other, heading inland on armed recce flights. Darlington's flight led by Lieutenant Kilburn took part in attacking junks and oxcarts, one of which exploded and disintegrated into fine debris. One junk was blown to pieces as well.

Then tragedy struck when a Firefly was shot down by heavy flak during an attack on a barracks near Pyongyang. The aircraft crashed in flames killing the pilot, Lieutenant J. H. Sharp, and his observer, Aircrewman First Class G. B. Wells. "The wreckage was scattered over a wide area and unfortunately there can be no hope for the crew," wrote 804 Squadron's diarist. "They were apparently hit by flak while attacking barracks north east of Chinnampo."

On 29 June the Furies and Fireflies had a busy day. Two sorties saw the Furies racing over the coast, attacking junks and buildings with great success. Flying fast over Ongjin-ni airfield 14 Flight stayed high away from the flak while inspecting the airfield below. They flew several passes, noting that bomb craters had been filled in. "There are rumours this day that peace proposals have been put forward," wrote the diarist[9].

The next day, the Furies and Fireflies returned to the airfield hammering it and the villages around with bombs and rockets. By the time the attack was over, the area was covered by dust and smoke making damage assessment impossible. They returned to the ship, happy with the day's work.

The catapult broke later that day when the strap came off the trolley as Lieutenant Howard was taking off. Unable to get up enough speed, his Fury

---

[9] General Ridgway, MacArthur's replacement, offered to meet with the communist commanders to discuss peace plans. See *The Korean War*.

flew over the bows into the water. "After a considerable time he broke surface and was picked up by HMS *Constance* who returned him to us in a very short time none the worse for this very unpleasant experience."

On 1 July, the last day of the patrol, all aircraft leapt off *Glory*'s decks using RATOG because of the broken catapult. In all, forty-seven sorties were flown by both Furies and Fireflies using this method. "By dint of working ceaselessly in the two hours available between details all our commitments were met," wrote the squadron's diarist. "The only sortie lost was one aircraft returning with unserviceable instruments."

HMS *Glory*'s fifth patrol began with some unusual activity. Reports had been received of a downed Mig 15 in very shallow water forty miles north of Chodo in a narrow channel flanked by sandbars and blocked at the southern end by a minefield. They were keen to capture an example of the aircraft to study. As the salvage operation to bring out the Mig got under way, *Glory* set sail from Sasebo on 10 July and arrived back in Korean waters the next day when flying commenced again. While some Furies and Fireflies flew inland, other aircraft (including *Glory*'s helicopter) flew CAP missions over the salvage operation of the crashed Mig. The entire recovery operation lasted several days, ending on 21 July. Several Royal Navy ships moved into the area for the recovery operation. The Furies photographed the downed Mig, as the diary for 804 Squadron related: "Part of the fuselage of the crashed Mig was visible from the water today."

Waiting for tides to change and water levels to drop, the salvage vessels were vulnerable to enemy fire but none came. In fact, the enemy seemed to take little notice of the operation, as they were deterred by constant CAP patrols of low flying Furies. Darlington and 14 Flight started their fifth patrol flying CAP duties over the ships and recovery craft slowly pulling the wreckage out of the water. The Mig was broken into several pieces, many small chunks and some much larger pieces such as wings and fuselage were spread about the site. The tail section had broken off and was some distance from the main wreckage.

Also on 10 July, armistice talks began at Kaesong. By this time the war on the ground was much more static than it had been before. In the air, communist Mig 15 jet fighters were appearing more and more in North Korean skies and were being assembled over the border by the Chinese in great numbers, while the USAF attrition rate was getting higher and higher.

In the Yellow Sea *Glory* continued to operate in the southern part off the west coast of Korea helping to keep the western blockade strong while attacking the enemy in the Chinnampo–Haeju area. This area was a natural port and by keeping a constant blockade it forced the enemy to use long supply routes from Manchuria over rough terrain to supply his forces.

The second sortie for Darlington on 11 July was in foggy and cloudy conditions over the ship. The Furies of 14 Flight roared over the coast targeting buildings and junks with rockets near Chinnampo where the sky was much clearer. Early the next morning, 14 Flight rose into the summer Korean air, the Furies catapulting off *Glory*'s deck one after the other, and climbing rapidly away. They formed up on a formation of Fireflies then escorted the two-seat fighter-bombers to Kumsan-ni, which the Fireflies subsequently bombed. In the afternoon, Lieutenant Kilburn led 14 Flight on an armed reconnaissance to an area north of Seoul at the front where enemy troops were strafed and rocketed.

Over the next few days, the aircraft were attacking their usual targets. Junks and buildings were strafed and rocketed by the various flights from the carrier. A battalion of communist troops was attacked in the front line, 1,000 yards from UN forces. Throughout these attacks the Furies were met with light flak. At one point a 45mm gun fired at them from a junk. Once more the pilots enountered the frustrating use of apparently innocent civilian transport such as oxcarts as transport for military purposes.

Replenishment at sea took place on 15 July. Bemused crewmembers from the supply ship watched as aircrew and ship's crew of *Glory* held a hockey competition on the flight deck with the aircrew victorious by a whisker. Good fun, but work was never far from the minds of the men. All too soon – the following day – HMS *Glory* was again stationed off the west coast in the Yellow Sea, fully replenished. The sun crept slowly above the horizon and dawn spread its fingers across the early morning sky as the aircraft handlers prepared for the first sorties of the day.

The roar of engines upset the morning calm as Furies and Fireflies prepared to fly off. One after the other, engines achieved full power as the aircraft catapulted off the deck, climbing quickly away as the handlers bent low against the slipstream of propellers and wind whispering across *Glory*'s deck.

Flak was an increasing problem as the Furies and Fireflies attacked their targets. On 16 July, a Firefly was hit by flak north of Sariwon and crashed in a ball of flame. Both the pilot and the observer were killed.

On 17 July, Furies swept in over the coastline as Lieutenant Kilburn led 14 Flight towards the Chinnampo area. The target was a large formation of enemy troops. Flying in No. 2 position was Lieutenant Hart with Michael Darlington again at No. 4. The Furies cruised in at 7,000 feet, keeping well out of reach of flak. Over their targets, Kilburn dropped one wing rolling over into his dive. Behind came the other three Furies in a line astern formation. Darlington, in the most vulnerable position, hoped the flak gunners would still be asleep by the time he reached his pullout and firing height.

Rockets and cannon fire ripped into the ground around the troop emplacements as the Furies attacked. Once Kilburn's rockets had gone, he pulled back sharply on the stick climbing quickly away – the flak was already strong. Lieutenant Hart was not so lucky. As he released his rockets the growl of his engine abruptly changed from a purr to several choking coughs as shells from ground fire slammed into the aircraft. Heading towards the sea, the engine getting worse with every passing moment, Hart ditched near some friendly islands off Choppeki Point and was later picked up by a ROK frigate. From there he was transferred back to *Glory* by helicopter. The remainder of 14 Flight got back to ship safely.

The last two days of the patrol saw the Furies attacking more ground targets but three Furies were lost over the two days. Two pilots were safely rescued but another one was shot down in flames and exploded on impact, killing the pilot.

"While searching the Ojan-ni area two aircraft were hit," wrote 804

Squadron's diarist. "Lieutenant Young had a shell explode in the cockpit behind him and Lieutenant Davis was forced to ditch further south. Davis had trouble with his Mae West and dinghy and was only rescued after a long and difficult time in the water. Young got back OK but Sparke was hit by flak and reported his aircraft on fire. A short time later his aircraft dived into the ground and exploded. There can be no hope of his survival and we must accept the loss of another great friend."

On 21 July, HMS *Glory*'s aircraft were coming to the end of the salvage operation as 804's diarist relates: "At 1545hrs four Furies were flown off, two to provide cover for the ships already assembled near a Mig and two to escort our helicopter (flown by Lieutenant O'Mara of the US Navy) from Chodo Island to the scene of operations.

"At dead low water the body of the Mig was sighted and marked by the helicopter with a buoy. The tail was marked with a life jacket and dye. The helicopter was then escorted back to Chodo and landed with its tanks pretty empty. The two Furies then went back to the Mig and watched the boats arriving and the activities on the mud whilst the Mig was picked up. After three and a half hours the Furies landed on having been relieved by four Corsairs from USS *Sicily*. After refuelling the helicopter arrived back on board and the ship set sail for Kure."

While the salvage operation was going on peace talks were well underway with a military demarcation line being the first item on the agenda for agreement. The area of Ongjin and Yonan south of the Chinnampo to Haeju area and south of the 38th Parallel on the western side of Korea was agreed by both sides to be controlled by the UN. The trouble was that the communists held it!

To reinforce this agreement, the UN decided to demonstrate a show of strength around the Han estuary, close to Kaesong. The Han River runs south from Yongjong-ni and Seoul sits on its banks. This political decision meant that all naval activities on the west coast of Korea would contribute towards this demonstration.

Late in July, a UN naval force arrived off the Han estuary into the approaches to the Han River to blockade it. These approaches are shallow and include many islands surrounded by shifting mud flats in low tide, making navigation risky indeed.

The demonstration of UN might began on 27 July, as the guns from frigates and other ships opened up on enemy positions. When aircraft were available for spotting, bombardment would take place, usually twice daily. This operation in some form or another lasted well into November while the peace talks continued on an on-off basis.

Because of this need for a show of strength, *Glory* left Kure in a hurry minus replacement aircraft that were being flight-tested. Some aircrews were also left behind when *Glory* sailed and rejoined the ship several days later. Poor visibility on 27 July, when *Glory* arrived off the west coast of Korea, restricted flying to a few flights in the afternoon.

The next morning was the same. Low cloud restricted flying to CAP duties over the ship, but by the afternoon the weather had improved and 14 Flight swept inland heading back up to their old hunting ground in the Chinnampo area.

The following day the weather cleared and aircraft from *Glory* attacked enemy positions in the Han estuary area. On Darlington's second sortie that day his flight attacked villages, railway boxcars and a tunnel. More than 40,000 enemy troops were reported to be in the area, but 14 Flight like the other Furies saw little evidence. The 804 Squadron diary records: "So far they haven't been very conspicuous and today is no exception. Many people were seen in the fields and may or may not be peasants. For this trip we are working with USS *Sicily*, the American aircraft carrier, and the chatter on the R/T is quite deafening."

By the end of the month the weather turned again. On the early afternoon of 30 July, high winds ripped across *Glory*'s decks. She was rolling in the heavy seas making flying very difficult. 14 Flight managed to get in some spotting and photography for the frigates navigating the Han River channels while bombarding shore targets. For the month of July the total number of flying hours was 989[10] for *Glory*'s aircraft.

The first day of August 1951 saw bad weather and low cloud in the morning covering the Han River approaches, so *Glory* headed out to sea to rendezvous with the tanker for replenishment. After several hours taking on fuel, she steamed back into Korean waters, off the west coast near the Han River estuary. That evening the Furies attacked several villages in the area but the low cloud made assessment of damage very difficult. Darlington was on station over the estuary flying CAP duties for the frigates. Throughout this time the enemy was quiet.

Weather curtailed most flying duties, but on 2 August, 14 Flight flew inland under the low cloud into the Kumsan-ni area. Rockets and cannon fire ripped into several enemy rafts and boats, destroying them. The following day the Furies, coming in fast and low, caught more than sixty enemy troops in the open. The fighters unleashed their weapons cutting into the enemy troop formations, destroying their vehicles and causing several casualties.

On 4 August, bad weather kept the Royal Navy aircraft from heading inland so they flew along the coast catching enemy soldiers in the open. Darlington's guns blazed as he dived behind his No. 3, whose rockets were already hitting the area. Dust and debris shot from the explosions. His own rockets quickly followed adding to the confusion and chaos on the ground. Thumbing the firing button, he tore over the target as his cannon belched shells in quick bursts; then he climbed and turned away, forming up with the rest of the flight. "It is a rare and welcome sight to catch troops out in the open like this in this area," said the diarist. "This lot probably thought they were safe with such a very low cloud base."

The last of the Furies and Fireflies landed on as the light was beginning to fade. One by one, the aircraft hit the deck as the batsman gave the 'cut' sign. Arrester hooks grabbed the wires, engines shut down and aircraft were pushed

---

[10] This is according to the squadron's official diary.

quickly forward of the barriers. With the light almost gone, and the aircraft lashed down to the deck, *Glory* turned away from the coast and headed back for Sasebo through rough weather. USS *Sicily* relieved her.

The seventh patrol for the British carrier group was short indeed. HMS *Glory* arrived off the coast on 14 August, and began flying operations the next day. Darlington, still attached to 14 Flight, began this patrol with CAP, but on 15 August was bombardment-spotting for frigates still operating in the Han River estuary even though there was a dearth of targets.

Elsewhere, rockets from low-flying Furies destroyed two junks, one bursting into flame as the aircraft pulled out of their shallow dives heading for other targets. Two Furies were forced down: one, flown by Lieutenant McNaughton of 17 Flight was hit by flak and beached on Chodo Island; the other lost Fury was due to a burst tyre.

The patrol came to a sudden and abrupt halt the next day as Typhoon Marge slammed into the west coast. High winds tore across *Glory*'s decks for two days and nights as the ship rolled and heaved under fierce swells. The heavy seas kept the ship in constant movement, corkscrewing badly. The vicious 60-knot wind covered everything with salt as it rocked the ship. Wind and flying rain hampered any movement on deck as aircraft handlers worked hard, in vain trying to clear the aircraft of the sea salt. Each time some portion of the aircraft was cleared it would soon be encrusted again as the sea water whipped up by the wind crashed over the ship.

After the battering from Typhoon Marge, *Glory* finally arrived in Kure on 25 August. Six days later with the remaining aircraft serviced and ready to fly it was again off the coast of Korea for another patrol, with operational flying beginning on 2 September.

Like all the other patrols, the targets were the same. The frigates were still attacking targets in the Han estuary. Junks, buildings, railway lines, and villages were all targets for the rockets, bombs and cannon of *Glory*'s Furies and Fireflies. Troops were strafed and buildings targeted as the aircraft attacked from Taedong Gang to Yonan. "The Furies rocketed two camouflaged buildings on 3 September," wrote 804 Squadron's diarist. "One disgorged about fifty bodies who were well and truly strafed."

The same day a flight of Furies attacked targets identified by friendly guerrillas – several troops in villages. "The only trouble with these targets," wrote the diarist, "is that by the time we get them they are a few days out of date. However, on several occasions good results have been reported."

On 5 September, 14 Flight climbed away from *Glory* heading towards Taedong Gang where they rocketed several buildings. "An unwelcome increase in flak," was recorded in the diary.[11]

The following day was taken up with replenishment, and *Glory* was back with operational flying on 7 September, although due to a faulty catapult launches were made by RATOG. Targets over these two days consisted of troop positions and several junks. Two were destroyed and six damaged, with a headquarters building receiving the brunt of the rocket and cannon fire from

---

[11] There is no further explanation of this in the diary.

several attacks by the Furies, including 14 Flight.

"Most of today's trips were guerrilla targets and in one case where a headquarters building had been hit by rockets a report came through that about sixty casualties were caused," wrote 804 Squadron's historian. "How reliable these reports are nobody knows."

The last day of the patrol, 9 September 1951, was a record day with eighty-four sorties flown, beating the record of sixty-six flown in a single day by aircrew from HMS *Theseus*. "At one point every aircraft was airborne," says the diary. "This is a record for the carrier and a fine example of first class maintenance. Several pilots flew three sorties during the day and congratulations are still coming in by signal."

Darlington was up twice that day; his first sortie was in the north where his flight attacked several junks. Furies escorted Fireflies to Suichon, attacking flak positions while the Fireflies bombed several buildings that included an enemy headquarters. American Harvard Mosquito control aircraft directed the Furies onto camouflaged vehicles, which were duly rocketed and strafed. Intense flak made the raid difficult with one Firefly going down. Both the pilot and observer were later rescued.

The following day, 9 September 1951, HMS *Glory* steamed away from Korea, ending her eighth patrol of the conflict and arriving in Kure two days later.

While Royal Navy pilots overflew the west coast keeping up the blockade of communist ports, operations on the eastern coast of Korea were also heating up as the UN forces struggled to keep the Wonsan area open. Throughout the summer the communists had increased their forces in the area trying to push the UN out and gain a firm foothold on the islands. Inside the town of Wonsan itself enemy defences were intensifying as the communists hoped to hold on to the harbour. A force of destroyers, three US and three Commonwealth and other ships were sent to counter this threat. HMS *Glory* was part of this fleet.

She left her usual hunting ground off the west coast of Korea in the Yellow Sea and headed for the east coast, arriving in company with the rest of the fleet for her last patrol on 18 September 1951. Flying began that day with Darlington's flight mounting attacks on Wonsan. The Furies swept in over the town, rocketing and strafing targets in the harbour area before wheeling away back to the ship. "At sixty-four rockets at a time quite a bit of damage must have been done," wrote 804's diarist. "Anti-flak fire was ordered before each strike went in and throughout the day no flak was seen." That day, *Glory*'s aircraft flew sixty-eight sorties.

The next day, 19 September, flying was delayed as high winds buffeted the ship. *Glory*'s bow smashed into strong swells as the waves crashed across her decks. This kept her nineteen aircraft lashed to the deck. Faces strained the sky for signs the weather was clearing and by the afternoon she sailed into the lee of the land where the wind was much softer and the seas calmer. But disaster struck as the catapult again refused to function. "A bitter and most disappointing anti-climax as this was our first and last time on the east coast and yesterday had been quite up to HMS *Glory*'s standard," the 80 Squadron diary recorded.

Most pilots flying off the carriers mistrusted RATOG and some simply loathed it. But, without the catapult it was the only way to get the aircraft airborne. 14 Flight was no exception to the trepidation of RATOG launches and was up spotting for destroyers bombarding enemy positions around Wonsan. However, the ship was very low on the equipment needed for RATOG launches and had to leave the east coast and head west for Japan to replenish its stocks.

After two days in Sasebo taking on stocks and supplies *Glory* returned to her familiar position off the west coast of Korea near the Chinnampo–Haeju area and began operations again on 22 September. Aircraft were still being launched by RATOG so the number of sorties flown was less than usual. "But in the afternoon the catapult was tested and pronounced cured," wrote the diarist. "A source of great relief to everyone."

While *Glory* had been gone enemy junk traffic in the Chinnampo area had increased, as well as on the railways. 14 Flight strafed a group of enemy soldiers with rockets and cannon fire as well as attacking buildings and villages in the area. Several junks were attacked and destroyed by the Furies on the same day.

On 23 September, Michael Darlington wrote in his diary: "Flew armed reconnaissance on my first sortie of the day." The targets were again several junks, many receiving the attentions of the Furies' rockets and cannon. As Darlington pulled out of his dive, forming up with the rest of his flight, he watched one junk explode; orange flame shot into the air scattering debris everywhere.

The next day, 14 Flight flew two sorties and on the first one attacked several villages with rockets and cannon fire, setting several huts on fire. Smoke and debris covered the targets as the fighters dived on the buildings below. Darlington's rockets ripped into huts and the ground around them sending dirt, dust and smoke everywhere.

The final day of operational flying for HMS *Glory*'s first tour was 25 September 1951. By now the catapult had been fixed and the aircraft flew their final strikes of the tour. Furies destroyed seven junks and damaged several others and the Fireflies bombed targets in the Chinnampo area before touching down on deck.

All her aircraft collected, she turned away from the west coast of Korea and steamed for Kure. HMS *Glory*'s replacement, the Australian aircraft carrier HMAS *Sydney*, was already berthed at Kure. Throughout the following day, *Glory*'s aircraft handlers worked hard servicing the aircraft, preparing her Fireflies for transfer to *Sydney*.[12] Suffice it to say that the Australians performed far and beyond the call of duty.

The Fireflies were transferred over, with all their stores and on 30 September *Glory* set sail for Hong Kong, ending her first tour of Korea.

---

[12] The account of HMAS *Sydney* is extensively covered in *With the Yanks in Korea*.

Chapter Six

HMS *OCEAN* AND THE IRISHMAN

Lieutenant Paddy McKeown

In the autumn and winter of 1951-2 during HMAS *Sydney*'s tour in the Korean War, Operation Strangle was still the main priority. When HMS *Ocean* arrived in May 1952, the focus switched to targeting the enemy's power by attacks on plants and dams, in order to put maximum pressure on the communist delegations at the armistice talks, which had begun again in October 1951 at Panmunjom, but by May were deadlocked again over the question of voluntary repatriation of prisoners of war. In July and August, the North Korean capital Pyongyang was heavily bombed by the UN air forces. In retaliation, the Chinese and North Koreans launched an offensive against UN forces.

Late in the autumn of 1951 four new Royal Navy pilots were appointed to 802 Squadron. They were on their way to Korea when one, whose wife had just given birth to twins, decided he couldn't go. In his place came a young Irishman Lieutenant Paddy McKeown, a Sea Fury pilot: "We sailed from Portsmouth in early January. HMS *Theseus* had already sailed from Devonport and we rendezvoused with her off Brittany in very bad weather. A signal came in telling me to transfer from HMS *Indomitable* to 802 Squadron on HMS *Theseus* forthwith. Both ships were going to Gibraltar. It could easily have waited a couple of days as both ships would be there and all I had to do was walk down onto the jetty, along the jetty then up to the other ship. The sea was very rough."

Aboard *Theseus* was a Dragonfly helicopter, which was to be used for search and rescue duties in Korea. "It was blowing a real gale. Normally, if there was a very strong wind you'd start the helicopter in the lee of the ship's island. But the helicopter was right up at the forward end of the flight deck with little shelter. The Commander Air insisted we start up the Dragonfly on the spot where the wind was a gale. The pilot and I got into the Dragonfly and it started up and suddenly one rotor blade broke off and wrecked the rotor head."

McKeown believed that they had now lost their only helicopter, but a never-say-die spirit was on hand: "The Commander Air (Old Wings) wasn't to be beaten. He said, bring in the Barracuda." The onboard Barracuda aircraft acted as a delivery service for mail and people from ship to shore. "A very experienced pilot flew it," McKeown continued. "I climbed into the observer's seat at the back and away we went.

"We approached HMS *Theseus*, but the weather was too rough and we got a wave-off from the batsman. On the fifth attempt Bill, the pilot of the

Barracuda, just ignored the batsman, put the stick forward and put the damn thing on the deck and taxied forward towards the barrier. I started getting my stuff out of the back. The Barracuda's wings are folded manually and a team of aircraft handlers started folding the wings, but they suddenly dropped the wing. I could see their faces and I realized something was happening behind me.

"A Sea Fury had missed the wires and was bouncing up the deck about to hit the barrier. We all went diving for the side and got off the flight deck. And sure enough the Fury slammed into the Barracuda. So one Barracuda down and one helicopter down just to transfer one idiot from one ship to another."

That was McKeown's introduction to 802 Squadron, en route to war. Once there, he was deployed to HMS *Ocean*. She had replaced the Australian aircraft carrier *Sydney* that had taken over duties from HMS *Glory*. *Ocean* relieved USS *Sicily* every ten days, giving the aircrew and ship's complement ten days on and ten days off.

When *Ocean* arrived in Korean waters on her first patrol of the war in the spring of 1952, Lieutenant McKeown flew a mount that bore his name. "The policy was to fly your own aircraft if you could, but sometimes it just didn't work out," McKeown told me.[1]

Weapons had been changed aboard the aircraft, as experience had proven that the Sea Fury was better suited to the dive-bombing role, because it was steadier and more accurate in steep dives than the Firefly. Also, the clear bubble canopy of the Sea Fury gave the pilot far better visibility; the Firefly's window struts and panes made it much less accurate for precise bombing of the target. "When we got out to HMS *Ocean* it worked out that the Furies dropped the bombs and the Fireflies fired the rockets."

Ocean's first patrol saw her aircraft flying across the static boundary of the 38th Parallel. The fractious fighting of previous battles was gone, as the peace talks ground on, still held up by the question of prisoner of war repatriation. The UN air forces were carrying out interdiction strikes on enemy positions and communications targets. Railway lines, dirt roads, bridges, tunnels, junks, buildings, huts and gun positions were some of the targets hit by UN forces. While the armies fought from dug in positions, in the air US and UN forces roamed the Korean skies hitting the communists' long supply routes and stopping them from mounting any major offensives.

McKeown's first sortie was on the morning of 11 May 1952. Catapulting off the deck, the Furies formed up over the ship then roared inland, climbing steadily. Over Sariwon, they turned towards their target, a railway bridge not far from the town. One by one the Furies rolled into their attack dives, McKeown flicked the master switch to 'On', watching the target grow in his sights. His eyes glanced quickly over the instruments as the Fury screamed towards the bridge.

Tracers from ground fire laced up towards the aircraft. McKeown kept the aircraft steady, his thumb over the firing button as the height slipped away, then he flipped the switch, and the two bombs dropped from his wings as he pulled

---

[1] An aircraft bearing his name now resides on permanent display in the Fleet Air Arm Museum at RNAS Yeovilton.

the stick back, kicking the rudder hard and taking the Fury into a fast climbing turn.

Bombs from the Furies rained down on the target, exploding on the railway line and adding to the destruction and confusion, fracturing the line in several places and making the bridge unsafe. The squadron returned to *Ocean* and a warm cup of tea. The afternoon's sortie saw McKeown over Haeju where he bombed another railway line.

The next day, on Tactical Air Reconnaissance and Combat Air Patrol (TARCAP) sorties flying No. 3 position, McKeown followed his leader in a line astern formation inland to attack railway bridges in the Chinnampo area. One by one they pulled out of their dives as their destructive cargo devastated bridges and other vital arteries of track. Heading west of Chinnampo, the Furies climbed swiftly away from the target back towards the ship. Reaching 4,000 feet, they dropped into strafing runs, destroying road targets and buildings with their cannon fire along the way.

On 14 May, Lieutenant K. McDonald was killed, a sad day for the Furies. He was attacking a notorious gun position on the Amgak peninsula. The AA fire from this gun was deadly, and had earlier damaged several aircraft from HMAS *Sydney* and HMS *Glory*. It needed to be put out of action.

McDonald had rolled into his dive ready to destroy the gun with his two 500lb bombs. Behind him was the rest of his flight, peeling off into their dives. The fire coming up from the ground was murderous and a shell ripped into the Fury. "I'm hit," he shouted over the radio. Fighting the aircraft, he tried everything he could to stabilize but it was now spinning out of control and his efforts were futile. The Fury spun into the ground and exploded. "Lieutenant McDonald was one of the sprog flying engineer officer pilots transferred from 801 Squadron with me," McKeown told me. "Amgak was at the end of a headland opposite some islands which were occupied by the US. A lot of guys were shot down or damaged over Amgak."

The current record number of sorties flown in a single day stood at 106 by HMS *Glory* in her previous tour. The men of HMS *Ocean* wanted to beat that record, and 17 May was the day when it happened. In fine weather, flying began at 0430hrs and continued throughout the day. The total number of sorties flown reached 123, a record for a light fleet carrier.

Everything worked perfectly and as the sun dipped below the horizon, McKeown's Fury, one of the last to come in, flew steadily in its final approach as he made a textbook deck landing: "I did five sorties on that day and that was more than anybody else. I got a nice little letter from the Captain. Everybody else flew three or four but I managed to squeeze in another one." By the time *Ocean* had recovered all the aircraft, twenty-eight out of the full complement of thirty-one remained serviceable for the next day's flying.

Once the crews had proven they could beat the record they settled back into their normal pace. On the afternoon of 18 May 1952, during the last sortie of the day, McKeown catapulted off the deck and climbed steadily and quickly forming up with the rest of his flight ahead of the carrier. They wheeled away at high speed towards Hanchon. Dropping into their 45-degree dives several minutes later, the Furies bombed anti-aircraft batteries and gun positions, their cannon spitting fire, sending soldiers flying in all directions.

The last day of the first patrol (19 May), saw a new weapon introduced to the Furies – the 1,000lb bomb. Normally, two would be carried with drop tanks but to get off the ship with the extra weight RATOG would have to be used for launching the aircraft. It was McKeown's first attempt at RATOG.

He stood on the deck with his fellow Fury pilots early in the morning waiting to see the first of 802 Squadron's Furies fitted with the bombs take off under RATOG power. A little audience had gathered in the shelter of the ship's island to watch the event.

At the controls was Lieutenant Commander Fraser Shotton. The Fury's engine sparked into life as Shotton put on full power. This was not just a demonstration but also a mission and Shotton would form up with the rest of his flight and head inland towards their target. But first he had to get off the deck.

Slowly, ever so slowly, the Fury seemed to roll down the flight deck, gathering speed. Bracing themselves for the roar of the rockets that would shoot the aircraft into the sky, the little audience clustered by the island waited. But there was no whoosh of rockets. Instead the Fury trundled right off the flight deck disappearing over the bows towards the sea below.

Working the controls quickly, Shotton managed to use the little speed he'd gained from dropping off the flight deck to gain precious height. On full power, the engine strained and the aircraft slowly began to accelerate as it burned off fuel. Ten seconds ticked by. On the deck all the faces turned towards the bows waiting to see the Fury reappear. Shotton pulled the stick into the pit of his stomach as the Fury hugged the waves with spray from the propeller streaming water down the windscreen. Gradually he became airborne. Moments later, the Fury appeared above the bows climbing slowly away from the ship.

As the wheels retracted, Shotton realized he should jettison the bombs to gain height. However, if he did that, the mission would be aborted and he wanted to reassure his pilots that there was no problem with the RATOG as well as carrying and dropping the new bombs. So he pressed on with the mission.

After he landed back on the ship with the sortie over and minus his two bombs, Shotton cut the engine as the Fury's wheels touched down. Handlers pushed it forward and Shotton climbed out. The rest of 802 Squadron's pilots quickly crowded around him wanting to know what had happened. Sheepishly, he told them he'd forgotten to flip the master switch that would have fired the rockets. Did they believe him? No, but they certainly trusted him.

However, that day ended on sadness. The RATOG malfunctioned on one Fury, only the rockets on one side igniting, which sent the Fury overriding the chocks. The blast blew a naval airman over the side into the sea and his body was never recovered. Also, the Fireflies lost their senior pilot Lieutenant Commander Williamson-Napier[2] who was shot down near the front line. His plane exploded on impact.

Her flying finished and the aircraft lashed down, *Ocean* turned away from Korean waters and headed for Sasebo in Japan. Her first patrol was over.

---

[2] This incident is related in Chapter Nine of this book.

For McKeown, this day had been a milestone. He'd done his first RATOG, used the two 1,000lb bombs to smash a bridge in the Hanchon area and for good measure destroyed three oxcarts. Unfortunately, not every oxcart carried military goods and some were attacked that were totally innocent. The North Korean tactic was not dissimilar to that of Iraqi soldiers putting on civilian clothes to attack allied soldiers during the Iraq conflict of 2003.

HMS *Ocean* arrived back for her second patrol nine days later and flying began on 29 May. The weather was fairly clear but during the first few days there were periods of low cloud and fog over the coast. Flying an armed recce that morning, McKeown and the rest of his flight ran into a storm of flak over the Hanchon–Chinnampo area.

The next day, on his first sortie, McKeown tucked in behind the No. 2 as the flight formed up over the ship, then they turned inland. The flight of four Furies was led by the CO of 802 Squadron, Lieutenant Commander Donald A. Dick, DSC, RN, and they headed towards the railway yards at Chinnampo. "The flak was intense," McKeown recalled. Over the target, the Furies spread out into their battle formation, a single line of four aircraft, as Lieutenant Commander Dick peeled off into his dive. A moment later, McKeown's wing came up as he rolled off, nosing the Fury down into an attack run. Ahead, he could see dirty black puffs exploding all around the lead Furies as they pulled out of their dives.

Below, the bombs from the CO were already creating havoc. Smoke and debris rose from the ground and railway trucks lay smashed on the tracks. McKeown hit the release button, pulled back on the stick and pushed the throttle forward, climbing as fast as he could away from the flak; his Fury was much lighter without the two projectiles. His bombs connected, destroying more railway trucks, lifting the remains clear from the tracks, which knocked them onto their sides.

On 1 June, McKeown was on his final approach to the ship from a long sortie when his engine started playing up. Flaps down, wheels retracted, coming round and lining the aircraft up with the deck, he watched the batsman adjusting the controls according to his signals. Suddenly, the batsman waved him off, and McKeown realized he was too high. Pushing the throttle forward, alarm filled him as his engine coughed, spluttered and died.[3]

Instead of the deafening roar of his engine, the silence was loud and ominous. Rapidly losing height he had no choice. No going back around; he knew he wouldn't make it. It would be touch and go if he made the deck. Radioing his predicament, McKeown had only moments to get the aircraft lined up as the forward momentum carried him towards the ship. Onboard the batsman was quickly signalling him to adjust his speed and height. The deck appeared underneath his wing and he landed hard, the undercarriage taking a terrific pounding. But he was safely down.

At dawn on the morning of 3 June, the Furies swept in low over the coast turning towards Hanchon. Bombs hung from their wings as they roared up the coast at 400 miles per hour, keeping low. On the ground, life was just stirring

---

[3] This incident was recorded in McKeown's logbook.

as the Furies shot overhead. Catching three sampans in the open, the aircraft dipped into shallow dives; they dropped their bombs on the vessels and then raked them with cannon fire. Pulling away McKeown could see them burning slowly and sinking below the water. He grinned to his great friend Nick Cook, the flight's No. 4 behind and beside McKeown.

On 6 June, blasting off the deck using RATOG, McKeown followed the rest of the flight, climbing slowly with two 1,000lb bombs slung under his wings. Heading for Chinnampo the flight slipped into battle formation over the target and one after the other the fighters peeled off into 45-degree dives onto a railway bridge the communists had rebuilt over the previous few days. Both his bombs were direct hits and several spans were destroyed. Later on *Ocean*, her aircraft lashed down, sailed for Japan, ending her second patrol off the western coast of Korea.

After ten days of rest, HMS *Ocean* began her third patrol in her familiar hunting ground off the west coast. She was still enforcing the UN's western blockade of North Korea. This forced the communists to rely on supply lines coming from Manchuria that US and UN air forces attacked with relish. American Thunderjets and Shooting Stars were pounding communist railway lines, roads, gun and troop positions all across the north, far behind the static line of the 38th Parallel in the hope that it would strangle the communists' ability to fight. But, as we have seen, it didn't stop the supplies from getting through.

On 20 June, McKeown's flight attacked a railway line with 1,000lb bombs completely destroying whole sections of track. Two days later, McKeown was in the cockpit of his Fury seeing *Ocean* became smaller and smaller as he climbed quickly. The beat of the huge piston engine in front of him was steady and even. Fully armed with two bombs, two drop tanks and a full load of cannon ammunition, the aircraft seemed fine. Suddenly, with the ship in the distance behind him, the perfectly running engine cut out.

With the advantage of height, he quickly released both bombs into the sea. Then he released the fuel tanks and turned the aircraft towards the ship. Height quickly dropped away as the aircraft glided towards the carrier. Again, luck was with him and he managed a hard emergency landing onboard without having to go into the water and be rescued.

On 24 June, the flight, led by Lieutenant Commander Dick, attacked a transformer at Chaeryong[4]. On the way back, McKeown dropped low destroying four oxcarts with cannon fire.

July 1952 was a busy month for the Furies and Fireflies. The Furies flew strikes supporting Commonwealth forces bombarding enemy troops on 7 July. "There were a couple of times when we were doing close air support with the Commonwealth Division," McKeown recalled. "There was pretty solid cloud all the way up so we couldn't do our normal visual ground attack. We flew in close formation guided by the Americans on their radar and they told us

---

[4] By this time in the war a ban that had previously been in place on transformers had been lifted and North Korea's hydroelectric system was a legitimate target.

the course to steer and the height to fly at. We were in level flight and they told us when to drop our bombs."

On 9 July McKeown's flight flew bombardment-spotting for HMS *Belfast*. "There was a big electrical transformer picked out as a target. It was to be a maximum strike by Sea Furies and Fireflies from HMS *Ocean*. There were four known gun positions A, B, C, and D on tops of hills."

Both Lieutenant McKeown and his wingman Sub Lieutenant Nick Cook, flying in the No. 4 position, flew the aircraft detailed to do the bombardment-spotting for the American battleship USS *Iowa* and the *Belfast*. "Nick and I were sent off ahead of the strike to direct the two ships' guns onto one of the gun positions. They shoot and the pilots examine it and correct them. Then they could shoot at the other three gun positions. We just had to put them on to one. We put them accurately onto gun position A then pulled to one side to watch the show."

Leading the Fireflies into rocketing the target was Lieutenant Commander 'Chico' Roberts, CO of the Firefly squadron on HMS *Ocean*, 825 Squadron. "He comes along with all these Fireflies," McKeown said. "When Roberts pulled up to gain altitude and then go into his dive with the rest of the battle formation, he would call up the ships with the code 'Out Lights'. That told them to start shooting while the aircraft were gaining height so they could start their diving attack," McKeown explained. "Nick and I were watching this. Chico Roberts pulled up and executed 'Out Lights'. We looked out to sea and there were USS *Iowa* and HMS *Belfast* with puffs of smoke as they opened up with their big guns."

Both pilots cruising high above the flak expected the shells from the two ships to hammer the enemy gun position. "They all fell exactly halfway between the target and the ships. In the meantime, the Fireflies were already in their attack and none of the enemy gun positions had been hit and they were all blazing away." In the mayhem of the attack the Fireflies and Furies unloaded their ammunition then headed straight back to the ship, out of harm's way.

"What happened was that a midshipman on HMS *Belfast* had put the wrong setting on some instrument that was vital to the whole operation," McKeown recalled. "So I came up on communications with HMS *Belfast* and asked them if they would shell the gun positions anyhow. They said negative, operation cancelled." McKeown again asked the ships to fire on the communist position and in the end they did.

In the afternoon's sortie, McKeown's flight, led by Lieutenant Commander Dick, shot off the deck using RATOG, two 1,000lb bombs slung under the wings of each Fury. During the sorties the Furies attacked and destroyed two bridges and five oxcarts before landing on the carrier again two hours later.

On 10 July McKeown had a busy day. He flew three sorties, the first in support of Commonwealth forces,[5] and in the second he strafed a gun position with his cannon. However, the third sortie was the most eventful, as the Furies formed up and headed down the Chinnampo estuary to destroy two loaded

---

[5] In April that year the British Commonwealth Overseas Force had changed its name to British Commonwealth Forces Korea (BCFK).

barges and gun positions. Not far from the Furies, the Mosquito controller vectored the fighters towards their prey. Peeling off quickly the Furies dropped onto the enemy like angry wasps. Their bombs and cannon raked the area, hitting the barges and gun positions and sending smoke, dust and flames into the air.

The following day's operations were a combined strike on rail yards at Pyongyang (outlined in Chapters Seven, Eight and Ten). Twelve Furies and eight Fireflies attacked; braving murderous flak all of the aircraft came back in one piece.

This patrol ended on 12 July. McKeown's flight, with Dick leading, bombed a radar station, then raked several sampans with cannon shells, sinking most of them. Once all aircraft had been recovered and lashed down, HMS *Ocean* headed away to Japan for another rest before starting it all again on the next patrol. On these ten-day rests they would spend their time reading despatches about the progress of the war or the peace talks. During the day they would continue to train while at night they would go into town.

Flying for the next patrol began on 22 July, with the Furies flying several Tactical Armed Reconnaissance and Combat Air Patrol strikes that day. McKeown's flight bombed and attacked two oxcarts and several sampans.

The next two days were the most eventful. During an A/R with two 500lb bombs the flight destroyed one bridge, sank five sampans and one motor junk. Tragedy struck on 24 July, when they lost Lieutenant Commander Dick, DSC, RN, who crashed and sank in the Taedong-Gang River whilst strafing a sampan. "He was hit by flak on the attack on the bridge," McKeown said. "And he came up on the radio. He broke the rules. If you think you've been hit by flak you should immediately turn back to base. He was a super bloke too, won a Distinguished Service Cross during the war flying Corsairs.

"He called me on the radio because I was his No. 3 and said I think I've been hit, could you have a look under my aircraft. So I did. I couldn't see any damage to the aircraft but that doesn't mean there wasn't damage. A bullet just leaves a hole, but inside is where you get the damage.

"When I was flying Sea Hawks at Suez I came down and I was told a bullet had gone through the fuselage just underneath the tail. Right behind it was my elevator control rod and there was just a small hole in the tail plane. But inside, half the control rod had gone.

"So we couldn't see any damage. I pulled away and my friend Nick Cook pulled underneath the CO's aircraft and he had a look and he couldn't see any damage so the boss carried on."

Seeing the sampans the Furies prepared to attack. McKeown watched his CO's wing come up as he rolled into a dive. "We were in a circle and went down strafing in order – leader, followed by Nos. 2, 3 and 4. When I pulled up to go around again for another attack, I looked down and all I could see was a great big brown mark on the river. The boss had gone. What had happened was when he tried to pull out of his dive something went wrong with his controls and instead of pulling out he went straight into the river creating this great big splash with no sign of the aircraft. It was high water and quite well inland from the coast."

Stunned, the remaining three Furies headed quickly back to the carrier raking more sampans with cannon fire along the way. As the handlers pushed their Furies beyond the barrier, McKeown quickly jumped out heading up to the bridge straight for the captain. "I suggested that we went back again at low tide to see if there was any sign of the aircraft. The captain agreed."

A few hours later, McKeown led a flight of Furies away from HMS *Ocean* in search of wreckage from the CO's aircraft.[6] Pushing the stick forward into a shallow dive he dropped down to 4,000 feet and cut back on his power, his eyes searching the landscape below. Suddenly, he saw it. Sticking high out of the mud was the tail of Commander Dick's Sea Fury. "If he suspected he had flak damage he should have flown back to the ship. That was really the worst incident I personally saw," McKeown remembered sadly. I asked him how he felt about the war. He explained: "It's what we were told to do. We lost a lot of good friends."

The next day, the flight was sent to bombardment-spot for HMCS *Nootka* but the operation was cancelled due to fog. Vectored by controllers onto other targets, the Furies headed for a road bridge north of Chinnampo, which they knocked down. The next sortie of the day McKeown's flight took part in a six aircraft attack on enemy gun emplacements at Kyomipo. Sampans were sunk on this raid. The last sortie of 25 July saw McKeown and Nick Cook flying together again. Peeling off from formation, Cook attacked a railway bridge, accurately placing his bombs on the bridge and destroying it.[7] McKeown bombed and strafed between thirty and forty oxcarts, his cannon shells ripping into the flimsy vehicles, some exploding from hidden ammunition inside them, others catching fire. The Furies climbed away quickly back towards the ship as the light began to wane.

On 27 July McKeown's flight successfully bombed a road bridge with 1,000lb bombs. The huge bombs sent debris in all directions as they shattered the bridge. As they dropped into their dive-bombing runs, three Migs swept down on the Furies at 5 o'clock. "My flight were the first ones to see them," McKeown explained. "I was entering my 45-degree dive when Nick came up on the radio calling 'Migs, Migs.' I was at the point of dropping my bombs and then I pulled up. We'd never seen the Migs before up until that time. They'd made a pass and gone off." For each carrier the Army had a liaison officer who debriefed the pilots after every sortie. "At the end of the debriefing we casually mentioned these Migs and they didn't believe us."

In fact, McKeown hadn't seen the Migs himself. "They stayed away from me but they created a lot of problems. There were several more attacks and three or four aircraft damaged by Migs had been forced to land on Chodo[8] (not too far from Amgak), which was occupied by the Americans."[9]

---

[6] This was the first time McKeown led the flight on operations.

[7] Cook also led another pilot of the flight down onto the bridge, but McKeown did not follow, according to his logbook.

[8] Chodo Island was a search and rescue base held by the Americans. It had a helicopter and a radar station.

[9] The story of the Migs, 27 July, is outlined in Chapters Seven and Eight.

After several days off in Japan, HMS *Ocean* was again back in Korean waters to start a new patrol and on 9 August McKeown was flying the first armed reconnaissance sortie of the day carrying 500lb bombs. One of the other pilots, Lieutenant Chris Jenne, destroyed a bridge with both his bombs: "He was one of the four transferred from 801 to 802 before we got to Korea and he'd bought himself a very expensive camera in Japan. It was beautifully stitched and he was very proud of it. After several days off in Japan, *Ocean* was again back in Korean waters to start a new patrol and on 9 August McKeown was flying the first armed reconnaissance sortie of the day carrying 500lb bombs.

"Jenne wanted to take photographs but he didn't want to take his camera in case he was shot down. The very last day he took his camera. As he went off the catapult he had engine failure or something and he ditched. He was in the water, holding his camera high above his head. And it had gone into the water and instead of being this beautifully stitched camera case it was all stuck together and peeled off. He was very upset about that."

The same day, on a strike on an electrical sub-station at Namchonjom, McKeown's Fury shuddered from a hit by flak. Flames licked around the shell opening in the port main plane as fire began spreading from the fuel tanks. Immediately, McKeown jettisoned both the fuel tanks hoping the flames would go out. He felt the sensitive aircraft buffet slightly as the tanks fell away. Dropping the aircraft into a sideslip to fan out the flames, he looked out the canopy to port and relief swept through him. The flames had gone out. Turning the Fury, he headed back towards the ship when the controls became sluggish and heavy and he realized the flak must have ruptured the hydraulic lines for all hydraulic pressure was gone. Determined not to ditch in the sea he nursed the aircraft back towards *Ocean* and made an emergency landing on the carrier. The same day other aircraft from the carrier engaged Migs.[10]

For the next few days, flying was routine, as the flight carried out a number of CAS and CAP sorties. On 16 August 1952, the new CO for 802 Squadron, Lieutenant Commander P. London, took over the squadron and assumed the position of leader of McKeown's flight.

HMS *Ocean*'s seventh patrol began on 26 August 1952, when she arrived with the usual destroyer screen off Korea's western coast with excellent weather for the first six days of flying. Right up to September it was all pretty routine. The Migs were back up fighting with the Sabres, whilst the Furies were concentrating on knocking down bridges, strafing villages, buildings, roads and railways.

On 28 August, McKeown's flight, led by the new CO, London, attacked a railway bridge near Chaeryong. Watching the first two Furies peel off into their dives and drop their bombs, McKeown rolled his Fury after them. His sights filled rapidly as the ground rushed up to meet him. At 1,500 feet he pulled the stick back, released his bombs and rocketed quickly away, climbing hard. The bombs struck the bridge, destroying it.

September began with strikes on gun positions at Hosa Dong, but one

---

[10] These are detailed in Chapters Eight and Fourteen.

incident on 2 September gave McKeown some cause for concern. While he was flying on a strike with 1,000lb bombs one of the bombs failed to release so he had to do a quick landing at the airfield at Suwon that was held at the time by the Americans. "They tugged and worked at the weapon and managed to get it free of the aircraft," he told me.

The rest of the Furies were busy destroying bridges. In fact, three were destroyed between Simak and Haeju in one mission. The next two days saw Typhoon Mary sweep through the region, creating high swells and rough seas and forcing all flying to be cancelled. The wind buffeted the aircraft on the flight deck, as the ship rolled desperately trying to miss the main part of the storm by steaming north.

By evening, they were so far north they could see the Chinese province of Shantung and the worst of the storm had missed HMS *Ocean*. During the night, the carrier steamed quietly back to her normal operating area in the Yellow Sea off the western coast of Korea. The next day was the last of the patrol and by then McKeown had flown ninety-five offensive sorties and twenty-nine defensive sorties.

Ten days later the ship began its eighth patrol. Flying began on 14 September, when McKeown's flight was on armed reconnaissance. That day he flew three sorties and on the last one, with Nick Cook as his wingman, they attacked a bridge at Sinchon. Bombs from Cook's aircraft hit the target, smashing the spars and blasting the structure to bits. "Scratch one bridge," recalled McKeown.

Bridges were now being destroyed faster than the communists could rebuild them, and several lay in ruins in the western part of Korea, direct results of the furious attacks by Furies and Fireflies. It didn't seem to matter. The communists often floated bridges under the water to be surfaced at night.

More and different targets were needed, so 16 September was a day of search and reconnaissance. By the day's end, three sluice gates had been identified in the mouths of rivers in the Haeju and Yonan. Whether they were for keeping fresh water for adjacent rice paddies or for keeping seawater from getting to the rice paddies didn't really matter. Increasing the number of targets was part of the UN's programme of putting real pressure on the North Koreans to start negotiating at the peace talks in good faith, rather than adopting the delaying tactics they'd been using up to that point. Simply put, rice was a staple diet not just for peasants but also for the North Korean Army, so flooding the rice fields could hasten the end of the war by denying the enemy food and fresh water.

The following day the Furies devoted almost the entire day to attacking these sluice gates. They roared off the deck one by one, some carrying 500lb bombs, but others like McKeown with 1,000 pounders. The angle of attack was 20 degrees along the line of the sluice gates where the hydrodynamic force of the bombs would breach the wall. Led in by Lieutenant Commander London, McKeown followed his leader down, rolling into the dive, ready to drop his bombs. Tracer from small arms fire whipped past the aircraft. He had to keep it steady and get as close as he could. Ahead, he could see some of the bombs skipping and missing the wall, while others were just breaking up on impact.

Each of the bombs had 30-second delay fuses so it needed to be done correctly. A few moments later he was over the first sluice gate and quickly released his bombs. One by one they fell but as he climbed away he couldn't see if they'd landed properly or skipped away. In fact, fifty per cent of the bombs skipped along the water, while another twenty per cent simply broke up, but during the morning missions two out of the three dams were breached. Eventually, during the afternoon's strikes, the third dam was breached.

The next day, McKeown's flight attacked and destroyed two lorries, seven oxcarts and one transformer station. During the afternoon's sortie McKeown successfully knocked down another bridge.

There was some feverish activity on 21/22 September, with the Furies hammering four loaded barges and raking them with cannon fire; they came in low, their guns blazing, then quickly whipped up into the sky and away too fast for ground gunners to get a fix. Then using the remaining 500lb bombs the Furies turned on Hanchon, damaging the bridge near the village before wheeling away back to the ship.

On the afternoon of 22 September, the Furies one by one catapulted off HMS *Ocean*'s deck, on a strike and photographic mission. McKeown's flight, led by the CO, rolled into a steep dive, with each aircraft levelling out at 1,500 feet before dropping its bombs on the target. As McKeown climbed rapidly away he glanced over his shoulder through the Fury's bubble canopy at the bridge below. It lay in ruins, a useless wreck. Grinning, he knew the communists would take some time rebuilding it.

The next day, in a pre-dawn raid McKeown's flight attacked three lorries and four oxcarts, destroying them with cannon fire and bombs. The lorries exploded, knocked on to their sides from the bomb blasts, while cannon shells ripped into their fuel tanks setting the vehicles on fire.

Ocean's ninth patrol began on 4 October 1952 and McKeown again climbed steadily away from the ship to form up with the rest of his flight. On the first sortie of the day, the CO, Commander London, was hit by flak but landed back on the ship safely. The next sortie that day they bombed and strafed 37mm AA guns in support of the Commonwealth forces and ran into a storm of flak but managed to get back to the ship relatively unscathed.

Two days later, the day on which the Chinese and North Koreans launched a new and heavy offensive, the Furies caught a train out in the open near Pyongyang on a pre-dawn armed reconnaissance led by McKeown. Dropping low into a strafing run, he went in first expecting to be greeted by a storm of flak. The gunners below must have been surprised because the fire wasn't as bad as it could have been. But he knew by the time his Fury had gone overhead that the gunners below would be awake and very angry.

McKeown flicked the firing button on the control column, keeping the locomotive in his sights as his speed increased. He watched his height, then pressed the button as the locomotive loomed ahead of him. Immediately the Fury's four cannons spat out their shells, ripping into the locomotive and stopping it dead on the tracks. Quickly he pulled out of his dive, climbed away and circled watching the other Furies attack.

Machine-gun fire from the ground reached up as the Furies came in and

Nick Cook was hit in the wing and fuselage. However, they all made it back to the ship without incident. Later that day, in the last sortie, McKeown's bombs destroyed another bridge, this time at Sinchon.

Over the next two days the Furies attacked several sampans, a stores dump and oxcarts while, in a sortie on 13 October, McKeown's 500lb bombs struck home on a bridge near Sariwon in a combined strike. By this time he had flown 170 operational sorties, 133 of which were offensive and thirty-seven defensive.

After ten days' rest, HMS *Ocean* was back for her tenth patrol and on 26 October McKeown's flight carried out an armed recce with 500lb bombs knocking down a bridge at Sokkyo-ri. On 27 October he acted as the link for a rescue mission over Lieutenant 'Pug' Mather who had been shot down at Kungsan-ni by flak:

"Pug joined us about halfway through the tour straight out of flying training. New pilots would join us halfway through the tour and replacement pilots would join through the whole thing. Pilots would do three months in one carrier then transfer to the replacement carrier and do another three months. When we arrived in Hong Kong at the beginning of our tour we took on about a dozen pilots from HMS *Glory*. Likewise when we got back from the end of our tour some pilots were transferred to HMS *Glory* and Pug was one of those. When Pug joined us he was given to me to introduce to operational flying. He did fine but he tended to fly too close to me. Most flak falls behind you so most of your damage is in the tail end of the aircraft because of the deflection.

"I explained to Pug that when we were flying battle formation he should stay a hundred yards or so behind me to protect my tail and not get too close. They shoot the leader and if they miss the bullets tend to fall astern and you don't want to be in that area."

After a few sorties McKeown could see the new pilot was still flying too close to him, so once on the ship after the flight he explained the procedure again. "Stay with your leader and just don't get too close." But he remained too close and was shot down and landed in the sea. He was picked up by helicopter and brought back to *Ocean* where he resumed flying for the rest of the patrol. When the ship returned to Hong Kong on its way home, Lieutenant Mather was one of those transferred to HMS *Glory* to continue the rest of his tour. "But he was shot down again," McKeown told me. "Only this time the target was well inland and the Chinese got to him before the American rescue helicopters could. I think he was a headache to the Chinese because he was mentioned in despatches due to his conduct as a prisoner."[11] McKeown is certain that Mather ran into a hail of bullets because he was still flying too close.

The last two days of October were busy for McKeown as he flew several missions in support of a guerrilla landing and the Commonwealth Division. One of the sorties on 30 October 1952 included the destruction of a railway bridge shared between McKeown and Nick Cook. The total of operational sorties stood at 178 at the end of Paddy McKeown's war.

---

[11] Detail of Mather's capture and treatment can be found in an appendix to this book.

Chapter Seven

HMS *OCEAN* AND COOK'S WAR

Sub-Lieutenant Nick Cook

Nick Cook flew alongside Lieutenant Paddy McKeown from May 1952 to October the same year, and gave me a fascinating account of life onboard HMS *Ocean*. "There were about 100 maintenance ratings on each squadron and by the end of 802 Squadron's stay in Korea there were twenty pilots," he told me. "That was an enormous strength. The air handlers, the chief petty officers, and the engine men generally did their apprenticeship at RAF Halton. They were unbelievably skilled so the serviceability was fantastic. There would be the engine man and the airframe man and one of them would be the chief of the squadron reporting directly to the air engineer officer."

Cook had joined the Navy as a National Service pilot and was one of the few in Korea: "I'd done eighteen months as a rating packing parachutes and after that I was selected to be commissioned as an ordinary seaman officer.

"I didn't know quite what to do. My brother had been in the RAF and my sister had been a Wren officer during the war, attached to the Fleet Air Arm. When I joined for my National Service, I had to go along and register. The man asked me if I had a preference and I said I wanted to go in the Navy, purely because my sister had been in the Wrens. He said they don't take anybody. When the call-up papers arrived, they happened to be the Navy. Changed my entire life."

Halfway through his training course on a training ship in Portland Harbour the Navy realized they needed more aircrew. "They re-opened the pipeline that they ran in the war so I volunteered for a two-year course learning to fly," Cook recalled. The course consisted of three months pre-flight training, then twelve months flying training at a RAF station. "The RAF always trained naval pilots up to wing standard, flying training command." For the first six months Cook did his flying training in a primary trainer, the Percival Prentice, which replaced the Tiger Moth biplane trainer used throughout the Second World War. "Bloody awful aeroplane," Cook remembered.

For the second half of the training period he moved up to the North American Harvard trainer. Thousands of these venerable aircraft were built and used during the Second World War, mostly in Canada and America. After that he went back to the Navy for the first part of operational flying school, which lasted three months, then did another three months for the second part at

Lossiemouth, flying Seafires. "You did mostly flight drills and learned to fly in formation. Then in those days one went to Culdrose in Cornwall where the fighter pilots did Operational Flying School Two, which was weapons training culminating in deck landings on the Sea Fury.

"There are several watersheds in flying, I think. The first one is the first solo in the Seafire because it really was unforgettable. You had a tiny bit of dual in a Firefly trainer but nothing prepared you for the Seafire. It was absolutely extraordinary. The Harvard was noisy but the Seafire was much rougher. You got all the heat from the exhaust stubs that came into the cockpit. The power of the Seafire with the 39 litre Griffon engine was extraordinary."

The first solo in a Sea Fury for the young pilots was a different experience again from flying the Seafire. The Fury was a larger aircraft to start with and had much greater visibility for the pilot. "The engine was much quieter, like a sewing machine," recalled Cook during our interview. "It was very sensitive after the Seafire because the stick was so light and marvellously harmonized, like driving a car with power steering when you'd been used to a manual car."

The last part of the training was on Sea Furies practising deck landing after deck landing. "Of course the first deck landing really is the watershed of all. You depended a lot on the training batsman. There were guys who were really good at taking people to the deck and there were guys who weren't. Luckily we had a fantastic fellow who was unflappable. If you got on the deck the first time he climbed up on the wing and spoke to you. Then they pushed the aircraft back; you took off and did four more immediately, which is rather like an actor going off on the first night. Then you had lunch and then you did sixteen deck landings on the carrier during the training period and that was it. This was on a carrier steaming off the Channel."

Before the days of jets and tricycle undercarriage, landing on an aircraft carrier flying with a piston-engined aircraft took great skill. "You couldn't see the deck because of the nose," said Cook, describing the procedure. "The batsman got you in the correct position and you just cut the engine and pulled back on the stick. You knew you were over the flight deck at the right speed. Then the wire would catch. There would be a drop. You'd stalled and caught the wire all in a second. But you didn't see anything except the mast. You were looking at the batsman who gave you the cut and went past and you instinctively picked up the horizon, which was out either side and then you just eased back on the stick. If you didn't get the stick back, the main wheels would hit first and the aircraft would bounce and the hook wouldn't catch. You'd go straight into the barrier."

Parked beyond the barrier were aircraft readying for take-off, waiting for all the pilots to finish landing. "If you went into the barrier the main wheel would catch first and you'd flip over," Cook recalled.

After his National Service in 1951 he rejoined the Navy as a volunteer. "I was then just a sub-lieutenant RNVR. All the chaps I trained with were going off and joining front line squadrons. So I volunteered to rejoin on the condition I could join 802, which I did in January 1952 and went to the Far East. I did the whole year with 802 Squadron and came back at the end of 1952. 802 Squadron re-mustered in 1953 and I did another year with them in the Med, still on Furies.

"In the middle of '52 three guys who had been flying in the reserve arrived. In those days the reserves used to fly on the weekends both in the RAF and the Navy. Three guys volunteered to come out and were thrown into the deep end flying with us young guys who were absolutely sharp as hell and they had to pick up deck landings, do everything, catapult, rocket-assisted take-off and dropping bombs. I forget how many sorties they did but they never got much credit for it. Today it would be an absolute federal case."

Cook's first commanding officer on HMS *Ocean* in 1952 was Lieutenant Commander Fraser Shotton. After Shotton's stint as his flight commander, a new CO of 802 Squadron arrived in the form of Lieutenant Commander Donald Dick. "He was killed in the middle of the Korean campaign," Cook recalled. "I was his No. 2 that day and Paddy was the section leader, the No. 3. The CO Lieutenant Commander Dick would call a battle formation when we went into our dives which had been developed at the end of the Second World War."

The Chinnampo–Haeju area was the main operating zone for the British carriers at that time. "Our missions were to fly up the Chinnampo estuary where we attacked bridges and railway lines time and time again. The idea was to stop the movement of goods down the coast. You couldn't deck-land at night. We started doing pre-dawn take-offs in the dark, forming up in the dark, and attacking when dawn broke and you'd catch a lot of stuff that way."

Trains, oxcarts and lorries were just a few of the many targets the Furies would surprise on their dawn raids. "They used to put the trains in the tunnels during the day and bring them out at night so you'd catch them just before dawn. You'd catch oxcarts on the move and lorries too. You'd swoop in on these wonderful summer mornings. Unbelievable."

At the time, North Korea was a primitive place by western standards. At least, that's the way it appeared from the air. The North Koreans were excellent at hiding what limited assets they had. The railway, for example, had been built by the Japanese and was mercilessly bombed by the British and Americans. But, just as quickly as the railway lines were cut, they were operating again the next day. "When they say you knocked down several bridges it was probably the same one because the enemy rebuilt them overnight. Then when they couldn't get across, they'd push a wagon up to the bridge, try to transfer the goods on foot and put a wagon on the other side of the bridge."

Cook pointed out that the rivers weren't very deep which made the repairs to bridges and crossing much easier for the North Koreans. Standard dive-bombing for the Furies was at a 45-degree angle making the procedure very accurate. "You've only got to look at the Stukas in the Second World War," Cook said. "Dive-bombing accounted for 150 Royal Navy ships in the Mediterranean and swung the battle of the Midway."

In early July, Sub-Lieutenant Nick Cook had his first really frightening moment. "We did this strike on Pyongyang, the headquarters of North Korea, the capital city. Everybody went.[1] The flight took one hour and forty minutes. The Americans sent a mass of Corsairs, Panthers and Sabres. The flak was very intense, persistent and very accurate. There were all these stores there at the marshalling yard. When we dived it was bloody hairy."

Cook was beside and slightly behind section leader Lieutenant Paddy McKeown as they dropped into their dives on the railway yard. Black puffs of accurate and withering flak exploded all around the aircraft as they screamed down on the targets.

Suddenly, a flak burst went off between the two aircraft. "It was so unexpected. They had proximity fuses and these black puffs, like the movies, were following you down. It was so unnerving. You could see it, unlike the small arms fire. I was looking across at Paddy following him down and this thing went off right between us. We just looked at each other."

Cook remembers the attack of 14 September on the railway bridge at Suichon, when he was flying as Paddy McKeown's wingman. Rolling into his dive he saw the bridge loom rapidly in his gun sight. Levelling out, Cook dropped his bombs and climbed quickly away, He saw smoke, debris and dust flying in all directions as his bombs found their mark and the bridge was destroyed. Over the R/T he heard Paddy McKeown's comment: "Scratch one bridge." The flight formed up and headed back to the ship as the sun was dropping low on the horizon.

One of Cook's lasting memories of Korea was the first sight of the Mig 15 by his flight on 27 July. He was nearly shot down when the three Migs came swooping down on the Furies. Paddy McKeown had just gone into his diving run on a bridge when the enemy jets shot past.

Cook called quickly over the radio, "Migs, Migs," and then yanked hard on the stick and rapidly turned the Fury. The jets were already shooting away into the distance as they made their pass. But it was enough. "My wing caught fire," Cook said. As the flames licked across it he jettisoned the hood ready to bail out. The wind whistled all around him. He pushed the stick forward, into a dive, heading back towards the ship. Looking over at the wing, he saw to his surprise that the flames had gone out. Presumably fanned by the wind as it whipped over the wings.

With no hood, and the sea air blown back into his face from the propeller wash, he did an emergency landing on HMS *Ocean*'s deck. Satisfied the fire was out, the emergency crews managed to quickly get the aircraft parked beyond the barrier to begin repairs later on.

In the middle of July 1952, the Furies of 802 Squadron had begun flying with two 1,000lb bombs, one under each wing. "We did several details with these things," Cook recalled. "You drop one of those and they could do a lot of damage. We started doing 1,000lb details off the rocket booster because we were flying them over the maximum all-up weight of the airplane. You couldn't

---

[1] Cook recalls that the Americans sent 1,000 aircraft to Pyongyang over the course of a day while British naval fighters attacked twice on the same day, 11 July 1952. The heaviest raid on Pyongyang was on 29 August, however.

catapult with 1,000lb bombs and full internal cannon ammunition."

According to Cook, they originally began flying with the bigger bombs using the catapult, but it very quickly became apparent that some of the main spars were twisting. Afterwards take-offs with 1,000lb bombs were always by RATOG. "It's interesting," recalled Cook, "because when we started doing RATOG the first was done by the CO, Fraser Shotton, who'd been a squadron commander since 1942. Although he was only thirty-three we called him God. When Donald Dick was killed after taking the squadron over in 1952 it upset Fraser terribly."

Like Paddy McKeown, Nick Cook has never forgotten that dramatic first take-off. Cook was airborne at around 5,000 feet when Shotton demonstrated how to take off using the RATOG equipment. Over the radio he could hear the chatter between the ship and the pilot as Shotton did his last checks then pushed the throttle forward. High above, Cook watched the CO roll down the deck. He waited for the rocket boosters to go off but nothing happened. Instead Cook saw the CO's aircraft go off the front of the ship. "He managed to accelerate the aircraft very slowly, so much so that there was spray coming from the tail plane area from the propeller wash," Cook said. "He dropped the rockets and gradually got flying speed riding the cushion above the water and got away with it."

Over the radio, Cook heard the captain say to Shotton. "Well done, you did it the hard way." Shotton radioed back that he'd forgotten to throw the master switch. "He didn't blame anybody else," Cook said to me. "That was the CO showing us all the way and nearly bloody well killed himself. Then there was the time the three volunteers arrived from England and the captain said to one of them, Nobby Clarke, 'You've done RATOG before, haven't you, Clarke?' He said, 'Oh yes, sir.'

"For RATOG, you started up, you went along the flight deck literally only 80 feet and there was a man there holding a flag. Very primitive. When you passed him you fired the RATOG button. Well Clarke fired the button, and had full power on with the tail up but didn't hold the stick forward enough. The aircraft went into the vertical and went right over the top of the island with the engine still flat out and went vertically into the water.

"He was under the water for a full minute and a half, right aft, with a helicopter waiting and he bobbed up, very badly bruised. Amazing that he got away with it. He completely lost control and the rockets took him straight up. Of course he had two 1,000lb bombs on."

The first successful raid using the 1,000lb bombs came late in July when Cook's flight attacked a road bridge. Watching McKeown's Fury go in after the CO had pulled out, Cook quickly checked his instruments and rolled into his dive on the structure below. Reaching the right release height he quickly yanked the stick back and hit the bomb release button as the Fury started levelling out. Small arms fire from troops on the ground whistled around his aircraft as he pulled it into a steep climb. Below, both his bombs had hit the structure, smashing two spars and shattering the bridge.

On one occasion Cook remembers being hit by 20mm flak in the tail plane while covering a photographic run by Paddy McKeown. Calling McKeown on the radio, Cook told his section leader he'd been hit. Immediately, McKeown throttled back and dropped in beside Cook, examining the Fury for damage. The smooth delicate controls had become rough and sluggish from the hit. McKeown saw the hole in Cook's tail plane and immediately radioed for him to return to the ship. Gingerly, Cook turned the aircraft back towards the coast, and then heading out to sea, he nursed the Fury home. "I managed to land safely on," Nick recalled.

His most alarming incident was during one sortie when a shell from small arms fire shot right across the back of his shoulders when it hit the hood rail. His concentration was shattered by a sudden bang as the shell ripped across the Fury, hitting the rail and smashing a hole in the canopy behind him. "It just went straight through across the back of my shoulders. The other close call I had was in the elevators. It went through the crease where the elevator was and if it had hit the stanchion the tail plane would have come off."

Pulling out of a dive was the most vulnerable time for the Furies when the belly of the aircraft was exposed to enemy gunners. They made the most of those few seconds when the fighters were vulnerable. "One bullet went through the starboard wing and came out through the roundel," Cook exclaimed. "All the metal just mushroomed up."

The one aspect that sets naval flying apart from any other is the deck landing at the end of every sortie. The challenge is always there at the end of a flight no matter what has taken place. "You've always got to get the thing back onboard," Cook said. "The great moment in the Navy was the initial deck landing. The approach speed was quite fast, 92 knots, which is about 105 miles an hour. You did it instinctively but you could never take a liberty with it."

The flight decks on the British light carriers of the day were small by comparison to their American counterparts so trusting the batsman implicitly became something every Royal Navy pilot had to do to get down in one piece. "In a rough sea it was quite hairy. Lots of guys didn't make it or they had a terrible pile-up and didn't do it again. The guy was either taken off flying or given the chance to be an observer."

Bad accidents on deck landing can destroy a pilot's confidence very easily. As an example, Cook talked about another fellow pilot Lieutenant Graham 'Oggie' Swanson: "He had to force-land during his operational flying school training. The aircraft went through about four Cornish stone walls and all he was left in was his seat. How he got away with it I don't know."

Cook remembers how one of Swanson's deck landings ended in near disaster. "He got over to the left and tore the hook out and went straight into the barrier and somersaulted over it." Swanson was shot down twice in Korea but he managed to survive both of them. "He was a remarkably robust guy," Cook said. "The first time he was shot down he managed to make one of the friendly islands and the second time he was badly burnt and picked up by an American helicopter."[2] He remembers flying with Swanson when he couldn't clear a

---

[2] A fuller account of this appears in Chapter Eight.

1,000lb bomb on the right side of the Fury. The bomb on the left side had been dropped but the right one was hung up. "You couldn't get back on board because of the terrific weight," Cook said.

Slipping in underneath and beside Swanson's Fury Cook gently tried to nudge the other aircraft's wingtip in the hope it would dislodge the bomb, but the interference from the slipstream over the upper wing was too dangerous. "In the end we went to Kimpo airfield. It was one of the big American airfields full of Sabres and Thunderjets where the runway was so wide you could probably land across it.

"When we landed all the Americans turned out to photograph us. As we went down the runway there were about a thousand guys standing on these bunkers and dunes taking pictures. Of course when we stopped and switched off the engines they all came across to look at the mighty Fury. They were looking at it and the pilots wanted to get in and sit in it. They thought it was the ultimate. It looked so good."

For Nick Cook there was nothing like the Sea Fury. Flying that aircraft was wonderful: "It was such a remarkable aircraft, the Fury, it was the ultimate piston-engined aircraft. You were so at home you could do anything with the aircraft. It was extraordinary. You didn't have to think, you were so instinctively involved. Flying with these great guys you knew what your section guy was going to do." Often Fury pilots would drop down to wave-top height as they roared down the coast sweeping in low strafing runs on targets or just having fun on the way back to the ship. "Doing a few aerobatics on the way back you just didn't realize how lucky you were to have that amazing aeroplane. The Fury took roughly twenty seconds on full throttle on take-off before getting up to a cruising speed of nearly 400 miles an hour," recalled Cook.

In ten patrols he flew 360 hours in eighty days. "One got very tired," he explained. "You didn't realize how tired you were. I had sixty-two deck landings before starting in Korea and 257 when I left." Looking back, Cook described his time flying and fighting in Korea as great fun. "We took it all for granted and didn't think. The comradeship is unbelievable and I still see nearly all of them from time to time. Even Oggie Swanson said that was the absolute period of his life. He said that being in 802 Squadron was like music, that you couldn't fake it. If you're the third violin and you're not up to it the other guys know."

Life aboard the carriers in the 1950s was sparse and uncomfortable. "At night you just had dinner and a couple of drinks," Cook said. "The fifth day was replenishment day when an oiler would come alongside and there would be no flying. So the fourth night was a real piss-up everybody got drunk. Then you had the next to saunter about the flight deck.

"The junior officers lived in a dormitory called the Kasbah, which was pretty squalid I can tell you. I was just an ordinary sub-lieutenant in a dormitory. Young lieutenants shared a cabin, a two-berther. It was pretty grim. None of those ships were air-conditioned. The humidity below decks was bad. You just slept. When you're young you can do anything. You spent as little time as possible below decks."

British carriers rotated with American carriers off the west coast. In HMS

Ocean's case she was relieved by USS *Sicily*, an USMC carrier, which flew Corsair piston-engined fighters. Life in Japan during the eight day break for aircrew was spent lounging around in the officers' club in either Sasebo or Kure. "The officers' club was very well run while the food on the ship was terrible," Cook remembered. "We were just having a good time, shopping, going around and up country. A lot of guys whooped it up more than I did. A lot did the town in Japan, which was easy to do because it was dirt cheap. It was martial law, you couldn't wear civilian clothes ashore, you had to wear uniform always. There were servicemen everywhere, jeeps, and American army. They were pouring money into the place. They were building ships in Kure. You could buy a set of china for two pounds but most people bought cameras."

Despite the life away from the fighting, HMS *Ocean*'s pilots and crew were always aware of the war. Many times, when the ship turned back towards Japan she would be missing aircrew that had been lost somewhere over Korea. Many pilots ditched and were rescued by helicopter but several never returned. "Ken Macdonald was killed on his first day in Korea, a young engineer pilot shot down," Cook said. "We lost five aircraft in five days. Chico, the Firefly CO, lost coolant and had to ditch. Tim Williamson-Napier, senior Firefly pilot, was shot down over the front line and killed. His observer screamed all the way down to the ground. Williamson-Napier's replacement, Bob Hunter, was eaten by sharks after having to ditch and Harry Hawksworth took his place."

The list goes on. Ten per cent of the Royal Navy's Fleet Air Arm aircrew lost their lives during the Korean War. Thirty-three young men never returned from it: "In the first sixteen days in operation in Korea the ship lost an aircraft a day. Fuel trouble, shot down with oil leaks and things like that. Charles Evans, the captain was hauled over the coals but he didn't take any notice. There wasn't a pilot lost every day because people were picked up and so on." The Fireflies had the higher death toll because they generally flew with an observer, which seemed unnecessary. "It was absolutely absurd," Cook said with disgust. "They just don't think laterally."

In Korea the Australians lost more pilots than the Fleet Air Arm did, as Cook explained: "77 Squadron was equipped with Mustangs and they re-equipped with Meteors which was the worst day's work anybody ever did. They lost the CO and flight commander while flying from Kure to Japan. They obviously collided in cloud. The Meteor began to be used for ground attack but it was paved with tragedy. The Meteor was a good aircraft but it was slow."

After Korea Cook stayed in the Navy up until 1956 when he left to become a pilot for BOAC: "Most squadrons were disbanded after coming back from Korea and reformed after a rest. I was reformed with 802 with a different commanding officer. I did the whole of '53 in the Mediterranean fleet in [HMS *Ocean*'s] sister ship HMS *Theseus*, still flying Furies. There was no fighting, it was just great fun."

Nick Cook has fond memories of his days flying over Korea. The friends he made during those tense, exciting and hectic days have stayed with him for life – as have the memories of the friends he lost in that far away war.

Although he describes the war he fought against the North Koreans dive-bombing targets in the superlative Sea Fury as 'fun', in reality of course it was full of danger and tension. Aircrews were always reminded of how close death was to them by the number of empty spaces at mealtimes. Perhaps, looking on it as fun was the main way for them to get past the loss of friends and colleagues, as well as forgetting the tragedy of civilians killed during the war.

Chapter Eight

WHEN THE MIGS CAME OUT TO PLAY

Lieutenant Peter Carmichael, HMS *Ocean*

No book about the air war in Korea would be complete without an account of a Mig getting shot down by Sea Furies. It makes an interesting story, as a Sea Fury is a piston-engined fighter and a Mig is a jet. It shouldn't happen. The jet, being much faster, should easily outrun the British fighter and shoot it down. The only defence Sea Furies really had against Migs was to go into a series of tight turns because the jets could not turn as tightly.

Nevertheless, on one occasion during the war a Sea Fury succeeded in shooting down a jet. The man credited with that amazing feat is Lieutenant Peter 'Hoagy' Carmichael who, like Paddy McKeown and Nick Cook, was flying Sea Furies onboard HMS *Ocean*. He was in a different flight to McKeown and Cook however.

Lieutenant Carmichael was no stranger to operational flying as he had joined the Royal Navy in January 1942 as a naval airman. Unlike many of the other pilots in this book who did their training in the UK and worked up in the Mediterranean, he went to Pensacola in the US for his flying training. In 1944 he was flying Seafires from Atheling in the Bay of Bengal with 809 Squadron. Later that year, during the final stages of the Second World War, he traded in the Seafire for the big radial-engined American fighter-bomber (the Chance Vought Corsair), flying with 834 Naval Air Squadron from HMS *Victorious*. Over the next four months, from October 1944 to January 1945, Carmichael's Corsairs swept in from the sea targeting oil fields in Sumatra, and later, as the war came to a close, pummelling Japanese airfields near Okinawa.

When the Second World War ended, Lieutenant Carmichael flew several different aircraft, the Blackburn Firebrand from the carrier HMS *Impeccable*, Sea Furies from HMS *Theseus* and Barracudas from St Merryn in Cornwall. By April 1952 he had joined HMS *Ocean* and found himself attacking Malayan bandits before the ship sailed to Korea. *Ocean*'s second patrol in Korea began on 29 May, when she arrived back off the western coast. This patrol was to last until 6 June and would prove to be an eventful one.

On 1 June, the Furies and Fireflies flew in support of Operation Billhook, covering the landing of South Korean guerrillas from junks at Ponghwai in the Han River. The guerrillas were going in to harass the North Korean army and gather valuable information, as well as supporting UN guerrillas working in the area.

Unfortunately, the wind was against the junks and the enemy was able to mount a strong opposition on the ground making the operation unsuccessful. Attacking the enemy from the air, the Furies and Fireflies hit villages, troop bunkers and trench systems to neutralize their effectiveness. In the afternoon, the aircraft flew back over the beaches to harass the North Koreans as the guerrillas withdrew.

Coming off these strikes, Lieutenant Carmichael made a routine landing. As his engine shut down, however, he was horrified to see another Fury taxiing towards him. Sub-Lieutenant Haines had landed just behind Carmichael and was now headed directly for his aircraft. Carmichael jumped to safety as the propeller from Haines's Fury bit into the rear of Carmichael's aircraft.

Handlers, aircrew and engineers dived in all directions to escape the mayhem. As the propeller blades ripped into Carmichael's aircraft the rear fuselage broke away. "Haines took my tail off," wrote Carmichael in his logbook.[1] From the deck, Haines's white face could be seen in the cockpit of his Fury, as the aircraft ploughed into Carmichael's, destroying it.

On 3 June, Carmichael's flight of Furies flew two armed reconnaissance missions each carrying 1,000lb bombs. Both sorties during the day were against bridges, with mixed results. This was the same day that Sub-Lieutenant Oggie Swanson was shot down in flames for the second time. Lieutenant Hallam radioed in that Swanson had been hit by flak. The Furies had been attacking a gun position and Swanson, flying close behind his leader, flew into a hail of shells from the gunners below. At 1,500 feet, Swanson levelled off when the aircraft was hit. Fire swept through the aircraft from stem to stern, as Swanson fought for height. Flames licked around the cockpit as he struggled to keep the aircraft level and jettison the hood. An almighty crash ripped through the aircraft as the tail plane fell off. Immediately, the Fury went into an uncontrollable spin. Swanson had seconds to get out, or he would surely perish.

Above, Hallam watched the burning aircraft spin towards the sea. Suddenly, the canopy flew away as Swanson jumped free of the aircraft. The fireball spun into the sea, breaking into pieces then disappearing below the waves. Pain must have been racking Swanson's body from the burns he'd sustained trying to get out of the doomed machine, as he clung to the parachute. Seconds later he was in the freezing sea.

Circling in his Fury above Swanson, Hallam saw his wingman drop into the water near the enemy-held island of Chongyang-do. Almost at once, fire from the island was directed onto the unfortunate pilot. Touching his rudder pedals, Hallam put the Fury into a dive, spraying the enemy troops on the island with cannon fire as he waited for the helicopter to arrive.[2]

"He was very badly burnt," Nick Cook told me. "His parachute opened after the aircraft hit the water. He landed in the sea, not knowing where he was but he could touch the bottom. The enemy came to the shore and started machine-gunning him." Minutes later, Hallam's Fury was joined by four USMC Corsairs, which kept the enemy gunners at bay while an American helicopter

---

[1] This is well documented in *With the Carriers in Korea.*
[2] See *With the Carriers in Korea.*

fished Swanson out of the water and took him to USS *John A. Bowle*.

For the next two days Carmichael and the rest of the Furies flew armed reconnaissance while Fireflies rocketed and strafed targets with great success. Carmichael averaged two sorties a day, mostly bombing bridges. On the first sortie of 5 June, he was hit by flak after dropping his 1,000lb bombs on a bridge. The aircraft bucked as each of the bombs left the moorings under the wings. Levelling out of a dive at 1,500 feet was the point when the aircraft was most vulnerable. Small arms flak peppered Carmichael's aircraft.

As he climbed rapidly away, the aircraft seemed sluggish, and the controls a little heavier than usual. He headed back to the ship and managed to land without incident, however. A few hours later with the damage from the flak repaired, Carmichael's flight was again in the air bombing bridges and shooting up villages.

Carmichael flew three sorties that day, helping to destroy part of a bridge north of Chinnampo. Over the course of the patrol the Furies destroyed nine bridges.[3] The Fireflies rocketed and strafed several ammunition dumps, troop concentrations, a brigade headquarters, and a telephone exchange, which erupted into a massive blue flame shooting into the air. Junks, sampans and oxcarts were strafed with great success.

Operations for the third patrol began on 16 June 1952, with the Furies flying reconnaissance of roads, rivers, military installations and railways. The Fireflies rocketed several buildings including an oil storage area and a vehicle repair installation near Chaeryong. Carmichael's flight strafed villages and a sampan and bombed a bridge on the third sortie during the afternoon. The next day, Carmichael led his flight towards two gun emplacements on the north bank of the Taedong estuary. Boring in on the target at 4,000 feet, Carmichael led with Sub-Lieutenants Haines and Ellis in formation with him. The Furies swept over the land, turning as they headed towards the target. Quickly checking his instruments and making final adjustments on the rudder, Carmichael peeled off into a dive with his flight behind him. One by one, they dropped their bombs, destroying the guns.

The next major milestone for Carmichael came on 22 June when he spotted more than 400 troops concentrated in some woods. Pushing the Fury into a dive, he radioed his flight. Belching fire, his four cannons poured shells into the area as he shot in low over the troops. Bullets from the ground came rapidly up as the soldiers returned fire but the Furies were too fast.

As he climbed away with the rest of his flight he called the ship, requesting a strike on the troops. Quickly changing its tactics, a flight of Fireflies currently heading towards targets in the Han River area were directed to Carmichael's troop concentration. When they arrived over the area the Fireflies sent their underwing rockets straight for the troops in the woods creating so much damage that the soldiers ran in all directions.

In June 1952, the third year of the war began. By now it was static again, with the front lines well defined and unmoving. On the east and west coasts, UN naval forces used the big guns from destroyers and frigates to pound enemy

---

[3] According to Nick Cook.

positions close to the coast while the UN air forces continued to hit communist targets deep inside North Korea.

June was the month when strikes on North Korea's electrical network intensified. There were four main power grids that became fair play for the UN forces. Three, at Chosin, Fusen and Kyosen, were on the east coast and the other, the huge hydroelectric plant at Suiho was on the west coast. The east coast grid supplied power from the Soviet frontier down to Wonsan and right across the peninsula; while Suiho, at the time the fourth largest in the world, was on the north side of the Yalu River, only thirty-five miles away from 250 Migs based at Antung in Manchuria.

Destroying these plants would mean the end of North Korea's power supply as well as most of Manchuria's. It was hoped that by depriving not just the North Koreans but also the Chinese of power, progress would be made at the peace talks and the plants became prime targets.

At the beginning of July, HMS *Ocean* was back in Korean waters for its fourth patrol. Carmichael started flying on the 4th with two sorties that day. On his first, carrying his usual load of two 500lb bombs and two drop tanks, he climbed steadily away from the ship and circled as the rest of his flight formed up. Turning, they headed towards their designated target. However, weather was poor, and visibility for bombing severely restricted, so they headed for another target, north of Chinnampo. Their engines roaring, the Furies followed the railway line towards two bridges. The weather to the north had cleared, making bombing an easier prospect.

Climbing to their attack height, the Furies peeled off, Carmichael leading, and his finger touching the bomb release button. Two bombs on each aircraft rained down on the targets. All eight bombs from the four Furies hit the mark. As Carmichael pulled out of his dive after attacking the first bridge he watched the bombs smash the structure. More bombs hit the second bridge, destroying it completely. The Furies climbed quickly away, filled with satisfaction that the targets had been completely destroyed.

On their return, Carmichael's flight heard that Migs had been flying in the same area and shot down four USMC Corsairs. The next day, they bombed another bridge near Sariwon, severely damaging it. But, as it was a steel bridge, they failed to destroy it.

The next important event for Carmichael was the combined strike on Pyongyang, the capital of North Korea, on 11 July. The capital was a tempting target but it was defended by heavy flak. In this raid, aircraft of 5th USAF, TF77, 1st Marine Wing, 77 Squadron of the Royal Australian Air Force and HMS *Ocean* mounted attacks on the capital throughout the day. Coordinated by the Americans, 1,254 sorties were flown in all. Their targets were the railway marshalling yards, which were stacked with large wooden crates thought to contain aircraft parts. The Furies were to attack the north end of the railway yards because it had the most crates, all stacked tightly together. The Fireflies were to attack the south end of the target.

Led by Lieutenant Commander 'Chico' Roberts in his Firefly, a flight of seven Fireflies and twelve Furies made for the city. Just before the target, the Fireflies split away from the Furies and rolled into shallow dives, gaining speed down from their height of 12,000 feet to stay above the flak to 6,000 feet. Then they dropped into their attack dives.

Heavy flak bursts peppered the sky just below the Furies, reaching up to 9,000 feet. Carmichael watched the Fireflies peel away, braving the storm of flak as they dropped into their attack dives to rocket their end of the target. "We carried two 1,000lb bombs when we hit the Pyongyang railway," Carmichael wrote in his logbook. Below, the city was covered in a thick brown cloud of dust and smoke from secondary fires burning from earlier strikes by UN air forces.

One by one the Furies rolled into their dives, dropping in a steep angle towards the railway yards below. Carmichael's aircraft shuddered as flak burst all around him. Miraculously none of the Furies were hit. Bomb after bomb rained down on the railway yards, destroying the crates and causing widespread chaos. Even as the murderous flak kept up its barrage, the bombs came down as the Furies pounced on the target. Pulling out of his dive at 1,500 feet, Carmichael swept the railway yard with cannon fire strafing the remaining crates before climbing quickly away.

The afternoon's sortie was a repeat performance and again no Fury was hit. One Firefly got hit in the starboard nacelle tank by shrapnel, but it caused no problems for the crew. One by one, every aircraft from HMS *Ocean* landed safely, having braved probably the worst flak of the war and coming through virtually unscathed.

It was during the ship's fifth patrol that had begun on 22 July that the Migs came out to meet the Furies and Fireflies. The first day they appeared was 27 July, when not only McKeown and Cook's flight but other pilots such as Firefly pilot Lieutenant Hawksworth ran into the Russian-built jet fighters. His story is described in detail in Chapters Nine and Ten.

The same day, two Migs swept across a formation of four Furies, one mile south of Chinnampo. The jets opened fire at extreme range, their cannon shells missing the British fighters. Quickly turning from their attack, the Migs made off as the Furies opened up with their cannon also at extreme range. In a matter of seconds the exchange was over, but elsewhere, Fireflies too had engaged the enemy jets. Coming off a raid near the town of Kango, Hawksworth's No. 3 had been hit by flak and began losing coolant. The rest of the flight turned back towards the ship escorting the crippled Firefly home but when they were ten miles north of Chinnampo, the Migs struck from out of the sun. The result of the quick attacking pass of the jets was two damaged Fireflies. The Migs raced quickly away, disappearing into the low cloud without any damage to themselves. However, both the damaged Royal Navy aircraft ended up ditching west of Chodo Island. There were no more Mig encounters on that patrol.

Carmichael's Mig encounter came at the very beginning of *Ocean*'s sixth patrol, during which Furies and Fireflies flew an average of seventy-five sorties a day with over 600 sorties flown over the whole patrol. The Migs were protecting the Hanchon–Chinnampo–Pyongyang corridor so encounters were inevitable. *Ocean* arrived in Korean waters on 8 August and operational flying began the following day. Carmichael was now acting CO of 802 Squadron after the death of Lieutenant Commander R. A. Dick and the mantle of command fell on his shoulders.

Early on the morning of 9 August, the Furies rose into the dawn sky away from the carrier, heading inland. Flying armed reconnaissance duties, the Furies followed the railway line fifteen miles north of Chinnampo, checking the state of the bridges along the line when they spotted eight aircraft ahead. The aircraft were Migs and they had already spotted the British aircraft.

"Migs at four o'clock," called Sub-Lieutenant Ellis, as orange tracer shot past his aircraft. The Furies broke into battle formation, turning tightly in pairs as the Migs came straight on. Carmichael turned the formation to meet the attack and eight Migs flew straight at them. (This momentous event was recalled in Carmichael's obituary in the *Daily Telegraph* in 1997.)

The Furies were difficult targets for the Migs because they could easily out-turn the jets. Aircraft shot all over the sky. Carmichael saw one Mig streaking towards him, tracer pouring from its guns. He thumbed his firing button and the Fury's four cannons burst into life. Behind him, his wingman also fired at the jet that quickly broke away, then went head-on towards two more Furies who saw their cannon shells hit the enemy jet.

One came down behind Carmichael, its air brakes extended, intending to dogfight with the Fury. Turning tightly towards him, Carmichael got the Mig in his gyro gun sight, flicked the firing switch and pressed the button. Almost instantly his cannons erupted into a storm of bullets at the enemy jet. The Mig pilot suddenly retracted his dive brakes, accelerating quickly to get out of the hail of cannon fire. Pushing his stick forward, Carmichael followed, and with the Mig in his ring sight he pummelled the jet with cannon fire. He could see his cannon shells ripping into the wings and fuselage of the enemy machine. Suddenly it turned onto its back and crashed into the ground, bursting into flame.

Carmichael had achieved the unique distinction of being the only pilot of a piston-engined aircraft to shoot down a jet aircraft in combat. Although he got a lot of publicity, he maintained a lot of credit for the kill went to his flight, which was typical of his character.

For nearly five minutes, the Furies and Migs tangled with each other, and the Furies managed to fire several times at the jets before they broke off. Suddenly, the Migs climbed quickly away disappearing as fast as they could with one Mig destroyed and two damaged.

The next day, Carmichael's flight again ran into Migs. This time the pilots of these jets appeared to be much more skilful and attacking them proved to be difficult. Shedding their drop tanks, the Furies turned towards the enemy jets. Again, eight Migs attacked the British aircraft. Desperately, the Furies fought off the jets, trading fire with the Migs. Finally, after ten minutes the Furies managed to make cloud cover but Carmichael saw one Mig diving away, with thick black smoke pouring from it.

Although the encounters between Migs and Furies came out in favour of the Furies, had the Migs changed their tactics and been better trained the outcome would have been far different. The tactics they should have used were the ones used by the Germans flying the Me262 at the end of the Second World War: diving attacks followed by rapid climb, in order to return for another fast dive attack.

After these encounters, it was decided that HMS *Ocean*'s strikes should take place the same time as the American F86 Sabre jet fighters were doing their fighter sweeps over the Yalu area. Up until the end of the patrol, the Furies would escort the Fireflies on their missions.

Carmichael finished the rest of the patrols, bombing and strafing the usual targets such as bridges, villages and transformer stations.

On 12 August, Carmichael's flight catapulted off the ship, climbing rapidly away and forming up before heading inland for strikes north-west, where they destroyed two bridges then strafed sampans and oxcarts on the way back. Over the next five days he flew armed reconnaissance duties, bombing and strafing many targets of opportunity, mostly bridges.

Lieutenant Carmichael ended his sixth patrol in Korea and was sent back to the UK, considered too important to lose in operational flying. For his destruction of the Mig he won the DSC. He had several commands after the Korean War and saw operational flying on jets and ended up as the Sea Cadet Corps northwest area officer based in Liverpool. He died in 1997 at the age of seventy-three.

Chapter Nine

HMS *OCEAN* AND THE FIREFLIES

Lieutenant Harry Hawksworth

On 10 May 1952, Lieutenant 'Harry' Hawksworth[1] joined HMS *Ocean* for its first patrol of the Korean War. He had finished his flying training and was sent to his squadron at Culdrose ten days before they were due to sail. "I arrived in almost complete shame," he told me during our interview. "The amphibian[2] was bringing up my luggage and I went on my BSE motor bike. I got there about the same time as the amphibian just outside the squadron when I fell off into a puddle. The ground crew died with laughter."

His Firefly squadron was 824, commanded by Lieutenant Commander 'Chico' Roberts. Hawksworth described his experiences and impressions extensively in a diary, which he kept throughout the conflict.

In one of the entries he cast an opinion on arming a Firefly and attacking a target: "It was sensible that the Furies did the bombing because they had better visibility. I worked out the dive angle. Not too steep but not too shallow when going down." The Firefly was designed as a two-seater with a maximum take-off weight of 10,000lb. "We were flying them with slightly shorter wings at 16,000lb so it used to be quite a struggle to get above 4,000 feet to cross the coast."

Hawksworth's first operational sortie was on 11 May, when he catapulted off *Ocean*'s deck on a dawn raid over the Ongjin peninsula. In his diary he states: "0500hrs saw various emplacements and villages. Used the whole flight's rocket projectiles (forty-eight) on reported troop positions (120)." The troops were by two houses and the Fireflies plastered the buildings with all their rockets but the shooting was wide. The first house was derelict anyway, but the second house was not, and was made the main target. The last rocket fired finally destroyed it!

Later in the morning, at 1015hrs, the Fireflies were heading east of Ongjin when they spotted a very juicy target. Young, inexperienced in war fighting, they were desperate to attack real targets and on this occasion the flight turned and dropped onto a train, peppering it with rockets. When the last Firefly pulled up someone noticed the train had already been wrecked by rocket fire several days before.

---

[1] His christened names are Richard Denison Rome but he was called Harry by 2 Squadron after a West Country character in 'Widdicombe Fair'called Harry Hawke.

[2] Amphibian is a term for an amphibious aircraft that in Hawksworth's case also had wheels. It would be an aircraft very similar to the PBY Catalina.

Heading back to HMS *Ocean*, the flight strafed some oxcarts. "A nasty business any day," Hawksworth wrote in his diary. They headed for home, for lunch of oxtail soup, which was far from appetizing. He was back in the cockpit late in the afternoon, heading towards blocks of Nissen huts on the coast. "Bombs would have been the answer but we were carrying rockets anyway," he wrote.

Pulling out of a dive he banked sharply, looking back at the target and counting the explosions from his rocket attack: seven. There must be more, he thought. Then he realized the balance of the aircraft felt wrong. Five rockets were still hung under the wings. To shake them loose, he went round quickly, dropping into another dive that was high and too fast. He pressed the button. Nothing, no stream of smoke, no sudden whoosh as the rockets leapt from under the wings. Stubbornly, the 60lb projectiles remained hung up. Wheeling away, the flight headed back to *Ocean*. That first day, they had completed six hours flying time. "A pilot's maximum effort," wrote Hawksworth.

That first day's sorties were not without casualty. A Firefly piloted by Lieutenant Sid Gandy ditched in an estuary south of Haeju due to flak. Fortunately, a US amphibious air-sea rescue aircraft picked up both the pilot and his observer. Suffering from exposure to cold they were taken to hospital in Seoul.

Shortly after dawn (0645hrs) on 13 May, Hawksworth's flight headed for a reservoir north-east of Haeju. At 5,000 feet the CO gave the call sign and the Fireflies pushed their noses forward one by one, dropping into their dives, and heading for a group of very large buildings near the reservoir. Rockets smashed into the buildings over and over as each of the four aircraft dropped from the sky. Hawksworth thumbed the button and his rockets fell from the wings, shooting towards the target as he went into a tight climbing turn.

During the same flight, the CO spotted an area of flak where two guns were firing at the aircraft. Kicking the rudder over, he tore down on one of the guns and gave it a long burst with his four 20mm cannons. Other pilots also saw the flak guns but Hawksworth didn't.

Heading back for home they ran across an oxcart and strafed it in one run. The CO wheeled around again with the flight following, this time going into a much shallower dive to strafe the oxcart again. Again the CO pulled his aircraft around and strafed the hapless cart, killing the ox. "In this attack, the CO broke his own rules, doing something he said he would never do – three strafing runs," Hawksworth recalled.

Back on *Ocean*, Hawksworth discovered that all flying for the rest of the day was scrubbed. Somehow, water had contaminated the petrol and all the tanks on the aircraft had to be drained. The crisis had been sorted by the following morning, and Hawksworth's flight took off at 0800hrs. The mission was an attack on a group of four huts. "One of them was new," Hawksworth noted.

The CO, Chico Roberts, led the first attack, firing six rockets. Hawksworth followed, but each of his rockets missed its target. Detailed by the CO to try again, Hawksworth turned, climbed to diving height, his wingman and No. 4 Bob Brand backing him up. After a few minor adjustments to his dive Hawksworth found that his rockets were just high; but Bob Brand did much better. As Hawksworth pulled up he could see a crater by the front door of the first hut.

Further away, Roberts and his wingman Alf Wigg pounded some hill coastal defences with their remaining rockets. Directly behind them Hawksworth and Brand let loose a storm of cannon shells on an object they couldn't see because of the muck and debris from the attack by the CO and Wigg.[3]

By 1400hrs, Hawksworth and Brand were on their second sortie. At 4,000 feet they headed for a vehicle hideout reported to be west of Kaesong. Followed by Brand and checking his turn and bank indicator, Harry brought the wing up and turned into his dive, hitting the firing button. All their rockets shot out from under the two Fireflies' wings, slamming into the building, but there were no fires. Rockets spent, they headed away, searching for a reported flak position but instead found two houses. According to their intelligence, one was supposed to contain a small arms works and an officers' mess.[4]

Dropping quickly into a low dive Hawksworth's thumb touched the firing button and instantly the four cannons on the wings belched flame as he strafed both houses. They flew for two hours and ten minutes before finally landing on HMS *Ocean*'s flight deck again.

The next day – Friday – their luck was better. Hawksworth's flight took off at 0845hrs, heading for a group of huts on the coast that proved to be a radio station. Covered by a thin layer of mist it was difficult to see the target. Suddenly the CO dropped into an attack run from the sea, heading directly for the huts. Hawksworth followed, and diving at 30 degrees he could see the hills behind the huts were at least 1,000ft in height.

Rocket after rocket dropped from their rails as each Firefly attacked the radio station. All of them missed, ending up in a rice grove to one side of the largest hut. Undaunted, Roberts brought his aircraft round again for another battle run, but this time it was for his observer to get a photo of the target. The run was too high, so he pulled the stick back, touched the rudder pedals and pulled the aircraft around; he failed to get his photo.

Bang! The note of the engine suddenly changed. Liquid began streaming from under the cowling. Roberts gained a little height then dived out to sea announcing cheerfully over the R/T, "Mayday, mayday, mayday. My engine is rapidly packing up, ditching out to sea. No. 2 follow me down."

Streams of fluid poured from the engine as it skipped over the water, dropping lower and lower. Fire licked around the cowl. Four thousand feet above the stricken aircraft Hawksworth could see the flames disappear as Roberts switched off the fuel. The Firefly dropped quickly and Roberts made a perfect ditching five miles off the coast. "It looked bad from the air," Hawksworth said. Both the pilot and observer got out of the aircraft before it sank beneath the waves forever but from Hawksworth's height he "couldn't be certain they got out okay." However, twenty-five minutes later a US amphibious aircraft picked up the aircrew watched by Hawksworth and the rest of the flight

---

[3] A footnote in Hawksworth's diary comments that this was not a very productive strike.
[4] This is according to Hawksworth's diary.

circling overhead.[5] That afternoon Hawksworth and Brand attacked the radio station again. This time, Hawksworth led the flight and all the rockets successfully hit the target.

By 17 May, Hawksworth had flown 123 sorties[6]. Cruising at approximately 5,000 feet, his flight headed for a reservoir north of Yonan where it turned for its target, a tiny village which was reported to contain enemy troops.

Hawksworth pushed the stick forward, dropping the nose into a 50 degree diving attack. Speed was increasing, as the needle on the altimeter wound down towards zero. He pressed the firing button. Nothing! Frantically he glanced at the rocket projectile master switch and realized he'd forgotten to turn it on. Flicking it quickly he pressed the firing button and his rockets ripped into the village. Pulling hard on the stick, Hawksworth banked and climbed away watching the projectiles disappear into the plumes of dust and debris from the attacks by the other Fireflies. "We couldn't see if any fires had started because of the dust," he told me, "so we headed back to the ship and strafed an oxcart."

That afternoon, Hawksworth's flight was again in the air, leaving *Ocean* at 1230hrs for a flight that lasted nearly two hours. CO Chico Roberts (who had been picked up the previous day) and his wingman Alf Wigg took the port side while Hawksworth and Bob Brand took the starboard side, heading for a group of sampans drawn up on the beach.

The CO fired a salvo of rockets but they were too high. Hawksworth watched Wigg's rockets completely miss the target. Hawksworth turned, keeping the Firefly level, then pressed the firing button. The rockets streaked away into the huts, which instantly burst into flames. Three-quarters of an hour later, as the Fireflies turned for home, the remains of seven huts were burning fiercely. Seeing the results of their handiwork chilled them.

The third sortie of the day[7] found the flight attacking some light flak positions and 37mm anti-aircraft guns. The same targets had been attacked the previous day and Hawksworth's flight had a target photograph that made the attack easy. Nearly two hours later he was back on the deck, weary, tired and ready for bed. It had been a long day.[8]

As the sun rose slowly over the horizon on 18 May, the Fireflies climbed into the morning light heading for known flak positions near the Alyong Reservoir. Hawksworth pushed the stick over at 5,000 feet dropping the aircraft into a 30-degree dive. Tracer shot past the nose as the target shot back. He watched the height bleeding off the altimeter as his thumb hovered over the button. Tracers continued to fly by as he reached 2,000 feet. A slight adjustment to keep the wings level, a touch on the firing button then six rockets shot away to pound the gun positions. Immediately, Hawksworth levelled off, then climbed quickly away.

---

[5] Hawksworth concludes this event in his diary by writing "too much static on distress frequency."

[6] According to his diary this includes both defensive and offensive sorties together.

[7] Hawksworth's flight took off at 1445hrs.

[8] Hawksworth wrote in his diary that he was very tired. This was the day HMS *Ocean* set out to beat HMS *Glory*'s record for the number of sorties flown.

He didn't have time to see if his rockets hit the target as the CO was already heading inland at 5,000 feet looking for more "trade". Under their wings, each Firefly carried the remaining six rockets as they sped away from the coast going towards a group of buildings in a large encampment suspected of housing several North Korean troops.[9]

"Choose your targets," the CO called over the R/T. Spying a large L-shaped building ahead, Hawksworth pushed the Firefly into a shallow attack dive, waited until he was at the right height, then fired his rockets. Pulling up he glanced in his mirror at the target behind and below him. To his delight he could see the last of his rockets smashing squarely into the building and starting several fires.

Dawn broke on the Monday morning, the last day of the first patrol, with clear skies. The sun glinted off the Sea Furies and Fireflies sitting on the deck, their engines ticking over as *Ocean* turned into the wind. One by one, the aircraft took off on what would be a shorter than usual trip. Hawksworth was airborne at 0800hrs, carrying only one nacelle fuel tank because of the sixteen rocket projectiles slung under the wings. Every Firefly carried the same number.

They headed towards some new warehouses in Haeju. At 1,500 feet Harry Hawksworth levelled out from his dive and fired, expecting the aircraft to buck under the onslaught of sixteen rockets blasting off their rails. But only eight shot away. Hawksworth turned to go around again. Below he could see the CO, clearly having the same problem as he turned into his second attack on the buildings. Hawksworth wondered what the hell was going on.

He could see puffs from flak and heavy machine-gun fire arching up towards the CO's aircraft and decided to do his attack from a greater height. Pushing the stick forward, he lined the nose up onto the buildings, rolling into a dive. Again he thumbed the rocket release button. To his relief they shot away and hammered the target.

Heading back towards the ship, they ran across some sampans and strafed them. Diving on the vessels, Hawksworth could see men moving around the deck. Pressing the firing button he expected his four cannon to belch their deadly ammunition, but instead, only one of the four cannons fired.

Back on the ship, re-armed and re-fuelled, the Fireflies were in the air for their next sortie in support of a guerrilla landing from twelve sampans. It was a joint sortie by Fireflies and Furies carrying 1,000lb bombs. Before the attack began Bob Brand returned because of a faulty engine. The air coordinator for the attack was Hawksworth's CO, Chico Roberts, and Hawksworth could hear him speaking to the bombarding destroyer, HMAS *Bataan*. Then suddenly there was silence. The CO's radio had died at a critical moment when he was directing the final bombardment and as he gestured wildly in his seat, Hawksworth realized that Chico wanted him to take over the bombardment direction. Clicking on his radio button, Hawksworth began directing the ship's fire onto enemy positions.

---

[9] Hawksworth had wrote this had previously contained troops but whether it still did then isn't clear.

p: The first Fireflies in
...tion over Korea were the
...1s from 827 Squadron
...oard HMS *Triumph*,
...554/P 277 being seen here
...Iwakuni, Japan during a rest
...riod. *(Andy Thomas)*

...ddle: HMS *Triumph* in dock.
...A Museum)

...tom: A Firefly takes off from
...MS *Triumph*. *(FAA Museum)*

HMS *Triumph* with Fireflies and Seafires ranged aft. *(FAA Museum)*

Top: A Fairey Firefly from 827 Squadron crashing into the barrier on HMS *Triumph*. *(FAA Museum)*

Middle: A shot of the aftermath of the crash. *(FAA Museum)*

Bottom: Sea Furies of 807 Squadron conduct power checks on the packed deck of HMS *Theseus* before a squadron strike mission during her 1950-51 cruise. *(Chris Thomas)*

Left: Firefly FR5
WB415/T232 of
810 Squadron departs
Theseus in 1951.
(Andy Thomas)

Right: Firefly 5
WB417/T231 leaves
HMS *Theseus* to patrol
the Korean coast.
(Andy Thomas)

Bottom: A Firefly of
812 Squadron about to
catch the wire during
work-up training before
deployment to Korean
waters in *Glory.*
(Cdr J W Sleigh)

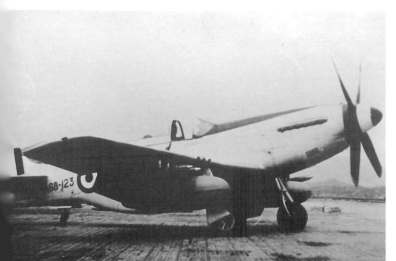

Top: The light fleet carrier HMS *Glory* anchored in Aden harbour while en route to Korea in 1951.
(Andy Thomas)

Middle: Pilots of 801 Squadron, HMS *Glory*.

Bottom: 77 Squadron RAAF entered combat over Korea flying P-51 Mustangs, though this one, A68-123, was actually an Australian-built example.
(RAAF via Andy Thomas)

Above: RAAF Meteor F8s aboard the carrier HMS *Warrior* whilst in Iwakuni harbour on 24 February 1951. *(RAAF via Andy Thomas)*

Right: Meteor F8 A77-616 forms a backdrop as 77's CO, Sqn Ldr J H Creswell, briefs his pilots before escorting US RF80s at Kimpo. Flown by Sqn Ldr D L Wilson, 616 had damaged a Mig on 29 August 1951. *(RAAF via Andy Thomas)*

Bottom: A USN S51 guard helicopter off the RAN carrier HMAS *Sydney* as 817 Squadron Firefly WB351/K202 prepares to launch in late 1951. *(Admiralty)*

Top: The men of 802 Squadron, HMS *Ocean*.

Above: Cdr J W Sleigh DSO DSC was Cdr (Air) on *Glory* during her Korean patrols in 1952. He received an OBE for his services. *(Cdr J W Sleigh)*

Left: Battened down and ship shape. HMS *Ocean* under sail with all her aircraft aboard and lashed down. The lead Sea Fury appears to be sitting at the end of the catapult. Note that the fighter carries only her underwing drop tanks and is not yet armed with bombs for a mission. *(Nick Cook)*

Above: A Sea Fury FB11 of 804 Squadron begins its take-off roll from *Glory* for a ground attack sortie in 1952. *(Andy Thomas)*

Right: A rocket-armed 804 Squadron Sea Fury is positioned onto *Glory's* deck in preparation for another mission over North Korea. *(Andy Thomas)*

Bottom: Firefly FR5s of 812 Squadron prepare for the final strike of the day aboard *Glory* on 17 March 1952. *(Cdr J W Sleigh)*

op: Chocked and with wings folded, a Sea Fury from
04 Squadron is brought up onto the deck of *Glory*
om the hangar deck below. *(Andy Thomas)*

Bottom: HMS *Ocean* anchored at Sasebo in Japan for a
replenishment period during one of her Korean patrols.
(Andy Thomas)

Top: Commissioned Pilot R M Brand brings an 825 Squadron Firefly onto *Ocean* for the ship's 1,000th accident-free landing on 10 July 1952. *(Andy Thomas)*

Middle: Firefly WB311 of *Ocean's* 825 Squadron is caught by the camera on the last day of their Korean operations on 30 October 1952. *(FAA Museum)*

Bottom: R/P armed Meteor F8s of 77 Squadron taxi a Kimpo for another ground attack mission. In the lead A77-446 in which Sgt K J Murray damaged a Mig 15 on 2 November 1952. *(RAAF via Andy Thomas)*

Top left: Aircraft in need of repair were usually unceremoniously hoisted off ship by crane whilst the ship was in Japan, shown happening to 807's Fury WF693.
(Andy Thomas)

Top right: A candid shot of Lieutenant Ted Anson who later went on to be the last captain of the old *Ark Royal* and a Rear Admiral with the Royal Navy.

Middle: The mighty Sea Fury in flight.

Bottom: Two airmen, one in flying gear, on the deck of a carrier.

Top: An 817 Squadron Firefly is cleared from the deck of *Sydney* after a landing accident off the Korean coast. *(Andy Thomas)*

Bottom: A North Korean railway bridge still intact. It would be an inviting target for dive-bombing Furie *(Nick Cook)*

Left: Two oxcarts are caught out on the road during the day. This was taken by aircraft from HMS *Glory*. The UN sanctioned attacks on oxcarts because the North Koreans often used this way of transporting ammunition. They became fair game to marauding Furies and Fireflies. *(Nick Cook)*

Bottom: This photo shows damage around a North Korean railway bridge after an attack by aircraft from HMS *Ocean*. *(Nick Cook)*

Top left: A North Korean railway bridge stands defiant against the bombing by aircraft from HMS *Ocean*. This photo, courtesy of Fury pilot Nick Cook, shows there could be some slight damage to the right spar.

Top right: The destruction of a bridge. It has just been bombed by aircraft from HMS *Ocean*. *(Nick Cook)*

Bottom: An inviting target of railway wagons parked on what appears to be a siding. However, these lone wagons would have been flak traps. The North Koreans were very adept at creating dummy railway wagons for UN aircraft to attack. When the pilots came down low the flak would open up. Many pilots were shot down this way.

Above: A North Korean road bridge still standing after an attack by Fleet Air Arm aircraft. *(Nick Cook)*

Left: This photo shows the results of bombing on a North Korean bridge. It was taken on 10 October 1952 by an aircraft from HMS *Ocean*. *(Nick Cook)*

Left: Taken from a Sea Fury, this picture shows a North Korean bridge the Furies were dive-bombing. *(Nick Cook)*

Bottom: This photo shows smoke rising (bottom centre), presumably from a bombing attack. In the distance (circled) another aircraft prepares to roll into its dive onto the target. *(Nick Cook)*

Finally, as his was the only aircraft with any ammunition left, he decided to attack two heavy machine-gun posts. Again, only one gun fired. He rocketed over the target, kicked the rudder to full power, climbed and pulled the aircraft around for another dive. Again, only one gun fired. Now he was furious and he went round again for a third dive.[10] This time he knocked out the guns and headed back to the ship.

Tragedy struck on a subsequent sortie when the senior pilot, Lieutenant Commander Tim Williamson-Napier, attacked the same target twice. The second time he flew straight into the ground exploding into flames. "His rockets didn't go the first time," Hawksworth told me, "so he went around again, but they knocked his tail off and he was killed." This tragic event turned Hawksworth into the 3rd Flight leader at the very end of his first patrol on HMS *Ocean*. "Not a job I craved," he said. "You get all the worst trips, and life is much easier as the CO's No. 3."

Ten days later, on 29 May 1952, *Ocean* was back in Korean waters for her second patrol of the tour. The weather that morning seemed ominous with reports of fog throughout the south. One of the Fireflies was unserviceable. As Hawksworth strapped himself into his aircraft he hoped there would be no more problems. Turning into the wind the carrier prepared to launch her aircraft. Hawksworth jammed the throttle up to full power then the catapult hurtled him down the deck and into the air. Behind him the remaining two Fireflies of the flight managed to get into the air. Heading north his wingman radioed that the nacelle tanks on his aircraft wouldn't transfer fuel. Hawksworth knew then that they wouldn't make the target, so he radioed back to the ship only to be told the target was fogbound.

Vectored onto a new heading by the ground-based controllers, Hawksworth and the other two Fireflies cruised towards a group of villages, which they had attacked in their first patrol. Touching rudder pedals and the stick to keep the aircraft level, he nosed into a dive, his finger hovering over the button. The rockets dropped away tearing towards the target. Suddenly, there was a loud thud and the aircraft rocked violently. Pulling quickly out of his dive, he recovered and checked his controls. Had he been hit by bursting flak? He couldn't be sure but decided enough was enough. His rockets had done little damage as had those fired from the other two aircraft.

Back on *Ocean*, with his aircraft parked behind the barrier, Hawksworth switched the engine off and jumped onto the deck. With the servicing crews he looked under the wing and immediately saw the problem. One of the rocket motors had exploded making a large dent in the leading edge and damaging the plate and underside of the wing. "On a couple of occasions I flew into bits of my own rocket because I couldn't see them," Hawksworth explained during our interview. "One piece went through the wing where the ammunition tank is. A much smaller one hit the 55-gallon tank, which was empty."

Poor serviceability dogged the Fireflies of HMS *Ocean* that day. Earmarked to lead a strike on railway wagons north of Chinnampo, only three Fireflies

---

[10] In his diary Hawksworth wrote he landed with a headache and shaking with rage.

limped off the deck at 1630hrs with a flight of Furies. Within minutes one of the Fireflies began experiencing fuel transfer problems but stayed with the flight. They droned on through rain and cloud climbing to 5,000 feet. Levelling off, Hawksworth finally spied the railway wagons. "As we were about to attack, a Fury pilot came over the radio saying it was the wrong target." Hawksworth said he was sure that they were the right ones. As if reading his thoughts, the pilot radioed again saying that indeed they were the correct wagons. Wasting no time, the Fireflies dived onto the targets one by one, releasing their rockets when they levelled off at 1,500 feet, and then climbing rapidly away to head for the coast.[11]

Back on *Ocean*'s deck, Hawksworth discovered the railway wagons that were attacked had, in fact, been the wrong targets. For Hawksworth and the rest of the Fireflies it was a disappointing start to their second patrol.

Two days later, the Fireflies prepared for an early morning raid on more railway wagons near Chinnampo. During a briefing the night before, photographs had shown heavy concentrations of flak in the area. As dawn approached, activity on the aircraft carrier increased in preparation for the attack, and Hawksworth had little sleep as a result. He was anxious about the flak positions too.

The roar of aircraft engines suddenly spoiled the morning calm and the first Firefly took to the air (0700hrs), followed minutes later by Hawksworth's. Not long afterwards, he realized one of his nacelle fuel tanks was failing to transfer fuel into the main tanks, and that disappointingly he wouldn't make the target. Rather than split the flight,[12] he decided to attack the alternate target, a coastal village housing anti-tank guns, which the enemy had been using to attack British ships. The Fireflies rolled into their dives and his rockets plastered a slit trench and several huts.

The afternoon's sortie was more successful. This time Hawksworth led the flight onto a village near the coast. Each Firefly sent six rockets into the huts and by the time the flight wheeled away towards the next target, the village was burning. Suddenly, Bob Brand's voice came over the R/T: "My engine's running rough so I'd like to stay near the coast, in case."

Acknowledging Brand, Hawksworth sent the remaining two Fireflies inland to attack a factory. They destroyed it with their rockets and headed back to the ship. Meanwhile, Hawksworth and Brand stayed near the coast searching for a truck hideout without success. Instead, they used the last of their rockets on a village they'd damaged before. This time their rockets finished the job.

The first two days of June saw a lower intensity of sorties. On the morning of the 1st, Hawksworth's flight attacked sampans near Yonan, as well as a beach gun position using six rockets and cannon fire for each target. 2 June was replenishment day, and the carrier steamed away from the Korean coast towards the rendezvous with the tanker that would provide them with fuel, stores and ammunition. "We all had hangovers from the whisky that had been put in our beer last night," Hawksworth wrote in his diary. "I felt depressed."

---

[11] 1,500 feet was standard height for firing rockets according to Hawksworth's diary.
[12] His flight was missing two observers owing to sickness.

The morning of 3 June broke with low cloud cover, the ship was back in position off the West coast, and while the aircraft were being serviced many pairs of eyes turned towards the sky wondering whether the clouds would lift. At 0830hrs Hawksworth's flight climbed into the air with a service ceiling at about 500 feet as they headed towards the Chinnampo estuary. "Here the cloud base was higher at 1,500 feet but still too low to my way of thinking," Hawksworth wrote. Instead of attacking the main target further down the estuary, Hawksworth fired his rockets into a group of huts by a canal near the coast.

Rain spattered his windscreen as he led the flight back towards the ship. Dropping his speed and wing flaps, he could feel the aircraft being buffeted by the wind and rain. He lined up his nose with the deck, his eyes fixed on the batsman off to the side waving him on. To lose sight of the batsman in such bad weather would have been a disaster. The batsman gave the 'cut your engine now' motion. Hawksworth flicked the switches, the engine feathered, and the aircraft dropped, landing with a thud on the deck as the hook grabbed the wire, stopping the aircraft from ramming the barrier. The rest of the day's flying was scrubbed as they waited for the weather to clear.

The next morning was a beautiful sunny day and Hawksworth's flight formed up over *Ocean*, and turned inland towards an ammunition dump in the Yonan area. Morning fog and mist covered the entire area so the whole flight continued westwards towards a village (and sampans) that supposedly had troops who had captured a friendly island.

Arriving over the village at about 5,000 feet, Hawksworth gave the signal and the Fireflies split into pairs, dropping into 50-degree dives. He kept the aircraft steady, making minute adjustments, waiting for the seconds to pass before reaching the right height. Firing, he saw his rockets rip into the village obliterating the huts and sampans. As the others attacked, he could see the orange and yellow glow of flames as a fire began to rage.

The third sortie that day found the Fireflies heading towards the Kushra Dong peninsula; they attacked a battery of NKA anti-tank guns, starting several large fires.[13] Fuel was getting very low as they roared out to sea towards their carrier and Hawksworth anxiously looked as his gauge. He needed immediate clearance to land but it wasn't coming. Down on the ship's deck there was a problem. As the Fireflies circled the ship Brand's voice came calmly over the radio: "Down to 15 gallons, skipper." Moments later Hawksworth watched Brand touch down on the ship's deck. His own fuel rapidly running out, he circled until he was cleared to land. When he finally did land on *Ocean*'s deck, his fuel tanks were virtually dry.[14] As he walked away from the aircraft he was soaked with sweat.

At 1800hrs on 5 June, the summer sun began setting as Hawksworth, leading a section of two Fireflies, climbed slowly behind Bob Hunter's section towards an installation beside the gutted Ongjin airfield. Circling the target, Hawksworth studied it and could see signs of repair work. Ahead, Bob Hunter's flight was already attacking a group of huts one mile north of the airfield.

---

[13] This sortie was at 1630hrs according to the diary.
[14] The No. 4 position pilot (unknown) had only twenty gallons left according to Hawksworth's diary.

They were losing light fast and were not rated for night flying, so Hawksworth knew they had to hit the target quickly and get out. Each Firefly carried sixteen rockets instead of the usual twelve, and Hawksworth was determined to make them count. Pushing the stick forward he dropped into a dive and fired all sixteen at the huts. Banking tightly, he watched the last two Fireflies follow suit, then they quickly formed up and headed out to sea towards *Ocean*, with the light almost gone.

As the aircraft carrier came in sight, Hawksworth realized it was too dark for a visual landing. The approach would have to be voice-controlled. He concentrated on the calm voice coming through his headphones, but the crackle from the R/T made hearing difficult. "Wheels down, flaps down, throttle back, nose up. Now steady, keep the speed down, keep the aircraft centred on the deck. Final approach. Cut!" Then suddenly the wheels touched with a thud, the arrester hook grabbed the wire and he was on.

After a quick shower and supper the flight was briefed for the next day's dawn raid at 0450hrs. The target was an ammunition dump north-east of Yonan and Hawksworth led the flight. Over the target area he spotted a very green strip which looked camouflaged. Rolling the aircraft into a 30-degree dive, he fired all twelve rockets at 1,500 feet and then pulled out. Climbing to get height he looked back to see the squadron follow his procedure, in a line astern formation. The shooting was excellent. Rocket after rocket ripped into the target area but there were no fires.[15] They were all back safely aboard *Ocean* just after seven in the morning.

More than three hours later, behind Bob Hunter's flight, Hawksworth led his section towards their target only to find that it no longer existed; the intelligence had been out of date! Cursing under his breath, he followed Hunter's flight along a river as the American air controllers directed them towards a large hut not far from the sea, and this time there was a result. His section went in first and he fired half his rockets at 1,500 feet. They raced towards the target but as he climbed away he couldn't see any results. However, the whoop of excitement from his section filled him with satisfaction. "Bloody great blue flash," said Brand. "Great shooting."[16]

Turning the aircraft round for another pass, Hawksworth could see smoke and flame billowing from the building below. Control hadn't told them what was in there but it must have been ammunition. At 1240hrs, the flight arrived back at the carrier. They'd been in the air just over two hours and ten minutes. It was the end of their second patrol.

The first day of HMS *Ocean*'s third patrol was 16 June, and at 1030hrs, Hawksworth's flight lifted off and headed towards Ongjin where they attacked a small island. Diving on a house surrounded by trees, each aircraft fired six rockets but there was no sign of life. They were then vectored towards what was reported to be a North Korean army headquarters north-east of the island. As

---

[15] In his diary Hawksworth suspected the target, an ammunition dump, had been moved because it had been attacked previously and there were no secondary fires.
[16] There is no indication what the blue flash was in Hawksworth's diary.

the Fireflies shattered the buildings with their rockets, Hawksworth could see green flashes amongst the smoke and debris. That made a good start to a new patrol.

That afternoon they were directed towards two villages. "We hit the first one squarely," Hawksworth told me. "But the second target was pretty nebulous and we ended up rocketing some houses west of the intended position."

In the early morning of 17 June, the Fireflies headed towards the Chinnampo area loaded with rockets to attack a hill position near the coast.[17] They then progressed to their second target: a line of huts and trenches further inland. On Hawksworth's second attack, his remaining rockets wouldn't fire so he headed towards the coast where he spied another hill position, this time with a network of trenches running in all directions. It was too good to be true. Hoping his rockets would work, he rolled the aircraft into a dive and smashed the target with projectiles and cannon shells as he bore down on them. Levelling out, he climbed away and headed home.

Three hours later, at 1230hrs, the final sortie of the day was complicated by thicker cloud. Hawksworth climbed the Firefly to 3,000 feet before he was above it. As he waited for the rest of the flight to form up on him, both his No. 2 and his No. 3 reported engine trouble and returned to the ship. Hawksworth pressed on with his No. 4, heading for the target. Suddenly, through a small opening in the thick carpet of cloud he caught sight of the coast. Dropping through the hole, they tried to find a clear area but the cloud base was between 500 and 700 feet. "There was nothing for it," Hawksworth told me. "I jettisoned my rockets and returned to the ship."

The weather was bad again on 19 June. While the area was covered in fog, HMS *Ocean* in company with HMS *Belfast* steamed north well beyond Chodo Island to brighter skies. By 1700hrs, Hawksworth was in the air with his wingman Bob Brand heading north-west of Chinnampo to attack two very large buildings. Rolling in at 5,500 feet for a 30-degree dive, Hawksworth could see a man run out of the building just as he released his rockets. Half the projectiles ripped into the buildings, engulfing them in smoke and dust while the other half went wide.

The next day dawned with the sun shining in a clear sky. Leading a flight of three Fireflies, Hawksworth was vectored onto some flour mills north of Chinnampo. He climbed to 9,000 feet because of the eight Bofors anti-aircraft guns that reportedly ringed the buildings. Waiting for the others to reach the same height he called, "Echelon break," and pushed the control column sideways rolling into a steep 50-degree dive onto the target far below.

As tracer streamed up at the Fireflies, Hawksworth's aircraft began pitching badly.[18] Alarmed, he held on for as long as he could, and then fired his rockets at 3,000 feet. Quickly pulling out of the dive, to his dismay he realized only half the rockets had leapt from their underwing moorings. Turning hard round to watch the rest of the aircraft attack he saw his No. 4 expend only half his

---

[17] The targets were reported by partisans to have enemy troop concentrations, according to Hawksworth's diary.

[18] In his diary Hawksworth wrote that the aircraft's trim was very bad in this dive. There is no explanation as to why this was.

rockets as well. All the projectiles smashed into the left-hand building, even though they were aiming at the right.

That afternoon the Fireflies attacked a coastal village filled with huts and boats. Using eight rockets from each aircraft, they left the village blazing, with flames licking high above the buildings. Spying a large barn, Hawksworth and Brand attacked it with four rockets, missing the target. Brand's projectiles set several more buildings on fire. Climbing away Hawksworth flew back towards the village, his observer photographing the several fires that now burned fiercely far below from their attacks.

Sunday 22 June was a good day for the Fireflies. The photo interpreter on *Ocean* had discovered several tracks leading to a group of new houses in the hills north of Chinnampo.[19]

So, at 0630hrs, the aircraft catapulted off *Ocean*'s deck and headed for the village. Climbing to 9,000 feet to avoid the new flak positions, they dived down to their release height at 3,000 feet. "We caught them sleeping," Hawksworth said. "All our rockets appeared to hit the village except some of Bob Brand's."

HMS *Amethyst* had been bombarding enemy troops massing on the coast opposite a friendly island when Hawksworth's flight of four Fireflies and two Sea Furies arrived for their second sortie of the day.[20] Looking down on the trenches, Hawksworth could see the puffs and explosions from *Amethyst*'s guns pounding the ground around the trenches. Suddenly the bombardment stopped.

Now it was their turn. "Break, break," Hawksworth called and peeled off into a steep dive. One by one the rest of the flight came down behind him, dropping bombs and firing rockets into the North Koreans. "I think we made life most unpleasant for them," Hawksworth recalled.

The next day, he led three Fireflies on a morning raid near Haeju attacking an enemy supply dump near a railway tunnel entrance. This would be a difficult attack because of the mountains directly above the entrance. Diving down in line astern, one behind the other, they fired half their rockets at the target. Hawksworth saw some rockets hitting the tunnel entrance and the railway lines. However, no fires were started.

The afternoon's armed reconnaissance flight was more eventful. Roaring off the deck at 1400hrs, Hawksworth headed south of the Chinnampo area to attack large barns. Several rockets found the mark with little damage but some of their projectiles hit a few houses starting two spectacular fires.

The sun was well into the morning sky on 24 June when Hawksworth's flight climbed away from the aircraft carrier, and headed towards a transformer at Haeju as part of the new air offensive striking at enemy power targets. "We used the 60lb rockets that worked pretty well but the trouble was the fuse," Hawksworth explained. "The big square fuse would come off and if you got one into your radiator you'd have five minutes of coolant coming out and usually about five minutes before the engine seized."

---

[19] This was in roughly the same area as they encountered on 20 June with the eight Bofors.
[20] They took off at 1230hrs according to the diary.

The Fireflies pressed on. On reaching the target, Hawksworth checked his instruments, made sure the master switch was set to 'on', and put the nose down. The ground came quickly up towards him as he fired two salvoes of rockets, which sped through the air towards the transformer. Levelling out he lost sight of the target as he climbed away. A huge ball of orange flame shot suddenly into the sky and thick black smoke began to pour from the building as the oil inside the transformer caught fire.[21]

Heading back to the ship, the flight of Fireflies strafed two villages in support of a guerrilla landing. Both were set on fire by the high explosive shells from the aircraft's cannon.

The final sortie of the day was at 1530hrs and this was to attack another transformer at Haeju.[22] As leader of the attack, Hawksworth sent two salvoes of rockets into the building then quickly pulled out. His second salvo hit the mark and a blue sheet of flame leapt into the air; sparks flew as the building was engulfed in smoke. Hawksworth was well pleased.

---

[21] He wrote that he was told his rockets had caused the orange fire by the rest of his flight.
[22] According to Hawksworth's diary Sea Furies had tried to knock out the other transformer but had had little success.

Chapter Ten

MORE STINGS FROM THE FIREFLIES

Lieutenant Harry Hawksworth, HMS *Ocean*

Their ten days of rest and relaxation in Japan quickly slipped into memory when HMS *Ocean* arrived back in Korean waters for her fourth patrol on 4 July 1952. The afternoon's sortie began at 1700hrs and again the Fireflies visited the transformers they'd attacked on 24 June. All the rockets carried by the Firefly were used on the target to make sure it was destroyed.

This day was marked with tragedy. Bob Hunter, who was the senior pilot, was on a test flight when his engine cut. He managed to ditch the Firefly close to the ship and both he, and his observer Blackie Taylor got out. Immediately, the air-sea rescue helicopter from *Ocean* was dispatched and plucked Taylor out of the water but there was no sign of Bob Hunter. Circling for some time, the chopper crew stared down at the waves, looking for the pilot but they saw nothing.

Dejected, they headed back to the ship. "They never found any sign of him," Hawksworth remembered. "We thought it might have been sharks, but his Mae West must have burst and he must have got cramp. Poor fellow had been his normal happy smiling self in the water," he recalled. "I now became the senior pilot over two dead bodies – not a very welcome job. As senior pilot you fly rather more than the others do."[1]

The weather was a problem on 5 July with poor visibility. The first sortie off *Ocean* at 0455hrs went in support of an evacuation of Wolfpack guerrillas from their normal raiding ground. "The Wolfpack were the pirates in the fishing war," Hawksworth explained. "They would do a landing in a particular place and identify enemy targets." The location of the targets would be radioed back to the ships for the aircraft to attack. "On one occasion a Canadian destroyer gave us a target that was a mortar position. I spotted it at exactly the same time as my No. 3 did. I told him and my No. 4 to attack and their rockets hit perfectly. The destroyer came through telling us to stop firing because they were 'donkeys'. Donkeys were friendly troops. But a few minutes later the ship came back again to say that they were indeed the enemy and well done."

Hawksworth's Firefly took to the air for the evacuation operation. Pulling the stick back he kept the throttle on full as the aircraft slowly climbed into the

---

[1] He was now senior pilot of the Firefly squadron.

blackness. Flames from his exhaust stubs danced brightly in the darkness.[2] Each aircraft carried its usual payload of rockets and Hawksworth made sure they were all used to stop the enemy from attacking the departing friendly forces.

The evacuation done, he wheeled the flight away and back to the ship. Suddenly, vibrations began to run the length of his aircraft and the engine was running rough at 2,400 rpm. In the south-east he could see increasing high cloud and fog approaching, but he landed safely, ahead of the weather.

A few days before Bob Hunter was killed, his flight had attacked a little outcrop overlooking a jetty. "His rockets took that out absolutely perfectly," Hawksworth recalled. "Bits of rocket were falling halfway between the boats and the shore. When the raiders got ashore they found everybody was dead and they were very impressed with the Fireflies and Sea Furies."

Later on the morning of 5 July, at 1110hrs, the Fireflies climbed above the fog, which was very thin over the ship but much thicker to the east. Hawksworth led the flight towards a railway line north of the Sinwan Reservoir. In a shallow dive, using the railway line as a sight, the Fireflies fired their rockets at a long line of wagons parked on the tracks. Watching the attack, Hawksworth felt very satisfied. "The shooting was good," he wrote, but he couldn't tell how many wagons they'd destroyed.[3]

The last sortie of the day began at 1630hrs as the Fireflies headed north-west of Chinnampo, rain streaming down their windscreens. The targets for this raid were two hills with a network of bunkers and some equipment. As they arrived over the target 20mm tracer shells arced up at them from ground fire. Flicking on the master switch Hawksworth rolled into a steep dive firing a full salvo of rockets into the hills. Tracers from small arms fire shot past his aircraft. Behind him his No. 2, Bob Brand, ran into a storm of small arms fire. The troops below had just woken up to the fact that they were being attacked and poured everything they could up at the marauding aircraft. One shell smashed into Lieutenant Brand's aircraft in the starboard wing just outboard of the nacelle fuel tank. The aircraft jammed on full power heading out to sea towards the safety of the ship.[4]

Poor weather on 6 July made flying difficult. Catapulting off HMS *Ocean* at 0930hrs Hawksworth led three Fireflies to the Chinnampo area. After a quick photo recce of a road the flight pushed on towards some huts on the island of Hwado. Each of the other three aircraft unloaded their rockets into the huts while Hawksworth concentrated on a series of trenches to knock out possible flak positions. He watched his rockets go, then suddenly a red warning light blinked on the instrument panel: "Hang-up!" Four rockets remained hanging under his wings. Turning north, Hawksworth attacked some hill installations

---

[2] In his diary he states that it "was rather dark for take-off".

[3] The captain of HMS *Ocean* was annoyed at Hawksworth because he couldn't provide exact numbers.

[4] Hawksworth wrote in his diary that they did not want to hang around and headed for the ship early.

diving on the targets, pounding them with his four cannon.[5]

The next morning at 0455hrs he led two Fireflies to attack enemy barracks near Haeju. The cloud layer covered the target, although the sun shone brightly above it. One by one the Fireflies rolled into their dives, dropping through openings in the clouds and firing their rockets. Later the same morning he was in the air again, this time leading one other Firefly flown by Lieutenant Arbuthnot, to search for a gun position they'd been briefed on. Below and above the sky was filled with a lot of cumulus cloud with sun shining brightly.

Spotting the target, Hawksworth called, "Break, break," and rolled into his dive with the other Firefly following suit. Hawksworth's thumb touched the firing button and the rockets were away, accurately pinpointing the enemy gun position as far as they could tell.

Less than three hours later[6] Hawksworth and the flight were back in the air again, heading towards a small transformer in the Schuwon Reservoir area. Partially obscured by clouds he led the attack badly and their rockets were wide of the mark.[7]

Fortunately, there were no pre-dawn raids scheduled for 9 July, although the morning strike was to be a big one. This time, Hawksworth flew with the squadron CO, Chico Roberts, for a combined strike on a peninsula west of Chinnampo. Off the coast, HMS *Belfast* bombarded known flak positions to keep enemy gunners away from the aircraft. Flying with the Fireflies were eight Sea Furies, each with two 1,000lb airburst bombs.

Dropping into a 35-degree dive, the CO fired his rockets first, with the rest of the Fireflies several hundred yards in a line behind him. Hawksworth saw the rockets hit everywhere except the targets. The Furies had more luck as one airburst bomb exploded over the target creating a huge orange ball of fire that lasted for several seconds before turning into brown smoke. They headed back to the ship after a raid that had been highly successful.[8]

The same afternoon, at 1445hrs, Hawksworth and three Fireflies climbed slowly away from HMS *Ocean* to the Sinwon area back to a small transformer that everyone had missed in previous attacks. Flying at 4,500 feet there was a thin cloud layer that slightly obscured the target below. Increasing speed, Hawksworth led the dive at 30 degrees, pointing the nose directly at the transformer below. The target grew in his sights as the aircraft rapidly lost height. The altimeter read 1,500 feet and Hawksworth levelled out quickly firing his rockets. The projectiles smashed into the transformer and more rockets hammered the buildings as the remaining Fireflies attacked. "At last, we've definitely hit it," Hawksworth reported.

On the way back to *Ocean*, with plenty of fuel in the tanks, the Fireflies dropped down to low level, strafing anything that moved; oxcarts and trenches bore the brunt of their cannon. Hawksworth's last entry in his diary for

---

[5] It is not clear whether his rockets remained hung-up or if they were released on this second pass.

[6] 1630hrs in the diary.

[7] In this diary entry he states he was annoyed with himself for missing the target.

[8] Hawksworth does not mention what the targets were but criticizes the CO for being too low at 6,700 feet.

this day was a single word: "tired".

Dawn on 10 July saw feverish activity on *Ocean*'s decks as she turned into the wind to launch her aircraft. One by one, Hawksworth's flight clawed into the sky, climbing for precious height on its way north-west of the salt pans at Han River. The target was a troop village on the coast. Hawksworth led the 30-degree dive on some huts a little to the north then turned towards the village, firing short bursts of cannon fire at the buildings and huts. Climbing he pulled around and dropped into a quick dive loosing off several bursts at some barracks and a nearby junk. The rest of his flight followed suit and then they headed back to the ship landing at 0640hrs.

Late that afternoon Hawksworth's flight headed towards more than twenty oxcarts and sampans south-east of Chinnampo. Arriving on the scene they found many of the oxen had been released from their carts. "Echelon, break," Hawksworth called. The Fireflies slipped into their battle runs behind him. Following along the riverside road, Hawksworth squeezed the firing button blasting the carts with his cannon. Pulling out of his strafing run he looked back and saw only one oxcart burning. "We claimed eight and that was conservatively," he later wrote. The others strafed the sampans and oxcarts but there were no more fires.

His ammunition exhausted, Hawksworth led the flight back towards *Ocean*. His No. 3, Pete Worthington, had a coolant leak from a stone in the radiator and a bullet through his wing. In the maelstrom of the attack Hawksworth hadn't even seen anyone shooting back. "He was going to ditch on a beach. The tide looked right from above but when he got down to around twenty feet there was a mist and he couldn't see so he tried to go around again with wheels and flaps down. I followed. There was an awful lot of nail-biting because the engine had been running for 15 minutes without seizing."

"He just got over a cliff," Hawksworth continued. "There was a bay over the other side and they ditched. There was an Australian landing craft there. He said it was more frightening afterwards because there were two rival groups of American Marines savaging his aircraft. Literally emptying their holsters."

The next morning, at 0745hrs, Hawksworth led the Fireflies on bombardment-spotting for USS *Iowa*, directing her 16-inch guns onto a coastal gun position on the Amgak peninsula. Circling at 6,500 feet, he could see the ship's huge shells hit the ground near the guns. "I gave the order to shoot when I was over the target. Each shell, they told us, cost as much as one Cadillac. They weren't terribly successful but we did knock out number three target[9]", commented Hawksworth. He was back on *Ocean*'s decks at 1015 that morning.

Four hours later they were involved in a big strike on Pyongyang, in which other aircraft from *Ocean* had been involved, as described in earlier chapters. Hawksworth led a flight of eight Fireflies and twelve Sea Furies to a mass of large crates in the railway marshalling yards. The flak had been severe in the morning's combined raid on the same target with the American Fifth Air Force, Marines, Australians and the aircraft from *Ocean*. "It was the first

---

[9] This was a Bofors type AA gun.

time I'd been up at 10,000 feet," said Hawksworth during our interview, "so I could go down and do a run in at 7,000 feet." He led the attack in as flak burst all around them. Hawksworth's No. 3 and No. 4 dived too fast, ending up ahead of him. Seconds later, rocket projectiles from another Firefly narrowly missed his starboard wing as someone had fired his rockets too early.

Concentrating on the target he unleashed his rockets with the flak getting heavier as he got closer and closer. Levelling out, he pulled the stick right back to climb away from the flak. The rockets and airburst bombs from the Furies sent large sheets of flame into the air when they exploded but did not ignite any subsequent fires.

As they headed back towards *Ocean*, Hawksworth thought about the trip, concerned about the reactions of his section. One of them had been in the morning's raid when the flak had been even worse. Hawksworth could only assume the previous raid had them spooked.[10]

On 12 July, Hawksworth led a strike on a very small transformer in the Chinnampo area. Diving on the target the flight ran into some sparse flak and his aircraft was buffeted by a few bursts. Losing height as the target loomed in his sights, he waited, thumbed the button and then watched his rockets streak towards the transformer. "They were far too high," he recalled.[11] It was the last sortie of their fourth patrol. Hawksworth was looking forward to the ten days in Japan.

The first day of HMS *Ocean*'s fifth patrol, 22 July, was not very successful because of poor visibility. Hawksworth's flight left the ship at 0700hrs and climbed to 5,000 feet where it headed inland. The target was a large number of vehicle garages. This was one of the furthest distances the flight had gone on a single sortie and would therefore be one of the longest at two hours and forty minutes. Hawksworth checked his fuel gauges for he knew they had enough for only a few minutes over the target. He hoped they could do a clear, straight shot and get out.[12]

The garages were covered in a fog bank but on the edge of the fog they could see some buildings. It would be enough. A quick call over the R/T and they split into their battle formations, diving on the targets. Rockets from each of the Fireflies shot towards the buildings, but whatever the result of the attack was, the pilots would never know as the fog rolled in obscuring the ground completely.

The second sortie of the day saw the Fireflies taking off from the ship at noon and climbing away in the direction of Songwha. Just outside the town they'd been briefed with photographs about a group of camouflaged troop huts. Ahead the cloud cover was well below them and he knew they would have to drop to 3,500 feet. Over the target, he wheeled the flight around and attacked, firing a full salvo of rockets at the huts spread out below. Each one missed and hit the hills. Dejected, he watched the rest of the flight do the same.

---

[10] In his diary Hawksworth wrote he was unnerved by the fact that his sub-section had got ahead of him, one of them being the pilot in the morning raid on Pyongyang.

[11] In his diary he wrote "damn it" regarding his overshooting.

[12] He recalled his concern about the time over the target in our interview.

They were back on *Ocean*'s gently rolling deck at 1340hrs but flying for that day wasn't over. At 1630hrs Hawksworth led the flight towards several different targets. The first was a large warehouse north of Changyong, which they blew into three pieces with a partial salvo of rockets.[13]

Despite the later sunrise on 23 July Hawksworth's flight took off when it was still dark to attack a transformer east of Chinnampo.[14] For ten minutes he circled over the sea off the coast, waiting for the sun to rise so he could see well enough in the dawn light to attack. Several layers of cloud covered the ground as he took the flight to 5,000 feet. Seeing the target below he led the Fireflies into their diving runs one after the other. Reaching release height he loosed off all his rockets and quickly climbed away.

In his mirror he could see bright blue flashes after the initial explosions of the rockets. The remaining Fireflies attacked the same target, hammering it with twelve rockets each and finally as they pulled away the building burst into flames, which rose high into the morning sky. Fires raged as the building burned.

They flew another fifteen miles up the coast heading for gun positions on which they'd been briefed on the evening before. Hawksworth went in first. He was boring in on the enemy when suddenly tracer shot past his wings, dangerously close. He could see the shells arcing up to meet him from three Bofors gun emplacements. He tried desperately to get the guns in his sights but didn't have the time and had to pull out. He knew the underside of the aircraft would be a tempting target for the gunners on the ground and felt the aircraft shake as more tracers sliced quickly by him. Nobody was hurt and the flight made it back to the ship unscathed.[15]

The following morning Hawksworth catapulted off HMS *Ocean* at 0830hrs with Bob Brand as his No. 2. Heading for the Chinnampo estuary, the pair climbed through low cloud cover and came out clear at 500 feet. As they gained height, however, the cloud was everywhere, above and below them. Hoping they would see the target through a gap Hawksworth caught a glimpse of a village known to have light flak emplacements around it. Diving through a hole in the cloud they unleashed their rockets and headed back for the ship, flying under the cloud cover.

Later that afternoon, Hawksworth was again in the air with his wingman Brand flying in clear, bright skies. Cruising at 3,000 feet the pair spotted a friendly island being shelled by North Korean troops from several gun positions on Amgak. Both Fireflies emptied their rockets on the gun positions and climbed away.[16]

The first trip on 25 July proved to be a washout. Hawksworth was leading the flight towards the Chinnampo estuary when black smoke started pouring

---

[13] Hawksworth stated they used half their rockets and that the building was empty.

[14] Originally, they were tasked to hit a transformer north of Chinnampo but due to bad visibility they hit one east of Chinnampo instead.

[15] In his entry in his diary he couldn't understand how the enemy could miss all the aircraft of the flight.

[16] In his diary he states that they had to climb to 6,500 feet and dive through a gap in the clouds to attack the gun emplacement but it was a successful attack nevertheless.

from his engine, so he quickly turned his nose around and made an emergency landing back on the carrier.

On Sunday 27 July, the usual early morning raid was delayed because of low cloud cover, but ahead of them lay an unexpected and dramatic turn of events. It was the day 'the Migs came out to play'and Hawksworth was among the pilots from *Ocean* involved at first hand. The ship steamed north to brighter skies and Hawksworth's flight, carrying a full load of rockets and ammunition, slowly climbed up to 8,000 feet above the cloud and headed for the target, a large factory.

The factory lay in a sizable town between Chinnampo and Pyongyang in the Chinnampo estuary. Checking his instruments, and listening to the even note of his engine, Hawksworth was satisfied all was well. Then he called over the radio, "Echelon, break." Touching the rudder bar, he flicked the aircraft over into the top of his dive and pointed the nose down at 50 degrees, tracking two large buildings in his gyro gun sight. Tom Clancy, his observer, was calling out the height as they roared down upon the buildings. Finally, at 3,000 feet, Hawksworth fired his rockets, which smashed into the buildings seconds later.

Suddenly, there was a shout over the radio: "Look out, Migs. I've been hit." Before Hawksworth could react Tom Clancy shouted over the intercom: "Yes. Dead astern. Jink!" Hawksworth saw a stricken Firefly, his No. 4, shoot by below him heading away while he had to contend with the Mig on his tail. "They were coming in low and astern. One place where we had very little chance."

He jinked hard to starboard and down, and as the Mig behind was too close and too fast to follow, it pulled up to port without firing. Just to starboard of Hawksworth's nose, however, he watched another silver swept-back jet with huge cannon spitting bright narrow flame on the tail of another Firefly. He had time to flick open his gun switch, reverse back and let fly with his cannon for about 200 yards.

The enemy jet swept past, increasing speed, and banked to port. What seemed like a two-second burst to Hawksworth was really ten rounds from each gun. "We counted them when we got back aboard," Hawksworth wrote. "It was a half a second burst."

His cannon shells never reached the jet, however, and he immediately reversed back, ducking under cloud. The radio was filled with chatter from the other Fireflies. Ahead was his No. 4 hit in the tail plane by a 30mm shell from one of the Migs. The stricken Firefly was lumbering along very slowly. His No. 2 (Brand) had a small calibre shell through his wingtip while his No. 3 had a tricky time when one of the Migs came around again. Coolant now flowed from his radiator as they headed home. Hawksworth commented: "If they'd had any sense they'd have come down and wiped us out."

The engagement was over in one or two seconds and the cost of the Mig attack was one Firefly lost and one damaged. Hawksworth's No. 3 ditched in the water near HMAS *Bataan* while his No. 4 made a wheels-up landing. "I was untouched," Hawksworth said, "but I missed the chance of a lifetime to shoot down a Mig. It would have been a lovely line to be able to say of course I'm not a fighter pilot but it doesn't look all that difficult." He holds the distinction of being the only Firefly that ever shot at a Mig.

Three sorties took place on 28 July and were all hampered by bad weather. On the early morning flight,[17] Hawksworth led a strike inland. The weather over the target area was so poor they couldn't see the pre-briefed target and ended up releasing their rockets on a coastal village near Ongjin. Later, the same morning they attacked another village where some camouflage netting had been placed over several trucks. As Hawksworth wrote in his diary: "No gain to the war effort at all." So ended an eventful fifth patrol.

The sixth patrol was routine, however, except for Saturday 9 August. The Fireflies climbed slowly away from *Ocean* at 0700hrs, the first time they were carrying bombs instead of their usual rockets. "You carry the bombs on the wing and you have a fusing wire that gets pulled out so the whizzer goes round and arms it. But the wires weren't long enough," Hawksworth remembered. "So they put two together. You're dive-bombing and one comes off and overtakes the aircraft. The bombs were going down safe instead of fused. The worst occasion I know of was four Sea Furies supporting a Commonwealth division. Using two 1,000lb bombs each they had five out of eight failing to explode. So I came up with an idea to use delayed action fuses.

"When you're attacking a bridge I said it would be a good idea that the bombs were dropped 30 seconds apart and one of them had a long delay so you could knock down the bridge. That night you'd blow it up again after they'd repair it and get the repair team as well."

Instead of the full flight, Hawksworth led only his No. 4, Pete Arbuthnot, towards their target. Bob Brand, his No. 2, left the ship with a rough engine, jettisoned his bombs in the sea and turned back while No. 3 hadn't been able to get airborne at all. "So I went with my No. 4 whose eyesight was quite incredible," Hawksworth recalled during our interview. "We were heading up the coast at around 4,000 feet when he let out a shout."

Something glinted in the sun off to port. A Mig! "He'd seen it just as a speck. I put on more revs and more power and I didn't want to jettison the bombs because they'd show up on the sea," continued Hawksworth. "I came down on him until I had him in my sights but he was going so incredibly fast that he was about 600 yards away and I hadn't fired. You could say the first time I fired on a Mig without aiming and the second time I aimed for a Mig without firing."

Either the enemy pilot never saw the Fireflies or just didn't care, it continued diving out to sea. This was the day that Carmichael earned his DSC by shooting down a Mig, a feat that Hawksworth recorded in his diary. Breathing a sigh of relief, Hawksworth turned inland in the opposite direction to the Mig. "I have to say when the 'Look out, Migs! I've been hit,' came through I thought 'those damn Sabres'. We'd never been shot at by aircraft except by Americans," Hawksworth said. So the Migs had been a real surprise. "And we had these great black and white hoops painted on our aircraft like the

---

[17] This was at 0525hrs.

Normandy landings so the Americans wouldn't shoot at us."[18]

The seventh patrol began on 27 August 1952, with Hawksworth's flight flying two sorties that day. They formed up over the ship at 1030hrs and headed inland for a photo recce of the Changyong–Sinchon area. As the flight rolled towards the target, high above them Hawksworth could see several aircraft. Worried, he wondered how long it would take before his Fireflies would be spotted.

He soon got an answer. Four aircraft dived down from the port side. He held his breath, flicking the firing button. Before he had a chance to take any action he let out a sigh of relief. The four aircraft were Sea Furies who waggled their wings and climbed quickly away.

That afternoon the Fireflies were back in the air, carrying bombs instead of their usual rockets. The target was a bridge north-west of Taeton. Instead of unloading both bombs on the target Hawksworth pushed the stick forward into his dive, heading for the port side of the road where the bridge began, in the hope of knocking out the spar.

The port bomb fell away, exploding on the road in a shower of flame and smoke. As he pulled out of the dive and came around to start his next one, Hawksworth could see the bridge had not been touched. The rest of his Fireflies targeted the structure but all of them were badly short. Finally Hawksworth brought his Firefly into the top of his dive, pushed the nose over and headed for the bridge. Because of the weight under only one wing, the aircraft skidded instead of slicing down through the air. He dropped the starboard bomb, but it missed the target completely,[19] and then they headed back to the ship.

It wasn't all hard flying and fighting. On one occasion Hawksworth flew some media people from the ship back to Seoul. "I remember flying through this brown rain cloud," he smiled. "This was at 700 feet and it was straight up the river in the peace treaty area you weren't allowed to touch. We landed at K16 and the airfield was closed. The wind and the sand got up and there were some Furies there as well. Being the senior man there I decided we should all go back to the ship the next day and that was very unpopular because it was replenishment night," laughed Hawksworth.

One by one the Fireflies catapulted off the deck just after dawn the next day carrying their usual rocket projectiles under each wing. Their target was a radar station previously missed by another flight. Leading the Fireflies Hawksworth climbed to 5,000 feet in clear, sunny skies. The drone of his engine purring happily away made him feel confident. This attack would work.

Near the target, he called out to the flight, "Echelon, break." They split into a line astern formation, and then Hawksworth dropped the nose, diving on the target. Thumbing the firing button the rockets roared away and plastered the radar station. Climbing, Hawksworth watched the other Fireflies bore in on the target. It was soon completely obliterated by smoke and debris.

---

[18] When he first saw the Mig he radioed in to see if it was a Sabre and heard one Sea Fury had been shot down in flames and another forced to do a wheels-up on Chodo beach.
[19] In his diary he wrote that he deliberately dropped one bomb on one side to straddle the structure. He also wrote that this day he flew his 100th offensive sortie.

Bad weather kept the Fireflies grounded for the next few days as a typhoon swept through the area. Life on the pitching deck was rough and Hawksworth preferred to be in the air.

However, on Thursday 4 September, the Fireflies headed towards the Ongjin transformers, which had been damaged in other attacks but not completely destroyed. Diving on the buildings Hawksworth fired a full salvo of rockets and watched each strike the transformer just before he pulled out of his dive. Rockets from the rest of the flight ripped into the structure. Turning tightly Hawksworth flew a quick photo run over the burning target, proving that the rockets from his aircraft and his No. 4 had done the trick.

Heading back to the ship, the flight dropped down low, strafing a village reported to house more than 300 troops.[20] Less than four hours later the Fireflies were attacking another transformer north-east of Changyong. This time, only half of Hawksworth's rockets fired but every one hit the mark.

Seeing a large white building nearby, Hawksworth attacked it with his remaining four rockets. The projectiles slammed into the building creating huge holes, but did not knock it down.

Turning the flight back towards home, they strafed a road, and some troops and installations in a field before finally landing an hour and forty minutes after take-off.

That was the end of Harry Hawksworth's war in Korea as he now returned to the UK.

---

[20] He does not indicate in his diary where the reports came from concerning the 300 troops.

Chapter Eleven

FURIES ASCENDANT

Lieutenant Ted Anson, HMS *Glory*

The ground war in late 1952 had come to a stalemate with little movement of the front line despite the bitter fighting. In November, President Eisenhower visited Korea, vowing to end the war, and examined both the military options and the possibilities of a truce. In April 1953, the armistice negotiations began again, while at the same time the possibility of having to widen the war with air attacks on China grew, and an escalation of the ground war in Korea was faced by the UN forces. The Chinese and North Koreans launched fresh offensives in June and mid-July, but they failed to win significant extra ground, and the armistice was duly signed on 27 July 1953.

Sea Fury pilot Lieutenant Ted Anson had arrived on HMS *Glory* during her third and last patrol in the Korean War in late 1952. Unlike Nick Cook, Lieutenant Anson was a Navy career man who went to naval college when he was thirteen. "It was a school as well. We had to get rid of Latin in order to make room for seamanship," he recalled when I talked with him. He left the college at eighteen to go to sea. "I did six months in a training cruiser. Seventy per cent of the crew were cadets and the remaining were professional trainers. We had to do every single job on the ship for six months. When you were at naval college you didn't mention you wanted to fly. The Navy was very snobby about aviation in the old days."

Flying was what he wanted to do, however, and before he could get near an aircraft, Anson had to finish being a seaman officer and get his navigation certificate. Next he took a series of lieutenant's courses in gunnery, mines, torpedoes, anti-submarine warfare and signals. "These were six to eight week courses and you were fully trained right across the spectrum," Anson explained. "At the end of that you went to sea to get a watchman's certificate so I went to sea in a destroyer."

Finally he found himself training on Prentices, Harvards and lastly Seafires; then he converted to Sea Furies at RNAS Culdrose in a very intensive course on air-to-air and air-to-ground weaponry as well as practising catapult launches. At Culdrose students learnt the art of dive-bombing onto their targets. Concentric circles were painted on the runway intersection and the new students would spend several hours diving on the circles. "When you got to the top of the dive your sight was more or less on the target," Anson recalled. "You then pushed the button that started the camera[1] that would continually take

---

[1] The camera was mounted either in the wings or fuselage and was a cine film camera.

pictures and when you got to the release point you pulled the trigger and that stopped the film."

When the film was developed, range assessors would project the images onto a tilting white board. "So when you were in the dive taking these pictures, the circles would come out as ellipses. When this was projected on the board, by tilting the board the ellipses became circles." The range assessors then read the degree angle printed on the side of the board, which would have been the precise dive angle of the aircraft.

Accuracy was all-important. "For a 45-degree angle you've got to be diving between 44 and 46 degrees," Anson continued. "If you are a bit shallow you can see you are shallow, so you aim over the top. Ideally you are trying to hit exactly 45 degrees. Believe it or not, after the hundreds of dummy dives we did you got a picture in your mind of running up to the target and where it should be in relation to your wing. If you wanted a 45-degree dive you doubled that for the target. You then rolled into your dive and you should have come out at 45 degrees. Then you had to be exactly at the right release height and speed."

On the Sea Fury there were red throttle settings for the diving speed. The aircraft was also fitted with a contact altimeter, which started screaming in the pilot's earphones when he rolled into his dive. Once the right release height was reached, the screaming stopped. "From the corner of your eye you can see the altimeter unwinding. You set your revs on the right setting and your throttles and you built up speed as you went down. If you're at the right dive angle, the speed should be right for the release height." In a crosswind, pilots were taught to aim upwind of the target and release their bombs. "It all sounds very complicated and it is very confusing when you start," Anson explained.

After the intensive training at Culdrose Anson went to 801 Squadron on HMS *Glory* in December 1952, for his stint in the Korean War. Before embarking, he and other new arrivals practised their flying skills on Furies out of Iwakuni in Japan. Here deck landings were the order of the day. Finally, as *Glory* was ready to go, he flew from Iwakuni towards the ship for his first patrol of the war. On his approach to the ship, however, despite all his practice Anson got six wave-offs from the batsman. "I thought to myself, they must be getting bored with this and are likely to divert me to Pusan which wasn't far," said Anson. Fortunately, on the seventh try he landed on safely.

His difficulty was that he should have been turning, as he explained: "It takes a little while to get a mental picture of where you turn when you're looking at the carrier. The ship is going one way and you're going another way, so if you turn too far you start coming in the wrong way. You should be in the turn all the way round. If you are angling, then at the last minute you have to do a very steep turn and so they wave you off."

He soon became an old hand at deck landings achieving 295 in the Sea Fury, most of them during his time in the Korean War. "Once you got the hang of getting the tail down, the Fury actually stalled and the tail wheel would still be about a foot above the deck. When you got the cut you whipped the stick back, the nose dropped and you got it through the stall and into three-point attitude[2].

---

[2] Three-point attitude is the two main wheels under the wings and the tail wheel at the rear of the fuselage touching down together onto the deck.

Once you got that in your mind you didn't have any problems."

By the time Anson joined HMS *Glory* in December 1952, she had already completed two patrols of her last tour of the war. Her complement when she began the tour in November was twenty-one Sea Furies of 801 Squadron, commanded by Lieutenant Commander Pete Stuart, and thirteen Fireflies of 821 Squadron commanded by Lieutenant Commander J. R. N. Gardiner. Four new volunteer reserve naval lieutenants joined HMS *Glory* on this tour. One of them was 'Pug' Mather.

The first patrol of *Glory*'s third tour saw new forming-up procedures introduced. Aircraft would form up at 500 feet on the starboard side of the ship instead of at 1,500 feet off the port bow ahead of the ship. This would avoid getting into the circuit of incoming aircraft.[3] The Furies carried bombs throughout each patrol while Fireflies often carried bombs for one part of the patrol and rockets for the rest. Bridges, tunnels, railway and road transport, transformer stations and troop concentrations were still their usual targets.

However, another harsh Korean winter was raging that hampered flying. Low cloud, high winds, snow and rain played havoc with operations during the first patrol in November. Faulty 20mm ammunition[4], which was to result in casualties in later patrols, reared its ugly head when a shell exploded inside a Firefly's cannon causing severe damage to the aircraft.

Nine Furies and six Fireflies were hit by small arms fire during the first patrol and one Sea Fury pilot, Lieutenant Neville-Jones, was lost on 18 November when he was hit by flak while dive-bombing a bridge over Chaeryong south of Sariwon.

Glory's operational area was carefully delineated owing to peace talks. These had been suspended in early October, after an impasse on the repatriation of prisoners. The Chinese and North Korean forces had begun a new and heavy offensive two days earlier, which lasted for ten days, while the UN air forces kept up the bombing pressure. Pammunjom, where the talks would be resumed in the spring, was a neutral zone and not to be attacked. The north and eastern limitation line was from Hanchonon on the west coast, south-east to Pyongyang, then south and east to Chungwha, Hwangju, Sariwon, Sohung, Kumchon and then along the river to the coast at Tosong-ni.

When the carrier and her escorts of destroyers returned to Korean waters on 28 November for her second patrol, the weather was even worse. High winds whipped snow across her decks as she rolled in deep swells. The aircraft handlers worked hard to keep the deck free of snow and ice, but for three and a half days the Siberian weather forced all flying to be cancelled.

By the time *Glory* began her third patrol, Lieutenant Anson was firmly ensconced in 801 Squadron as it was his fifth patrol. Flying began on 17 December and the Furies were set to attack bridges and tunnels. As the North Koreans would hide their trains in tunnels during the day and bring them out at night, the Furies' aim was to block off the tunnel, trapping the locomotives

---

[3] One wonders why it took them so long to introduce these procedures.

[4] 20mm ammunition was used in the Sea Fury's four cannon as well as in Firefly cannon.

inside. They used 500lb bombs with 30-second proximity fuses, and attacked at 200 feet. Dropping into their dives they screamed in on the target, following the railway line leading towards the tunnel, then they lobbed their bombs into the entrances and pulled out sharply. "It was not difficult," explained Anson, "You hit the button at the right moment and then pulled out quickly. One of our squadron released his bombs and just inside the tunnel was a locomotive with a full head of steam. His bombs hit the locomotive and the explosion flipped him [the Fury] over on his back."

Early one morning Lieutenant Anson's flight, led by the CO, Lieutenant Commander Stuart, was briefed to fly to an inland target. Catapulting off the deck, the flight formed up above the ship and headed for land. Over the radio Anson heard the controllers providing new coordinates. Minutes later, their course changed to head for another railway tunnel. The bombs under their wings didn't have the long delay fuses, so Anson knew the pull-out would have to be quick.

"Echelon go!" Stuart shouted over the radio as he peeled off, dropping into a dive and heading towards the target. The other Furies followed their leader, dropping low above the tracks and heading at high speed for the tunnel mouth.

As Anson rolled into his dive, he could see Stuart pulling up sharply; his bombs were skipping into the tunnel entrance and exploding on impact. "The CO was the only one who managed to drop the bomb straight in. They went off as he was pulling out and he got away with it. In a situation like that you built experience fast," said Anson. The average mission was one hour and forty-five minutes, with up to six scheduled each day.

The combination of flak damage, low fuel and bad weather made emergency landings onboard *Glory* difficult for any pilot. "If you knew you were going to hit the barrier during an emergency landing there was a technique that you used to get the tail up again and get the nose right in the middle of the barrier," explained Anson. "There were two wire strands going across with smaller wires crossed over each other, and when you hit that on either end there was a hydraulic mechanism, which pulled out and went from nothing to stopping you suddenly. If you did manage to get the nose into the barrier, the damage wasn't too severe because it would only be all around the cowling. The wings would be untouched, so it would probably be flying the next day."

Ted Anson always flew with Pete Stuart, the squadron's CO. Unlike most other flight leaders, Stuart would lead his flight around onto the target for a second attack dropping one bomb on the first run and the second on the next run. "None of the other flight leaders did that. They used to drop both bombs at the same time whereas we used to drop one and come round again and drop the other one.

"The other guys hit just as many targets as we did, so it was quite honestly stupid. If you've got to come back you come back twenty minutes later. On the first dive the enemy are drinking their cups of tea then suddenly this aircraft comes over and they've got to get organised. But the second time you come down they're ready for you." On this one, Anson was flying No. 4 when Stuart lost his No. 2: "So then I was flying No. 2 but then he lost No. 3 and I was flying No. 4, so it got pretty hairy."

On 18 December 1952, faulty ammunition very nearly cost the life of Sea Fury pilot Lieutenant Leahy[5] when a shell exploded inside one of his cannon. Fortunately, he managed an emergency landing at the airstrip at Paengyong-do, landing safely. However, Lieutenant Fogden, a Firefly pilot, was not so lucky. A 20mm shell exploded in one of his guns and he crashed into the sea, sinking with the aircraft. The faulty high explosive ammunition was ten years old and needed to be replaced. All strafing runs were cancelled until this problem could be solved and pilots were only allowed to fire their cannon in self-defence.

HMS *Glory*'s next patrol began on 4 January 1953 when she set sail from Sasebo. She arrived with her escorts off the coast of Korea in such bad weather that only seven days of flying were achieved instead of the normal nine. Thick banks of clouds between the ship and the coast, with snowstorms beneath the cloud, hampered flying operations throughout the patrol.

By this time in the war, the policy towards attacking railway lines had changed. Hitherto bridges and tunnels had been considered to be the most vulnerable part of the enemy's railway network. If those were knocked out the enemy couldn't use his railway. However, the North Koreans kept several large stocks of repair materials close to these areas, making it easier to repair the lines and get them working again. "They knew we were going for bridges and we were pretty successful in knocking them down," Anson recalled. "Once the pilots had been acclimatized there were very few cases when all four aircraft would have missed a bridge. But the Koreans had the bloody thing built the next day. So then we switched to going for railways."

The new plan was to attack and cut railway lines in the most difficult and inhospitable places far from roads or tracks of any kind to make it more difficult for the North Koreans to repair, and the policy proved to be very effective.

On 5 January, Anson watched his colleague get hit by flak and burn. Flying over the Chaeryong area in low cloud at 2,000 feet, Lieutenant Anson and Lieutenant Derek Graham Pug Mather attacked a railway bridge. "We knew it had radar-controlled AA fire," Anson said.

Mather went in first with Anson right behind him. The two Furies rolled into their dives, Mather gauging his release point as flak shot up past the aircraft; with his throttles set in the red position, rpm fine, he watched the bridge get bigger and bigger as the flak burst around him. Behind, Anson was dropping into his dive, and saw Mather's Fury pull up sharply, as its two bombs fell quickly away. Under a storm of flak he saw the lead Fury suddenly buck and weave. "I've been hit," called Mather. "Under the seat, I think."

At the bottom of his dive, Anson released his bombs, yanked the stick back into his stomach, pushed the throttles forward and climbed quickly away, as flak continued to burst around him. Over the radio Anson heard Mather's calm voice asking him to look over his aircraft for damage. Easing his Fury closer to Mather's, Anson watched in horror as the other Fury suddenly broke in half,

---

[5] This episode is mentioned in greater detail in Chapter Thirteen.

flames licking around the seat and armour plating as debris shot back towards Anson's Fury. "The whole back piece of the aircraft fell away. It caused me some consternation because I had to quickly get out of the way. I saw his parachute open and he was making himself comfortable in the straps, at which point I flew into cloud. We should never have been flying that day because of the low cloud base. Normally we flew above the ground fire.[6] But that day it was at 2,000 feet."

The optimum height for dropping into a dive was between 5,000 and 4,500 feet, which enabled the pilots to release their bombs at the correct dive angle, speed, height and at the right place. "Going in at 2,000 feet you've really got a very short space of time to get all those parameters right."

Anson climbed hard through the cloud layer, hoping to get above it. At 6,000 feet he levelled out, but below him was a field of almost solid cloud. He needed to find a hole quickly, so he could get back and protect Mather. Pushing the Fury into a quick circle he scoured the cloud for an opening. "I found one and went back down through it then flew back to where we'd been." But there was no sign of Mather.

Standard issue for the pilots among their emergency suits was a Smith and Wesson revolver. "The idea was when you are surviving behind the lines you can shoot game for food," Anson explained. "Pug had swapped his revolver for a .45 Colt with an American. As he was coming down he saw these guys firing at him and thought that was a bit unfriendly and started firing back at them. Before he landed he threw the Colt away and as soon as he landed they jumped on him and got his parachute off and sat on him in a ditch or something till we'd gone."

The North Koreans knew the drill. If a pilot was shot down, all other UN allied aircraft in the vicinity would stop what they were doing and start looking for the downed pilot. "The North Koreans were very quick in getting him out of sight," Anson continued. "They grabbed him as soon as he landed and he was a prisoner of war for the rest of the conflict."

Despite not knowing Mather's position, the rescue helicopter from Chodo Island had been called in and now clawed its way towards the area, escorted by two Furies flown by Sub-Lieutenants Rayner and Keates. The area was mountainous and covered in low cloud. Visibility was very limited as the helicopter flew on. The two Furies disappeared in and out of cloud as they throttled back to the chopper's speed.

Dropping low out of the cloud, Keates looked around for Rayner but saw no sign of him. Then he saw a large fire on a nearby hillside and wondered what it was. As Rayner wasn't answering his calls Keates felt a sense of foreboding spread over him. Rayner did not return to the ship. He could have been hit by flak or simply hit high ground in the low cloud visibility. It was later confirmed by partisans operating behind North Korean lines that Rayner's Sea Fury had crashed into the village of Chang Yang Dong, south of Chinnampo.

HMS *Glory*'s fifth patrol in Korea began on 21 January. The gun stoppages due to the faulty ammunition had been cleared by the time this patrol began.

---

[6] Above ground fire was between 5,000 and 6,000 feet.

The Furies and Fireflies now had new ammunition and the restrictions on strafing were lifted. "The cannon was very effective for different kinds of targets," Anson said. "After you'd dropped your bombs you still had a full ammunition tank. You didn't just go in, bomb something and come back. You'd fly up there, you got your targets and you dropped your bombs. Next you're doing your reconnaissance and looking for opportunity targets like trucks. You used your cannon on those targets."

The cloak of winter had set in over Korea with icy gales still bringing Siberian temperatures and snowstorms from the north. Temperatures were dropping so low that ice was forming between the island of Chodo and the mainland. The UN forces realized that if a continuous sheet of ice resulted the enemy could use it to invade Chodo and destroy the radio and radar installations there.

To counter this, ships of the blockading force acted as ice-breakers keeping the channel clear. While the destroyers, cruisers and patrol craft slowly hacked their way through the ice, overhead, *Glory*'s aircraft kept standing ice-reconnaissance flights in high gear. These sorties comprised more than just flying over ice, they were for checking the communist build-up of forces on the coast as a prelude to any invasion of the island. The aircraft were tasked on villages known to have heavy Chinese and North Korean troop concentrations and gun emplacements on the coast.

One morning, two Sea Furies formed up over *Glory* and headed for the coast. They were detailed to look at a gun position on the Amgak peninsula, which fired out to sea towards Chodo Island. After that they were to fly inland and bomb a bridge. Lieutenant Anson, flying No. 2 on this flight, roared up the coast. "We had two bombs each," said Anson, describing the action. "This gun emplacement was very low down and very steep. It was a Bofors type gun in a cave. I was flying with this other bloke. We were supposed to attack the bridge first and then do the gun emplacement on the way home but he chose to do it the other way round as he had the lead."

Visibility was better than in previous days as the two Furies rolled into their dives, Anson a few seconds behind the leader. He watched the lead Fury's bombs fall away and saw the aircraft pull up sharply because of the hills surrounding the gun. Screaming down onto the target,Anson pulled back on the stick, then released his bombs and climbed away. But nothing happened. "I couldn't pull the aircraft at all. The hill in front of me was climbing faster than I was because my elevators had jammed."

For a few precious seconds he fought the controls, trying desperately to pull the Fury out of its headlong plunge toward the hill. "It's moments like this where somehow you become very strong and I managed eventually to move the stick over and pull out." Climbing away, he radioed his colleague. "I'm going to get rid of my bombs over the sea because my elevators are jammed." Ditching his bombs in the sea the two Furies headed for the next target. "He dropped his bombs on that and we flew back to the ship. The elevators seemed alright and we landed back on board."

Back on *Glory*, the handlers crawled all over Anson's Fury to find the problem. Standing watching them work, the noise of aircraft taking off and landing all around him, Anson thought about what could have happened.

Finally, one of the maintainers[7] fished out something. "It was a bit of metal that had been left in during the manufacturing process; originally it was about eight inches long, now it was two inches."

Furies later targeted the Bofors gun positions, knocking it out of action for some time. For the rest of the patrol, roads and railways leading to the coast were regularly strafed and bombed by Furies and Fireflies. Then *Glory* steamed out of Korean waters back to Japan, her fourth patrol over.

Bad weather continued to play havoc with flying when the carrier left Sasebo in Japan on 5 February 1953, to start her sixth patrol. It was either little high cloud with 50-mile visibility on some days or low cloud, snow showers and poor visibility on others. Again the targets were largely troops and stores. Villages south-west of Chinnampo were said by partisans to be housing around 1,400 troops while more troop concentrations on the Ongjin peninsula were attacked as the enemy prepared for invasions of friendly islands and partisan subjugation.

The morning of 8 February, the aircrew stood on the windswept deck in darkness. The sun was still an hour away from rising and the low cloud cover would bring a murky grey light, which would make the Sea Furies hard to spot because of their grey camouflage. They'd been briefed for their pre-dawn mission. A convoy of trucks and other vehicles was moving along a frozen road between Hanchon and Pyongyang. The Furies were to demolish it as best they could.

Anson climbed into the cockpit, stiff with cold as the handlers began running up the Sea Fury. He checked the time, 0500hrs. Quickly, he ran through all the pre-flight checks, looking at his instruments and making sure everything was as it should be. Ahead, Lieutenant Commander Stuart was in position. Moments later his Fury catapulted off the deck and roared into the air, disappearing into the thick murky grey sky.

At 0520hrs, Anson's Fury shot off *Glory*'s deck and climbed quickly away from the ship. The flight of Furies formed up then wheeled around, heading for the coast. Just as light was beginning to show through the low cloud cover the Sea Furies arrived over the convoy. Headlights below stabbed through the murky gloom as the vehicles slowly rolled over the frozen road. "Echelon, break," was the call over the radio as the lead Fury rolled over, dropping into its dive. A moment later Anson flipped his Fury over, checked his firing button and bomb release and watched the convoy quickly grow in his gun sight as he lost height. When Stuart began diving on the convoy, the enemy vehicles shut off their headlights. His bombs hammered the lead vehicles before he pulled up. Behind him, Anson released his bombs further down the convoy, strafing the vehicles with cannon fire as he shot over the convoy and pulled away. As the fighters formed up they could see several of the hapless vehicles had caught fire and were burning brightly, but they had no idea how much of the convoy had been destroyed because of the poor visibility.

Several Furies were lost on this patrol. One of them, piloted by Sub-Lieutenant Hayes, was hit by flak while attacking a bridge near the Chaeryong

---

[7] This was Anson's word for aircraft handlers.

area. The shell split his oil lines and he noticed an oil leak but by the time he had reached Taedong-Gang estuary on his way back to the ship, the oil pressure had dropped, the temperature increased and the engine seized. He ditched the Fury in water clear of ice and was picked up two minutes later by the American helicopter from Chodo Island.

On 11 February, Sub-Lieutenant MacPherson crashed into a hillside after being hit by flak as he pulled out of a low level strafing attack on a stores dump near Chaeryong. Three days later, Sub-Lieutenant Bradley's engine failed. He called up on the R/T saying that he was going to ditch. Instead of slowing down and trying to stall the aircraft over the sea, however, he went in at high speed. The aircraft immediately broke up and sank, taking Bradley to the bottom.

"Getting hit by flak captures your attention," Anson said to me. Throughout his time in HMS *Glory* Anson was hit three times by flak. "If you flew with the CO you got flak. Once was with a larger calibre shell that made quite a hole. With rifle fire you don't really know you've been hit but with the larger gun there is no doubt whatsoever. But I was very lucky because whatever it was did not explode on impact but went in one side of the fuselage and out the other." Later, when the handlers put a rod through the hole it went between the tail plane trim wires inside the fuselage. "It missed them all so I was very lucky it didn't explode."

At the beginning of her seventh patrol, when *Glory* arrived back in Korean waters on 25 February 1953, she ran into the worst weather yet, meeting rain, snow, steep seas, heavy swells, high winds and low cloud. Only 371 sorties were flown on this patrol and twenty-three missions were cancelled because of the weather, accounting for 229 sorties lost.[8]

Fog was one of the biggest culprits; it began low over the coast and was swept out to sea by high winds. The wind speed would increase, pushing the fog up to a layer of cloud that over the land obscured targets. High winds and storms would make flying completely impossible for two days.

Throughout the bad weather two Furies constantly maintained Combat Air Patrol cover ahead of the ship. Briefed for a normal CAP duty one morning, Anson and the CO were suddenly diverted (while in the air) to attack an island north of Sunwido. The request came from the partisan guerrilla fighters who had identified several NKA positions.

The two Furies turned away from the ship, heading up the coast towards North Korea. Under each wing was a 500lb bomb and their ammunition tanks were full of 20mm rounds. Directed by the partisans, Stuart rolled into his dive first, under the low cloud cover. Pulling out, he released his bombs and climbed away. Behind him, Anson could see soldiers running in all directions as he screamed down on the targets. Watching the altimeter unwind he waited for several seconds, reached the right height, pulled the stick back and released his bombs as the Fury levelled out. Now at low level he thumbed the firing button, his cannon spitting into life as he shot over the target. No return fire came from

---

[8] This number is in Anson's logbook and also in *With the Carriers in Korea*.

the ground and the Furies did so much damage that a follow-up air strike was unnecessary. Then they headed back to the ship.

The 4th and 6th March were leafleting days, where British aircraft carried special American leaflet bombs. The bombs had been modified to drop the leaflets.

Now that the relationship between *Glory* and the partisans operating behind North Korean lines was closer, more accurate reports of damage and casualties came through. The 1st Partisan Infantry Regiment operating in the area confirmed the number of troops killed, installations destroyed and aircraft lost.

The eighth patrol for *Glory* and her escorts began on 15 March 1953, when she set sail from Sasebo. Again the weather was terrible with flying severely curtailed. Virtually every day of the patrol saw mist and fog at sea and in valleys, and a perpetual haze. Gale winds and heavy swells made flying difficult for the British. In Korea, the spring thaw was in full swing and targets such as railway and road bridges were attacked including tunnels. Because the rivers were running faster and higher due to the thaw the enemy found it much more difficult to repair bridges and railway lines than he had during the winter.

On the 17th Furies attacked a railway bridge heavily defended by enemy gun positions on an adjacent hill. One section of Furies separated from the other, heading towards the hill. Rolling into their dives, one by one the Furies went down, releasing their bombs accurately on the gun emplacement, destroying it. The rest of the Furies went for the bridge with bombs, successfully knocking it out of action without a single enemy shell being fired at them. This kind of operation was known as flak suppression and was very effective.

Another flak suppression operation took place on 22 March when Furies hit three anti-aircraft guns near a radio station in the Sariwon area. The guns were put out of action while Fireflies destroyed the radio station. "We were doing close air support for the Army," Anson said. "They would say, 'We want you to take out that target there.' They would get some smoke in its vicinity and they would say, 'Can you see the smoke, can you see this, can you see that? There's your target.' Just before you went in they (the Army) opened up with all their guns with airburst ammunition[9] over the Koreans. They all got their heads down. That's called flak suppression."

After her ten days rest in Japan, *Glory* set sail from Kure for her ninth patrol on 4 April to begin flying operations the next day. Again the weather was variable and 130 sorties were cancelled because of extreme conditions. One fine day, however, the captain, aircrew and ship's crew decided to try to break a record for the most number of sorties flown in a day. It was estimated that a carrier equipped with thirty-three aircraft and fifty pilots flying sorties of one hour and thirty minutes should be able to launch twelve sorties for every hour of daylight. This idea was put to the test on the 5th, the first day

---

[9] Large calibre ammunition designed to explode in the air over the target, which forces the enemy to take cover, thus suppressing enemy fire.

of the patrol. Over eight hours more than 100 aircraft were hurtled one by one down the deck by the powerful hydraulic catapult and into the air. The aircraft handlers and maintainers worked at fever pitch to keep maximum serviceability throughout the day, and but for an early morning accident where a Fury had to have its tail plane changed they would have managed it. Nevertheless, nineteen of the twenty Furies were kept airborne throughout the day, and the damaged aircraft flew later in the day. By halfway through the day 107 sorties had been flown with everyone working at maximum effort. Satisfied that they could do it, the pace was reduced.[10]

Fog coming in from the Yellow Sea in the early days of the patrol hampered flying, keeping it to a minimum. To get to clear seas, *Glory* steamed north, getting out of the fog banks to a place where she could turn in a clear sea space for launching her aircraft. At one point she was between two fog banks and was so close to one that one of the wing destroyers disappeared from view. As on the other patrols the Furies pounded road and railway bridges, cut railway lines with heavy bombs, smashed tunnel entrances, hammered troop concentrations, and strafed stores, warehouses and villages.

Perhaps the most remarkable point of *Glory*'s tenth patrol, which began on 20 April, was the beginning of the exchange of sick and wounded prisoners of war at Panmunjom, and a few days later the armistice negotiations began once more. It was a signal that hostilities might soon be over.

Anson spent much of his time during this patrol ferrying aircraft from Iwakuni in Japan to the ship. The usual strikes took place, however, with the Furies pounding targets in their area, concentrating largely on lines of communications and transportation. *Glory*'s final patrol began on 14 May, during which the Furies were busy hitting targets in support of the partisans. However, the situation changed slightly when restrictions were placed on her aircraft, because of heavy losses to USMC Marines on heavily defended targets.

For major attacks flak suppression would be done from shore-based jet aircraft. The target was only to be attacked once, with the pilot weaving the aircraft all the way up until his final approach to it. At the same time aircraft had to stay above 3,000 feet except when dive-bombing and all aircraft had to pull out of the dive at 1,500 feet. The aim was to give enemy gunners as little chance as possible to aim at diving aircraft.

Targets on roads and railway lines were only to be attacked where there were a lot of them together, not in ones and twos. Oxcarts, which were generally used for carrying ammunition under manure, could be attacked as seen.

The rivers were drying up as summer approached, so bridges became less important than coastal guns. Two radar stations were destroyed on this last patrol. The number of sorties flown per day averaged sixty while a total of 417 were flown during the entire patrol.

At the end of her eleventh patrol, as *Glory* left Korea for the last time, Ted Anson's war was far from over. Once in Japan he transferred with some

---

[10] This information is per John Lansdown's *With the Carriers in Korea*.

other pilots to HMS *Ocean* to join 807 Squadron, and saw out the last few months of the war flying his beloved Fury from her deck. Each time he climbed into the Fury's cockpit and the huge radial engine roared into life, adrenaline would shoot through Anson's veins until he touched down on the deck again and shut the engine off. "There was excitement, the thrill of flying an extraordinary aircraft, but there was also the loss of life, and the sadness at seeing your colleagues shot down in flames or taken prisoner," he recalled sadly.

HMS *Glory* had left the UK in 1951 and spent 530 days at sea. Over the course of her time on operations she steamed some 157,000 miles and spent fifteen months of war service with 316 days fighting off the coast of Korea. Her aircrew had catapulted off her decks or been launched by rockets for 13,700 flights, for a total of 9,500[11] operational sorties over North Korea.

Lieutenant Ted Anson went on to a full career in the Navy with the distinction of being the last captain of the HMS *Ark Royal* aircraft carrier before the arrival of the Sea Harrier and the smaller carriers. He became a rear Admiral. He summed up his time in Korea thus: "You went there to do a job."

---

[11] These numbers are published in Anson's logbook.

Chapter Twelve

THE COAL BURNERS

Lieutenant Anthony Skinner, HMS *Ocean* and HMS *Glory*

As did Lieutenant Anson, Lieutenant Anthony Skinner served on HMS *Ocean* and HMS *Glory*. His first operational sortie was flying from *Ocean*, which he joined on the last leg of her second tour of Korea. "It took about a week for us to fly out with BOAC," he told me. "The carrier was in Iwakuni and in those days it was quite a journey. We flew in some small plane from Malta to Rome and stayed for three nights because the aircraft we were due to take had broken down. BOAC put us up in a five-star hotel. We'd never seen such luxury." A week later he and three other pilots arrived in Iwakuni to transfer over to 825 Squadron onboard the ship.

On 4 October 1952, Skinner catapulted off the deck of the aircraft carrier in his Firefly Mark 5 and formed up with the rest of his flight on his first sortie, on which the flight pounded some huts near Chinnampo with rockets.

Light began creeping up over the horizon as the Fireflies climbed away from *Ocean* the next day. Armed with a full load of ammunition Skinner strafed several oxcarts before returning to the ship. "Every now and then you'd blast an oxcart and the thing would blow up," he said. "It was pretty clear it wasn't full of manure but ammunition."

On 6 October, 825 Squadron's Fireflies caught several enemy troops out in the open on a beach and let loose their rockets. Rifle fire came up to meet the aircraft but they were gone before the soldiers could get organised. "Rocketing and bombing was done at quite low level," Skinner recalled. "Occasionally you'd see a tracer coming up but most of it you didn't see when you bottomed out of the dive."

Anthony Skinner's second patrol began at the end of October. It was *Ocean*'s last in her second tour. On the morning of the 24th, the Fireflies headed towards the Haeju area on a photographic reconnaissance mission. "We'd take off and form up while we were heading ashore." Aircraft would form up at 500 feet on the starboard side of the carrier instead of the 1,500 feet off the port bow as had been done by other carriers in the war. The tactic was to keep forming up aircraft away from aircraft returning to the ship.[1] "Then we'd break into pairs."

On the morning of 26 October, Skinner was in the air on his first sortie of the day heading towards a transformer station. Climbing to 5,000 feet he did a

---

[1] This method was documented in John Lansdown's book.

quick check of his instruments, then pushed the nose forward into the dive. Reaching the release height, he fired his rockets, and climbed steeply away. He could see flashes as his rockets hammered the target in great gulfs of smoke and dust. "We'd gain height and look around to see if it caught fire. Generally the explosion would happen behind you."

The 27th brought routine flying for Tony Skinner. The early morning photo-reconnaissance flight of the Haeju area provided targets for later strikes. On the way back to the ship they strafed several oxcarts. The afternoon saw the Fireflies pouring their rockets into a village on the Ongjin peninsula.

The following day the Fireflies swept in on troops and huts, strafing and pounding the enemy with rockets, but in the afternoon their rockets only partially damaged buildings at Pungchon. Oxcarts, gun positions and bridges were rocketed and strafed the following day by the Fireflies while the Furies flew bombing missions in support of the guerrillas.

This was the end of the carrier's second tour, but Skinner wasn't yet going home. As *Ocean* returned to Japan Lieutenant Skinner said goodbye to her crew and transferred to HMS *Glory*, *Ocean*'s replacement. Lieutenant Anson was on *Glory* at the same time as Skinner, although Anson did not join until December that year.

Skinner's third patrol began on 11 November when *Glory* arrived off the western coast of Korea. Wind, snow and rain hampered flying, and low cloud and poor visibility cut the number of sorties. In grey overcast sky, Skinner's flight of Fireflies climbed away from the ship. They rocketed coastal gun positions embedded in cliffs, then headed back to the ship as the weather deteriorated. Two days later Skinner's Fireflies pumped rockets into an officers' mess in the Haeju area.

Climbing away from *Glory* on 16 November, the Fireflies turned inland heading for gun positions south of Haeju. Keeping low under the cloud, Skinner looked down past the aircraft's nose to the target below. Touching the rudder, he rolled into a dive. Pulling out at 1,500 feet he loosed off the rockets under his wings and climbed quickly for the next targets. On the way back to the ship, the Fireflies dropped low over some bridges not far from Haeju to photograph them.[2] Tracers from ground fire came up to meet the aircraft but the Fireflies were well out of reach and sped away.

The next morning the weather eased and Skinner's flight attacked a storage dump. Rockets flew from his wings as he bottomed out of the dive, his engine roaring. The projectiles slammed into the buildings, which erupted into flames seconds later. "You'd go in and have some fun," he said. "In those days war was war."

Though this might sound callous there was an element of excitement for these young men. They were flying at high speed at very low levels in very agile machines. They had to be focused on their jobs and to think of it as having fun was their way of coping with the death and suffering.

---

[2] During our interview Skinner remembered that wherever possible the Fireflies of his squadron would photograph prospective targets to be hit at a later date either before or after they attacked the main target.

The morning of 19 November saw Fireflies slowly climbing into the grey overcast sky to search for the surviving aircrew of an American B29 shot down the day before. As they criss-crossed the area, scanning the ground for any sign of the downed crew, one of the pilots caught sight of something glinting in the sun. Diving down to take a closer look, Skinner could see a piece of metal that looked like it was a fuel tank from the aircraft. There was no sign of the aircrew, and reluctantly, the flight turned back towards *Glory*.

In the afternoon, as the deck pitched in a strong sea, Skinner waited while the aircraft handlers re-armed the Fireflies. The rockets were being replaced with 1,000lb bombs. Showered, briefed and fed, the aircraft ready, Skinner climbed into the cockpit as engines began coughing into life up and down the flight deck. A few minutes later, with the engine running on full power and the aircraft attached to the catapult, Skinner shot down the deck into the air. The weight of the two bombs momentarily made the aircraft drop but with full throttle on the Firefly slowly climbed higher into the air and headed to the Haeju area. The target was a railway tunnel, which was bombed with precision.

"As soon as you got airborne you'd see the coast," Skinner remembered. "You were flying by a map and the targets were identified by grid references. If you were going for a tunnel you followed the railway until you came to the tunnel then you'd attack. We were briefed by army carrier-borne ground liaison officers and we might get intelligence photos of the targets." While operational flying was under way the ship rarely went further than thirty miles off the coast. "She'd come in a bit then go out a bit," Skinner said.

The grip of winter had hardened by the time HMS *Glory* returned for her next patrol on 29 November. Temperatures were now well below zero and with each breath the maintainers' lungs would ache as they sucked in the freezing air. The aircraft fared little better. Left out on the decks overnight, coolant pipes in the Fireflies contracted under the extreme cold, creating leaks that were difficult to stop. In those temperatures the oil would thicken so much that engines wouldn't start.[3] To solve the problem, small quantities of petrol were pumped into the oil to reduce the viscosity and keep the engines turning over.

Every morning on the carrier's deck park the aircraft handlers and maintainers ran the engines up on all the aircraft. The great Griffon 74 engines, with their diluted oil, would cough, splutter and burst into life on one Firefly after another. Because of the petrol in the oil thick black smoke would pour from exhaust stubs earning the Fireflies the nickname 'The Coal Burners'.

The icy fingers of winter not only affected the Griffon engines but also the propeller pitch on the Fireflies. Oil acted on a cylinder inside the front of the spinner. The pilot would set the revolutions while the oil pressure on the cylinder would automatically set the pitch. The extremely cold temperatures meant that the oil in this cylinder would get so thick it couldn't move fast enough to change the pitch, and that wrecked the engine, forcing several engine changes. To get round this, pilots would vary their airspeed on the way back to

---

[3] This is mentioned in greater detail in *With the Carriers in Korea*.

the ship and on approach, which would keep hot oil flowing through the spinner.

Despite harsh weather Skinner's flight managed to get into the air on 29 November to attack troops in a village north of Chongyang with rockets and cannon fire. That afternoon *Glory* turned into the wind to launch her aircraft again. Skinner's flight rocketed a radio station by Point X-Ray. In reality Point X-Ray was Choppeki Point, while the radio and radar installations on Chodo Island were codenamed Point Dog, Taechong Island was Point Able and Yonpyong Island Point Baker.

The worsening weather cut the number of sorties throughout the patrol, but that afternoon the flight of Fireflies swept north of Ongjin destroying a wooden bridge with its rockets. "If you knocked a bridge down you could expect a few days later that it would be up and running," Skinner said. "They'd get vast numbers of people working on it and then we'd attack it again to make life difficult."

In the afternoon of 5 December Skinner catapulted off the deck, climbing quickly into the winter sky. "Catapults were much more vicious in those days," Skinner recalled. "You had to take off under full power with your elbow in your groin so your hand was steady when you got the kick from the catapult. Everything was set for take-off, you only had to do the top winding of the trim and the aircraft would fly itself off. You just queued up for the catapult and it went whoosh and the thing would come back then the chaps would hook the wire strops onto the airplane under the belly. We'd wind the aircraft up to full power, give them the thumbs up then the chap on the side of the deck would pull a lever and the thing would go off."

The following day, 6 December, just as the Fireflies formed up off the starboard beam dawn began to bring light to the early morning sky. Armed with rockets and full ammunition tanks they headed inland towards Ongjin on an armed reconnaissance flight. Spotting a group of trucks below, the Fireflies peeled off. Following the flight leader, Skinner dropped his nose and dived onto the vehicles, raking them with cannon fire. As his Firefly shot over the trucks, he glanced into the mirror on the windscreen above him, watching the vehicles get caught in a storm of shells from the rest of the flight.

Climbing, he followed his leader towards another group of trucks, kicked the rudder and pushed the nose over again. The lead Firefly had just unloaded its rockets and was climbing away. Now it was Skinner's turn. Levelling out, he punched the release button, firing his rockets on the trucks, which were desperately trying to race away from the attack. Not wanting to stick around, he climbed the Firefly quickly away, forming up with the rest of the flight and headed out to sea.

On the last day of the patrol, 7 December, visibility was very poor over the ship. Carrying 1,000lb bombs instead of the usual rockets, Skinner's aircraft laboured under the extra weight as he headed away from the ship with the rest of the flight. Following the Ongjin-Haeju railway line they attacked a railway tunnel not far from the village of Haeju. Diving on the hapless soldiers protecting the tunnel, they dropped their bombs and turned back to the ship. Skinner had no idea if they'd been successful or not. "We were continuously cutting up the railways," he recalled. "We were given a lot of freedom. If there was low cloud and you couldn't see what you were doing you'd look for an area clear of cloud."

Skinner's fifth patrol began on 17 December,[4] with a simple photo-reconnaissance of promising targets in the Ongjin area. This was the only sortie he carried out that day. The next day was far different. The Fireflies were up early, pouring their rockets into targets near Point X-Ray. On the way back, Skinner teamed up with a Fury over Chinnampo that had had a shell explode inside the gun. This was probably Alan Leahy's.[5]

The 20th was a sad day. An explosion was seen in the wing of Lieutenant P. G. Fogden's Firefly while he was attacking some coastal targets. His aircraft crashed into the sea and sank immediately. That afternoon, the Fireflies pumped their rockets into a series of buildings reported to be a battalion headquarters.

The following day Skinner and the rest of his flight attacked several buildings near Ongjin using rocket projectiles. On the way home to *Glory*, the Fireflies dropped into low level strafing runs, hitting several oxcarts with their high explosive cannon shells.[6] There were no explosions to signify the oxcarts were carrying ammunition, however.

On 22 December an accurate attack took place, leaving Skinner feeling the effort was worthwhile. They'd been briefed on a target that was supposed to be a stores dump at Changyong. The Fireflies climbed to 5,000 feet, heading inland towards the target. Under each wing hung a full load of rockets.

As they neared the stores dump, the flight split into pairs in a line astern formation and rolled into their attacks. One by one, the Fireflies dropped on the target, their rockets shooting off the rails in clouds of smoke and ripping into buildings and sheds. At 1,500 feet Skinner pulled out of his dive and turned tightly, climbing as quickly as he could away from the target which was now engulfed in flames, debris and smoke. Forming up with the rest of the flight he headed back to HMS *Glory*.

Early the next morning Skinner was once again at the controls of his Firefly, this time without an observer.[7] The first target was a village near Son-Wido. For the inhabitants of the village it was a bad day indeed as the Fireflies pulverized it with rocket fire. On the way back they picked up the Ongjin–Haeju railway line and did some fast photographic runs. "As fast as the Furies cut the track the Koreans would rebuild it," Skinner said.

Unlike so many millions around the world celebrating Christmas Day 1952 snugly by the fire, or in churches, giving each other presents and kissing under the mistletoe, Skinner was up in the cold morning air, his flight grinding slowly towards a bridge west of Haeju. The usual load of rockets had been replaced by two 1,000lb bombs. Reaching the target he rolled the aircraft into the top of his

---

[4] This was HMS *Glory*'s second patrol.
[5] The incident is noted in greater detail in Chapter Thirteen.
[6] Their cannon carried a mixture of high explosive and incendiary 20mm cannon ammunition.
[7] During our interview Skinner recalled he rarely flew with an observer in the back because there weren't very many available.

dive. Screaming down on the target he watched the bridge grow larger in his sights. His thumb hovered over the button, and then suddenly he was at the right height. Hitting the button he felt the aircraft lurch as the two heavy bombs dropped from their moorings. Levelling out, he banked sharply watching great plumes of water shoot up into the air. He'd missed. Both bombs had straddled the structure.

Pulling the stick back he pushed the throttle forward climbing quickly away as shells came arcing up at the British aircraft from the enemy gunners below. Clearly the first Firefly in had given the enemy a surprise but now they were pumping everything they could at the Fireflies. Skinner wrote these three words in his logbook: "Barratt shot down." A tragic Christmas indeed.

The next day they attacked the same bridge again without much success. Skinner was glad of the next ten days away from the fighting as the ship headed for Japan, ending its third patrol. Skinner's sixth patrol began in dreadful weather. His first flight of 1953 was part of a group of eight Fireflies armed with 500lb bombs heading towards the Ongjin railway tunnel. They were determined to destroy it but once again the attack was not as successful as they wanted. They were a dejected bunch of pilots that returned from the sortie. Three Fury pilots were missing.

During the first few days of the new year one of the biggest air battles of the war took place over the north-western region of Korea when forty F86 Sabres and thirty-eight Migs clashed in wheeling, diving dogfights. Fighting on the ground was limited to small attacks to harass the enemy.

The new year also saw a new American administration with President Dwight D. Eisenhower taking over from President Truman. His philosophy was a little different than his predecessor's and the use of force on targets inside China was authorized. At the end of January General Maxwell D. Taylor took over command of the US Eighth Army from General Van Fleet. The opening months of 1953 saw the Chinese attacking front line UN positions with no results.[8]

On 6 January Skinner was involved in a Firefly raid on a village near Chaeryong, which was attacked with 500lb bombs. Turning towards Haeju the Fireflies became involved in a search for Lieutenant Rayner, (described in the previous chapter). On the way back they were bounced by American P51 Mustang piston-engined fighters and an ensuing fight occurred until the Mustangs realised their mistake and flew off.

On the morning of the 8th, Skinner pulled away from HMS *Glory*, with his 500lb bombs hanging from their moorings under his wings. This was a target he liked to hit – a train. Climbing to attack height he felt sure the Fireflies would destroy it.[9] Diving on the steaming locomotive, however, his bombs missed the target completely. Later, he learned Fury pilot Alan Leahy had destroyed it. That afternoon, flying in bad weather with a very low cloud base, the Fireflies attacked a village in the Ongjin peninsula with 500lb bombs. On

---

[8] This is mentioned in *With the Carriers in Korea*.

[9] During our interview Skinner mentioned that many of their sorties were frustrating because they didn't often hit their targets, so when they did they felt great satisfaction.

the way back to the ship they did a recce of a nearby storage dump.

Two days later Skinner had a much more satisfactory outcome. The first sortie of the day had two elements: the first was a rocket attack on a village near Haeju; then Skinner bombardment-spotted for USS *Sparrow* on the village. The little hamlet was razed to the ground with several fires started. "Not a bad day's work," he wrote in his logbook.

His seventh patrol began with an early morning raid to cut the railway line near Haeju with 500lb bombs. The Fireflies dive-bombed from 5,000ft, destroying several sections of track. That afternoon, the Fireflies were again armed with 500lb bombs and attacked a village north of the Haeju railway tunnel. East of Taetan two oxcarts and an ammunition dump were strafed by Skinner's flight before it wheeled away and headed back to the ship.

23 January saw the Fireflies attacking a village with rockets near the Haeju–Ongjin area. After the last Firefly had unleashed its rockets the flight headed down the coast strafing oxcarts wherever they saw them.

The following morning they were back again over the Haeju–Ongjin railway. The cloud cover was low making the attack more difficult than normal. Armed with 500lb bombs, each with long delay fuses, the flight followed the railway towards the target, another railway tunnel. Dodging just below the cloud, Skinner could see the tunnel entrance below. Checking his instruments, he flicked the aircraft over, following his leader down onto the target. The tunnel entrance grew in his sights as he dived. He watched the altimeter wind down, then quickly pushed the bomb release button and pulled away. The bombs skipped into the tunnel as the flight quickly climbed away heading out to sea.

Late that afternoon the Fireflies were re-armed with 1,000lb bombs. Strapped in, engine roaring, Skinner watched the Firefly in front of him catapult down the deck, drop out of sight and then slowly claw its way into the air. Snow swept across the deck as the engines warmed up. It was Skinner's turn. He pushed the throttle forward to maximum power, while watching the batsman beside him. The signal came, and then the aircraft rocketed down the deck and into the air. Spray from the tossing waves flowed down his windscreen while Skinner held the stick right back watching his airspeed slowly increase. Gradually, the Firefly climbed into the air, heading towards an ammunition dump west of Sinwon. Diving on the dump, the aircraft dropped their bombs and headed quickly away, leaving the target burning ferociously. The following morning the Fireflies tore up the coast towards Ongjin where they pumped all their rockets into a nearby village suspected of being troop barracks.

On the first days of Skinner's eighth patrol the weather was terrible. Low cloud cover made visibility very bad. On the first day of flying, 6 February, as Skinner climbed away from the ship, he was flying almost blind as the cloud base was so thick. "We ditched our rockets because the visibility was so bad we couldn't cross the coast." They headed back to HMS *Glory* for tea.

By the afternoon, the weather had cleared enough for a strike to take place. As the Fireflies climbed up to their usual height Skinner could see the coast just ahead. Inland, however, the clouds hugged the terrain like a blanket. This attack would be on coastal gun positions south of Chodo. Visibility was bad, and he could see the cloud was moving in quickly. Once again the Fireflies unloaded their rockets without touching the targets, more concerned with landing back on the ship under worsening conditions.

The following morning (7 February), as snow swept across the pitching decks of the carrier, Skinner sat in the Firefly cockpit waiting to go and looked at the ominously low clouds. The target was the gun position at Amgak, which had caused so many headaches for the UN forces. Once the Fireflies had taken off and formed up over the ship, they headed inland. Low cloud made it difficult to gain the necessary height, but they lumbered on. Over the target they wasted no time in attacking, unleashing their rockets on the enemy positions below. One by one, the grey-green British aircraft peeled out of their dives, turned into a steep climbing turn and headed quickly away, just as the gunners below were waking up.

Skinner watched the tracers just beginning to arc up from the ground as the fourth Firefly climbed away. The gunners were off that morning, but the main worry was getting back to the ship. Snow and rain poured down the canopy and windscreen as the wind buffeted the aircraft. Landing back on the ship was difficult in the terrible weather, but they all got down in one piece.

The following day the weather cleared in the afternoon and Skinner climbed into the air on his third sortie, heading for a reported brigade headquarters near Songwha. Each Firefly unloaded its rockets into the buildings, sending debris and smoke flying in all directions.

Heading back towards the ship, the flight diverted to the Ongjin-Haeju railway and did a quick low level photographic reconnaissance before climbing away towards HMS *Glory*.

The second sortie on 9 February was particularly remarkable for Skinner. "We attacked a gun position near Chodo Island," he told me, "but as I got closer to the ship my engine started to get rougher and rougher until by the time I landed on it was very rough indeed."

Poor visibility on the 11th kept the Fireflies on the windswept deck of the ship for most of the morning. It wasn't until the skies began to clear in the afternoon that Skinner climbed into the cockpit again. Catapulting off the deck, the Fireflies climbed to 500 feet and formed up on the ship's starboard beam then flew in pairs. Each of the fighters carried rockets, as they flew towards a village full of enemy troops west of Ongjin.

Tucking in beside the leader, Skinner watched the lead Firefly flick over into its dive. Moments later, as he followed suit the rockets from the lead aircraft shot from under the wings plastering the village below. At 1,500 feet he levelled out of his dive and flicked the firing button on his control column. Under his wings, the eight rockets dropped, their engines igniting and roaring towards the target. Pulling up quickly into a tight, steep turn, he had enough time as he climbed away to see that this rocket attack was very successful. The village was all but obliterated.

The morning of 13 February the aircraft were airborne early flying towards the Ongjin-Haeju railway. One by one they dived on the line, dropping their 500lb bombs and destroying whole sections of track. Turning towards

Songwha, they strafed enemy stores emplacements and several oxcarts, and then headed seaward. As Skinner circled over the ship watching his colleagues land he reflected on how successful the last few sorties had been.They had made significant damage to the railway lines but come dawn tomorrow they knew the enemy would have repaired the lines and be using them again. It was very frustrating.

The last few sorties of Skinner's eighth patrol saw the Fireflies pinpointing various targets with rockets before the ship turned away and headed back to Japan. On 26 February, his ninth patrol began as the ship arrived again off the west coast of Korea to continue to impose the western blockade, and began operations the next day. Targets for the first sortie were several enemy trucks in the Haeju area and the Fireflies poured their rockets into the target zone.

Skinner shot over the trucks at 1,500 feet, turning and climbing tightly as explosions suddenly ripped through the vehicles below. Climbing, he watched the fire destroying the targets as the last of the rockets pummelled the area. "You couldn't think about the people down there," he said to me. "You just couldn't."

On 1 March Skinner flew only one sortie. Over a period of one hour and thirty-five minutes the Fireflies of his flight attacked a village with rockets west of Ongjin and strafed several boxcars on the Haeju-Ongjin railway.

The first flight of his ninth patrol on 4 April nearly ended in disaster. As he climbed away from the carrier, Skinner pushed the button that retracted the landing gear but nothing happened. Trying manually to pump the gear he found the undercarriage was stuck. "It wasn't coming up so I ditched my rockets in the sea and landed back on HMS *Glory*."

On the next sortie of the day things went better. This time the undercarriage came up and Skinner formed up with the rest of the flight. Nearly an hour later, they attacked a village near Haeju and Skinner saw his rockets plaster the ground near several huts before they were enveloped in smoke.

Skies were clear for the first early morning sortie on 5 April for attacking the Hwanghae reservoir.[10] Eight 60lb rockets hung on Skinner's moorings under the wings of his fighter-bomber, as the flight climbed to their standard altitude. He could see the reservoir below and ahead of them. The village near the edge of the reservoir was the target.

"Echelon, break," came over the R/T from the flight leader, and Skinner dropped into his dive, following his leader down onto the target. The rockets leapt from their moorings, tearing into the village. Flames suddenly shot up from the clouds of dust and debris as rockets pounded the buildings.

Back on *Glory*'s decks the Fireflies were quickly re-armed with rockets, refuelled and made ready to go. They were heading back to the reservoir, this time to target the sluice gates south of the village with rockets. One by one the Fireflies screamed down onto the gates, their rockets punching holes in the concrete as great plumes of water rose into the air.

After a quick meal back on the ship, while the aircraft were again re-armed

---

[10] The UN forces were still attacking communist dams to cause as much destruction as possible to the enemy.

and refuelled, Skinner took off from the ship heading for a village north of Changyon where his flight rocketed troop positions. The last sortie of the day was a rocket attack on gun emplacements at Chodo Island. Turning towards Pungchong the Fireflies headed south and destroyed a large house with cannon fire.

7 April was another very busy day for the Fireflies. The first attack was rocketing a reservoir, and then they strafed the railway marshalling yards on the Haeju railway. The last flight of the day was an attack on more enemy troops in a village north of Haeju. However, it ended badly. With an engine running rough, and fuel very low Skinner had to make an emergency landing at Point Y-Do.

On 11 April the Fireflies were loaded with 1,000lb bombs for attacking a railway bridge near Haeju. "There was a very strong crosswind," recalled Skinner. "My bombs missed the bridge entirely so we went and did a recce of Ongjin, again." A few hours later, his flight was again climbing away from *Glory*, but this time the 1,000lb bombs had been replaced by 500lb bombs. This target was another bridge at Taetan and in this attack Skinner's bombs hit the south end of the bridge.

Three new pilots had arrived on the ship and were working up when Skinner started his tenth patrol of the Korean War on 19 April. The first flight saw Skinner doing dummy dives on *Glory* with these new pilots before heading away for an actual attack on a village north of Taetan. Unfortunately, Skinner's rockets jammed so he turned back to the ship, managing to get rid of his rockets at last over the sea.

The afternoon's sortie was much more successful. This time, all the rockets worked and started several fires as the Fireflies hammered the village of Chaeryong. They hit the target with both rockets and cannon fire before breaking off and heading back.

On 20 April the exchange of sick and wounded prisoners of war began. The communists had agreed to this step as a preliminary measure, and armistice negotiations began again on the 26th. UN prisoners were transported by truck convoys along the enemy's main supply routes from camps north of Pyongyang towards Panmunjom in the neutral area, and air operations were severely restricted to ensure the UN aircraft did not attack the convoys.[11]

On 21 April Skinner took off from the ship in the early morning heading towards Kimpo airfield on a ferrying job, with Wing Commander Fison in the back seat. Exactly one hour and thirty minutes later he was back over the ship, ready to land on. Several hours after his morning's flight, and after his aircraft had been armed with rockets and refuelled, Skinner climbed into the cockpit. Sitting on the deck, he waited for the signal, and then pushed the throttle wide open as the catapult shot the Firefly down the deck. There was a sudden jolt as the catapult released the fighter and Skinner was quickly working the controls, putting the aircraft into a climb away from the ship. He formed up with the rest of his flight and they headed towards the coast. The flight poured rockets into

---

[11] This is well-documented in *With the Carriers in Korea*. One wonders why they couldn't simply tell the UN pilots not to attack those routes.

a village near Chinnampo leaving it shrouded in smoke and dust as it headed out to sea towards their ship, nearly two hours after taking off.

On one sortie on 22 April the Fireflies rocketed a village north of Sunwido. As each aircraft dived on the huts and buildings clustered together, their rockets pounded them and flames suddenly shot up from one explosion.[12] Pulling out, slightly low, Skinner's Firefly rocked from a series of explosions on the ground. "Several large fires were started. I think we hit a hidden petrol dump," he told me. On the way back to the ship, he had to hand-pump his wheels and flaps into the down position in order to land because debris from the explosions had jammed the hydraulics.

On 25 April Skinner's flight dive-bombed a bridge north of Changyong. "We attacked that bridge with all our bombs but both of mine missed," he recalled. The next day the Fireflies made two attacks. The first was bombing a village north-west of Changyon, and the second attack was on a supply dump at Yonan. Skinner strafed positions east of Yonan on the way back to the ship.

On 14 May Skinner had the distinction of flying on HMS *Glory*'s last operational sortie which was an attack on a village west of Taetan. The flight over, *Glory* steamed away from Korean waters for the last time.

---

[12] As there was now much greater cooperation between the guerrillas and UN controllers, intelligence on targets such as this one would have been provided by the guerrillas.

Chapter Thirteen

HMS *GLORY* AND LEAHY'S WAR

Lieutenant Alan Leahy

Volunteer pilot Lieutenant Alan Leahy's recollections of his time in Korea provide a colourful impression of life fighting and flying with 801 Squadron from HMS *Glory* during her last tour of the war. He told me that *Glory*, which was built in 1944, took part in the surrender of the Japanese at the end of the Second World War and that she was, "just the right size for the aircraft that were on it."

"At the beginning of the war we thought that fifty sorties a day was good," Leahy said. "Then the next ship did eighty-six, then the next ship did over 100, then HMS *Ocean*, which was before us, managed to do 124 sorties."[1]

Trained by the United States Navy during the Second World War, Leahy flew Corsairs with a British squadron, training in Brunswick, Maine. "We did our deck landings on an American carrier," he said. "We came back to the UK and were going to go onto HMS *Illustrious* to go out to the Pacific but the war stopped."

Leahy loved flying the Sea Fury, but of the Corsair he said. "It was affectionately known as the Bent-winged Bastard from Connecticut. If you got too slow with your wheels down and flaps down and you bashed on full throttle then the prop would just about stop and turn the aircraft around, which wasn't a good idea if you were about to land. Lost quite a few people doing that kind of thing."

At the end of the Second World War, the squadron was wrapped up and he was sent into the ferry pool to fly different types of aircraft. "I could fly the Corsair, the Hellcat, the Avenger, the Beech Staggerwing, Oxfords, Barracudas, Ansons, Seafires, and Firebrands." On one occasion near Carlisle in the UK two Seafires landed at the airfield and as they taxied onto the flight line and shut their engines off, Leahy and his colleagues decided to go over and talk to the pilots. "As we got closer one of the pilots stood up, pulled off his helmet and this long hair flowed down and we thought, bloody hell, we're not going to ask a girl how to fly a Seafire, so we turned around. They were jolly good pilots."

He was sent off to fly everything from Oxfords to Mosquitos. "It was a bit of an event when you arrived at an air station with your Mosquito. Not a lot of naval pilots could fly them."

---

[1] According to *With the Carriers in Korea* this figure was 123 set by *Ocean* on 17 May 1952, on her first patrol.

Originally an RNVR officer, he got a four-year extension after the war and was then granted a permanent position. "I stayed on because I couldn't see the point in going outside and working for a living when I was getting paid and enjoying myself flying airplanes."

In 1949 he left the ferrying service behind and went into 801 Squadron, flying Sea Hornets. "That was the baby Mosquito, single-seater," Leahy explained. "Went like a bullet too. The big thing about the Mosquito was if you opened the throttle hard the aircraft would swing because the two props would pull you around. The Hornet had them going against each other so you could open the throttle as much as you liked. It was a beautiful airplane and about two miles an hour faster than the Sea Fury."

From there, Leahy became a weapons instructor at the operational flying school at RNAS Culdrose until he rejoined 801 Squadron flying Sea Furies. Before going out to the Korean conflict in late 1952, he practiced RATOG on HMS *Glory* in Malta. On his first RATOG experience, the rockets didn't work. "I went off the front of the ship at a walking speed and hit the water vertically in front of the ship," he told me. Water poured into the cockpit as he hit the harness release button on his chest. The belts keeping him in the seat slipped away as the water reached his neck. "I kept my Mae West and got rid of my parachute, then tried to get out." The aircraft was sinking fast, however, and the pressure forced him into the canopy. "I had to go back into the cockpit, turn round and push myself out again."

Releasing the canopy, he felt the aircraft turn as it sank. All around him was the murky darkness of the water. Dropping from the cockpit as the aircraft turned upside down Leahy headed for the surface. He wondered where the ship was and thought about staying down so the ship would pass over him. "Then this little voice said, 'Don't be a bloody idiot you'll drown, so which way up?'"

Holding his Mae West in his hands he struggled to put it on under the water and then swam up to a point where he thought he would be safe. "I popped up a few feet from the ship's side where the starboard propeller was."

Swimming hard away from the ship, he inflated his dinghy and climbed into it as the huge ship moved slowly past him. Anxious faces, like little white dots, looked over the side far above him. "I was rescued by the rescue destroyer which used to follow the carrier around. That was not an experience I would like to go through again," he said. "The aircraft was gone and there was no point in trying to get it."

Though he was accused of not throwing the master switch to fire the rockets, Leahy believes it was a faulty connection. "I'm positive I did throw the switch. Anyway, I took off the next day and that was it. There were lots of stories of guys who got into trouble with rocket assisted take-offs onboard."

Catapulting off the deck gave the pilot a real jolt because it was much like a slingshot. "The aircraft was on absolutely full blast," Leahy recalled. "You told them you were ready and off you would go up to flying speed. In the Fury you had to hold the stick right in your stomach. If you were holding it any other way the G forces would pull you back. You had to hold her steady as soon as you went off. The wire that is hooked onto the airplane just drops off as the aircraft goes on past. It stops pulling, the aircraft flies away from it, and the wire drops into the sea. There was a wire gone every time we launched an aircraft."

His first sortie flying off *Glory* was CAP duty. "We flew over the carrier in case there was an attack from the communists," explained Leahy. Throughout the conflict the North Koreans did not attack any of the Royal Navy aircraft carriers, but the combat air patrols were kept up in case an attack did arise. "We would be given a primary target to attack. Then we would be given targets of opportunity."

Leahy flew with Lieutenants Peter Wheatly, Fiddian-Green and Sub-Lieutenant Baynes. "We would go off and at the same time the Fireflies would go off on another flight entirely separate from us." He remembered the scheduling of aircraft to be usually two Furies on CAP duty, four Furies on strike, another three on strike and six Fireflies also on strike duty. "So it would repeat. The first lot would come on and land; turn around and load up with ammunition all ready to go again. I was up in the first detail and the third detail, the fifth detail, the seventh detail and the ninth detail."

During a TARCAP mission over the Changyon area, the Furies hurtled towards the target but found it covered by low cloud and obscured. Carrying their 500lb bombs with full ammunition tanks, they searched for targets of opportunity. "We cut a railway on that sortie," Leahy said. "The next day, 17 December, was a strike on the same railway where it went into a tunnel."

Using the techniques perfected by pilots from previous tours, they would fly low along the railway line, lob the bombs into the mouth of the tunnel and then pull up quickly. Standard procedure but for young pilots such as Leahy, it was new. "I remember there was one day when we went off very early in the morning to attack the railway system," he continued. "There was a long line of smoke where a train had recently been before going into a tunnel. So we thought, right we've got you. We dropped our bombs and there was a hell of a boom and out came a load of smoke and goodness knows what. We didn't do that train much good. It was a bit dodgy because to do a low level attack you had to have 30-second fuses, whereas, if you did a dive-bombing attack you wanted an instant fuse."

During one attack on a railway tunnel the Furies used the skipping technique, dropping their bombs so they bounced into the entrance. "We had one set of fuses go off at 13 seconds which was a bit surprising for the guys coming up behind. We were very wary of that."

Alan Leahy was one of the victims of the faulty ammunition problems that occurred during *Glory*'s last tour on 18 December 1952, during her third patrol. "I was doing a strafing run and I was firing at the target when there was a hell of an explosion in my port wing. I looked out and could see right through the wing. I also could see my tail was shredded. I thought I'd been hit by flak."

Climbing hard, Leahy immediately got on the radio. "Mayday, mayday," he called, giving the standard distress call. Stabilizing the damaged aircraft, he turned towards the coast, hoping he could reach the ship. "I flew towards a friendly island with a beautiful big beach."

Pulling the stick back and dropping his speed and height, Leahy managed to land the Fury on the beach. Once the engine had stopped he climbed out of the aircraft and looked at the damage. Then he could see that it wasn't flak that had caused the damage. "A shell had gone down, one gun stopped and an explosive shell came up its chuff and went bang and blew the gun to bits, ripping the panels off the aircraft. I could stand up through the hole."

The same faulty ammunition on the Fireflies caused a few casualties because, as Leahy pointed out, the guns were more vulnerable on the Firefly than they were on the Fury and the explosion did more damage. One or two Fireflies had their wings severely damaged or ripped off when these explosions occurred.

Chodo Island was regularly shelled by coastal guns hidden in caves along the coast west of Chinnampo. "They'd come out of a cave and fire and then go back into the cave. Of course it was hard to dive-bomb the cave but we did it just to annoy them. Having done that we thought we'd go and look for targets. We bombed the railway and made two cuts. Then we thought we'd head north a bit and see what was going on but we made a balls-up of it and we went right up to Pyongyang." The Furies suddenly realized where they were when the anti-aircraft fire over the capital started firing at them. "So we turned round and beetled off," Leahy recalled. This was on 6 February 1953, the first day of HMS *Glory*'s sixth patrol.

Before they could get to the ship, enemy Mig fighters bounced the flight, their guns blazing as they swept down on the Furies. "We'd just got out over the coast when we were jumped by two Migs," Leahy said. "We were flying leader, three, four and two and we broke to port. As I got to 90 degrees this Mig was pointing straight at me. There was a great 37mm cannon underneath the intake and I remember thinking the bastard's missed me, because he's pointing directly at me and so he's not going to hit me. We reversed but they'd come in so fast they were disappearing off and they didn't come back again. They'd been bitten once before by Furies."

That experience taught Leahy and his colleagues not to go up to Pyongyang too often. Because there were no American Sabres in the area to engage them, the Migs could come down to give the British fighters a scare. "When a faster aircraft is attacking a slower aircraft the slower aircraft can always manoeuvre more tightly," Leahy explained.

On one pre-dawn strike, on 8 February, the Furies headed inland, to attack a convoy of trucks. "As soon as you fired at them their lights went out. You were then in mountainous country and not knowing where the ground was or where your wingman was. He didn't know where you were. You'd be on your own. We did quite a few of those."

During another pre-dawn attack on 14 February, Leahy and the rest of his flight strafed five convoys of vehicles. "The ship was way out in the water," he explained. "There was an American radar station at Chodo so as you came off the ship you'd check in with the radar station. I found myself well up north and thought what are all these lights around? It was China. So I came back again very quickly."

The North Koreans regularly moved their anti-aircraft guns around to protect important targets such as bridges, railway lines, dams and tunnels. "The balls would come up, boom and you'd see them coming, especially at night, but then they couldn't see what they were firing at."

To pick up downed pilots on friendly islands, Fireflies were sent to the rescue. "It didn't work one day when I was on CAP. A Firefly had to go in and pick up a pilot who'd put his aircraft down. I was watching from above. The Firefly landed, the guy got in the back and then they roared down the beach. But they put a wheel in the water and the airplane went whoosh up on its nose."

Over HMS *Glory*'s eleven patrols during 1952-1953, the ship would either put into the American base at Sasebo or the Australian base at Kure during its off cycle. "When we went into Kure the little Japanese hammered away and painted and the noise was terrible," said Leahy. "We did a lot of flying although we only flew half of the month."

It wasn't uncommon for bombs to get 'hung up' under the wings of the aircraft. "We didn't like to land on the ship with a bomb that shouldn't be there because it could come off at the wrong time," he explained. "So they would divert us to Kimpo where the Americans would take the bomb off for us. You'd never go alone, you always had your wingman. We had to stay the night."

Leahy recalled one incident in the middle of the harsh Korean winter where he and another Fury pilot, Pete Wheatly, were directed to Kimpo because of a hung-up bomb under the Fury's wing and the temperature was below freezing. "It got very cold at night," Leahy recalled. "We were hosted by an American fighter squadron who looked after us. We went into a Nissen hut and had a few drinks, a meal and few more drinks. About midnight Pete and I went outside to dilute the oil in the engines to stop them from freezing."

The procedure for that was to run the engine up to the proper temperature, push the dowler and pump petrol into it then shut down the engine and the following morning the engine should start. "We'd done all that and we'd shut everything down and were just shutting the cockpit when five Americans walked out to their aircraft. They were going to do a night flight over Korea in their B26 twin-engined bombers. This guy was walking along and his torchlight shone on the span of the Fury, which was painted pale greenish grey. The Fury had five blades and this guy went one, two, three, four and five. He looked at it and counted it again to be sure and then he called his buddies over and said, 'Look at this.'"

As far as targets were concerned Leahy maintained they attacked anything that moved. "We attacked troops in a village, where the houses were usually just shacks, covered in straw. The Fireflies did the rocketing and we did the bombing. If you saw an oxcart you went for it because that could be carrying ammunition. If you saw a man with an A frame on his back you went for him because he shouldn't be out in the daytime and he's probably carrying a weapon of some sort. But I never saw one even though we were told to go for them."

Intelligence about troop concentrations or why they were attacking targets such as villages was kept from the pilots most of the time, according to Leahy. "That was information we shouldn't have in case we were shot down," he claimed.

As described earlier, because the North Koreans could rebuild their bridges overnight, the UN switched their policy to attacking railway lines further away from the point where the enemy kept his repair materials. "It was certainly more profitable for us to knock the stuffing out of the railway five or six miles away so they had to cart the repairing stuff along," Leahy explained.

The attacks were fast and furious. Diving, one after the other, they dropped their bombs and climbed away. "You wouldn't come back there until near the end of the sortie, at a safe height to see what you've achieved," Leahy said. "If you went round and attacked it again then you were asking for trouble and that's why some people got shot down. We did lose quite a few. In my opinion it was because they went back again too soon or tried to do more than one attack on the target. That's not good news. In our squadron we lost five."

Light fire at low level accounted for many damaged aircraft and some casualties: "They used to lie on their backs and fire straight up as you came over," Leahy recalled.

Heading north was only viable when USAF Sabres were fighting with Migs. Under those dogfights, Furies and Fireflies pounded targets, rocketing and bombing where they could.

Leahy's flight did several strikes in support of the Commonwealth Division. "We'd check in with the Americans who were controlling the aircraft. They would hand you over to a small aircraft flying over the lines called a Mosquito. He would then contact the CO and start on an indicated target. He would fire a small rocket and say your target is just left of that. You would then attack that and come away."

On one strike the Furies damaged four caves and destroyed a mortar position in support of the ground forces. The next day they attacked the same area, this time wiping out five mortar positions. Leahy and his flight bombardment-spotted for the USS *Missouri*, the biggest battleship then in Korean waters. "We were to bomb-spot to make sure she hit the target," he explained. "She fired and the senior pilot couldn't see where the shells had hit." According to Leahy the ship's big 16-inch shells would be fired in clusters of six. "They were way down, about five miles away. So we told the 'Mighty Mo'[2] to come left a bit and she just shut down and wouldn't talk to us after that, too embarrassed."

Leahy had a near miss when bombardment-spotting on another occasion. Well clear of the line of fire, he watched the puffs of smoke coming from the ships off the coast. "My aircraft suddenly went whoosh and I looked to see what had happened. I could see a shell going away from me. The shock wave around it had thrown my aircraft up in the air as it passed underneath me. You could actually see the shell disappearing. I didn't like that at all. If it had hit me that would have been the end of Mrs Leahy's little boy."

At the very end of one patrol Leahy was diverted to Kimpo airfield as *Glory* had already steamed for Kure. He knew he would have to stay overnight then fly on to the bottom of Korea across to Japan and up to Kure to meet the ship. As he was approaching Japan, however, he suffered a sudden fifty per cent engine failure. "I had to do a forced landing on an airfield just inside Japan."

---

2 This expression is slang for USS *Missouri*.

The trouble was that a giant crane was coming towards him on the runway. Knowing he couldn't go round again, Leahy did everything he could to get the aircraft down safely before being hit by the crane. He made it with inches to spare. "We left my Fury there and a Firefly came from Kure, picked me up and took me back. When my aircraft had been repaired I went down, picked it up and flew back so they could put it back onto the ship."

Supporting the Commonwealth Division sometimes also meant exchanging officers or doing a stint for aircrew at the front line. "A few would come onboard for an operation. They appreciated this tremendously. They'd have hot baths, bar everything else. They'd have a real holiday. Two of us, the senior pilot and myself, went to the 3rd Royal Australian Regiment up on the front line. That was a bit startling. It was cold at the front. We were in little holes dug out on the side of the hill and their mess was another hole in the same hill. We were in thick army clothes and sitting very close to this huge red-hot stove, so close it singed the trousers but your back would be frozen. The first morning I woke up and the solider came in and put a cup of tea down and disappeared. I sort of shut my eyes and opened my eyes. The tea was steaming."

After Korea Leahy returned to the UK, going up to RAF Lossiemouth to train gunnery officers. "I wasn't there too long when I was back in a front line squadron of Seahawks on the first commission of HMS *Ark Royal*. In our squadron there was the CO who eventually became captain of the *Ark Royal*. And also the last captain of the ship was also in our squadron, Ted Anson."

Leahy then became the CO of the squadron at Lossiemouth converting naval airmen onto the Seahawk. He then spent six months on a frigate. "Then I went to the Royal Air Force flying college. We flew Hunters, Meteors, and Canberras and it was a jolly good course. After that I was a CO of a Scimitar squadron and had the first Buccaneer outfit up at Lossiemouth."

He went through a series of jobs in the Royal Navy, culminating in that of of air commodore in charge of the submarine base at Faslane. "I could do whatever I wanted, the whole of the west coast of Scotland was mine. I conned some of the guys at the RAF to let me come and fly in return for going to sea in a submarine." The Korean War seems a distant memory now, but for Alan Leahy flying and fighting over that strange country had been very real.

Chapter Fourteen

THE RAF AND THE RAAF

It has long been considered that the RAF's involvement in the Korean War was minimal. Certainly they did not fly ground-attack missions, as did the Fury and Firefly pilots, but a small group of exchange pilots did fly fighter sweeps with the USAF. Their other RAF colleagues could be found more in the transport and reconnaissance role. Almost from the outset the Americans used small, light aircraft such as the Cessna L19 Bird-Dog as spotter aircraft for artillery, naval bombardment and air strikes. These little aircraft, called Mosquito Controllers, would direct the air strikes onto specific enemy targets. The communists did all they could to shoot these aircraft down, because they knew after one popped up there would be an air strike or an artillery bombardment. The Commonwealth Division fighting on the front lines wanted its own Mosquitos so two flights were set up, ostensibly under the RAF, although they were flown almost entirely by Army personnel.

The first of these observation units was set up in June 1951 at Middle Wallop, flying the Auster AOP 6. Officially named 1913 Light Liaison Flight, the little aircraft were packed into crates and shipped to Iwakuni in Japan where they were later assembled and then delivered to Commonwealth airstrips. From the moment the Austers of 1913 Squadron arrived in Korea, visual reconnaissance quickly became their main task, completely overriding what should have been their primary task of liaison. Sometimes the squadron's aircraft would penetrate far into enemy territory looking for useful targets.

Pilots often flew up to seven sorties a day.[1] Staying alive meant listening for enemy gunfire and the whizz of bullets passing close to their machines, while keeping in constant touch with the ground by radio. Pilots achieved this balance by having only one ear covered by their headsets, and the other ear free to listen for enemy gunfire.

The only other RAF unit to operate from Korea was the second observation squadron, 1903 Independent Air Observation Post Flight, which had seen service against communist terrorists in Malaysia as part of the Army Cooperation Flight.

Detached to Korea, the flight landed in airstrips inside the Commonwealth Division's area via Hong Kong. The role of this squadron was a dangerous one, spotting enemy gun positions and directing friendly artillery fire to bombard them. Unlike some of the American Mosquito aircraft, which flew very low missions, the Austers of 1903 Squadron flew mostly above 5,000 feet to avoid

---

[1] Robert Jackson goes into greater detail in his book, *Air War Korea*.

enemy small arms fire. Though the Auster's cockpit was armour-plated, each pilot flew with a parachute. Racking up more than forty-five flying hours a month was not uncommon for the Auster pilots while flying their spotting mission over the lines. Once the two squadrons were operational over the Commonwealth Division they quickly became invaluable in helping to keep the communist forces guessing. Army pilots flying the little high-wing monoplanes behind the communist lines also helped to direct Sea Fury and Firefly pilots towards their targets.

Other RAF units in the Korean War included 88 and 209 Squadrons flying Short Sunderland flying boats in the patrol and reconnaissance roles. They were part of the Far East Flying Boat Wing based at Oppama in Japan and were used for mine-clearing as well as ferrying and coastal patrol. There were no other RAF units operating in Korea against communist targets but there were some pilots. RAF pilots flying with the USAF were very experienced men.

Early in 1950, Wing Commander Peter Wykeham was asked by USAF General Stratemeyer to go to Korea as an advisor on night intruder operations. A famous British Second World War ace followed him out, Wing Commander J. E. Johnson. Both these highly skilled pilots flew extensive missions on night operations, targeting enemy positions with bombs and rockets.

Out of this came the exchange programme that ultimately saw twenty-one RAF pilots flying with the American Air Force during the Korean War. The idea was to attach instructors and potential instructors to F86 Sabre wings flying and fighting in Korean skies. Many of these pilots went to the 335th Fighter Interceptor Squadron, which had the distinction of being led by the first Sabre jet ace of the Korean War. Captain James Jabara of the USAF was flying with the 335th during May 1951 when he scored his fifth kill, thereby giving him that honour.

It was into this illustrious company that the RAF pilots on exchange found themselves in the early part of 1952. Before they arrived the 335th had been stationed at Suwon, where in the middle of June 1951 they had received an unpleasant reminder of the war. On the 16th two old Russian Po2 biplane trainers loaded with bombs appeared very low over the 335th's airfield which was brightly lit. Sabres were neatly parked along the flight line and the enemy pilots lumbered over them, dropping their bombs and causing havoc on the airfield below before turning for home. One Sabre was completely destroyed and eight others damaged. A few months later the 335th was moved to Kimpo near Seoul where the USAF Sabres took up residence with 77 Squadron of the Royal Australian Air Force, who were just working up on the latest version of the British jet fighter, the Meteor.

In this part of the air war the communists introduced an updated version of the original Mig 15, the Mig 15bis, whose improved turbojet made it more than a match for the F86A Sabre currently on strength with the USAF. By the end of 1951, enemy air activity over North Korea was increasing all the time. Migs were crossing the Yalu River in very large numbers, sometimes in excess of eighty aircraft. They would dash across the border from Manchuria at high speed and above 35,000 feet and turn south towards Pyongyang in the hope of catching Sabres and other UN aircraft low on fuel trying desperately to get back to base. The Migs would then head back towards Manchuria.

Into this situation came the first RAF pilots after Johnson and Wykeham. Like their two predecessors, the new British pilots already had experience flying Sabres in the USA while on attachment to the USAF. Flight Lieutenant S. Daniel was the first to arrive as part of the scheme and was attached to the 335th. Four others, led by Wing Commander John Baldwin, followed Daniel to Korea. They were split into pairs and sent to different units. Baldwin and Flight Lieutenant R. Knight went to the 51st Fighter Interceptor Wing while Squadron Leader W. Harbison and Flight Lieutenant B. J. Spragg went to Kimpo with the 4th Fighter Interceptor Wing. Under the 4th FIW was the 335th FIS.

It wasn't long before they were mixing it with Migs over the Yalu. Baldwin and his other British pilots added to the high success rate of their American colleagues but for Baldwin that success was short-lived. On 15 March 1952 his aircraft disappeared while flying a weather reconnaissance mission over Chinnampo. The flight climbed quickly out of the cloud at around 7,500 feet to find nothing but empty blue sky. There was no sign of any other aircraft. Baldwin's F86 had vanished. The flight leader desperately tried to reach him on the radio but static greeted his ears. After flying above the cloud for several minutes the flight wheeled away back towards Kimpo as the sun climbed higher in the morning sky. A few hours later a full-scale search was mounted but once again there was no trace of his aircraft and no evidence of wreckage seen in the near vicinity. His aircraft had simply vanished, possibly having exploded in mid-air with pieces scattered far and wide.

The British pilots were training at Nellis Air Force Base near Las Vegas, Nevada and by June 1952 another four arrived in Korea. By the time they arrived, however, the old F86A, which had proven to be less capable against the Migs, had been replaced by the newer version – the F86E.[2] This was a much better machine, which had virtually no vices and was described by its pilots as a joy to fly. The British pilots were posted to the 4th and 51st Fighter Interceptor Wings.

By the end of the Korean War, twenty-one[3] RAF pilots had gone through the scheme and several had been credited with damaged or destroyed Migs. One of them was Flight Lieutenant John Nicholls, who later became Air Marshal Sir John Nicholls, who was attached to the 335th flying the new F86E Sabre. He damaged three Migs and shot down two, making him one of the highest scoring RAF pilots. Fighting against the Migs was a frustrating business. They could dash across the Yalu back to Manchuria at very high speed and altitude[4] when the battles got too rough. Nicholls did a tour of 100 missions in Korea, and on two occasions his frustration was overcome when he was able to shoot down a Mig.

---

[2] Robert Jackson goes into greater detail in his *Air War Korea*.

[3] In *Air Mail, The Commonwealth's Air Contribution to the Korean War*, part 2, the author suggests this figure is closer to forty pilots, and that British pilots accounted for nine Migs destroyed and several damaged.

[4] Manchuria, part of China, was off limits for UN aircraft so they could not follow them home.

On 30 August 1952, Nicholls had a busy day. Climbing away from Kimpo he flew the No. 3 position of a flight of four aircraft and wheeled northwards. Heading towards the Sinuiju area, he tucked into formation as the jets headed for their first fighter sweep of the day. Before long, Nicholls and his fellow pilots encountered a large formation of enemy aircraft, as several peeled off to attack the Sabres. In the ensuing air battle, Nicholls sent a burst of machine-gun fire into one Mig. It dodged away from his Sabre as pieces flew from the wings and fuselage but it remained aloft, rolled onto its back and dived away for the safety of Manchuria. Nicholls was credited with his first damaged Mig.

That wasn't the end of it, however. Climbing, he fired his guns at another Mig, which shot across in front of him. Shells from his six 50-calibre machine guns hit the enemy jet but again it slipped away, heading for safety. Nicholls had no time to follow it but dived quickly away from the mass of enemy aircraft now rolling and twisting all around him.

The next time his guns damaged a Mig was on a fighter sweep over the Yalu River on 15 September. On 30 October, the flight of Sabres, escorting F84 fighter-bombers, was vectored to its targets over Pyongyang where it encountered large formations of enemy aircraft. On this occasion Nicholls damaged another Mig before breaking off the engagement and heading for home.

On 13 November, Nicholls and the rest of his flight were involved in another fierce air battle with enemy Migs over Sinuiju, which flew directly towards the Sabres. One Mig shot towards Nicholls in a head-on attack, guns firing. He felt his aircraft buck and shudder as the shells rocketed past him. Thumbing his button, the six machine guns blazed away as the two jets headed towards each other. Taking evasive action, he had to break off the attack, turning his aircraft. It was shuddering against the stress and the controls were heavier than normal. One of the Mig's shells had found its mark. Before he broke away Nicholls had fired another burst at the Mig as it dropped low and he saw pieces fly away from the enemy jet. Landing back at Kimpo Nicholls discovered his aircraft had been hit in the tail by a 23mm shell. He'd been lucky. The damaged aircraft crashed into the ground but was never officially confirmed as a kill for Nicholls.[5]

Over his first confirmed Mig, however, there was no doubt. Flying at 15,000 feet in the No. 3 position in a flight of four he sighted enemy aircraft near Sinuiju in December, on his ninety-ninth mission, his last but one. Calling up the rest of the flight, Nicholls peeled off, climbing quickly before attacking the enemy formation. The Migs immediately went into evasive action to shake off the Sabres. Locking onto one aircraft, he followed it as the enemy plane twisted and turned, trying desperately to shake him off.

Lining up the Mig in his sights, Nicholls fired a long burst of machine-gun fire. Tracer shells ripped into the rear fuselage of the Mig, pieces flying in all directions. Almost immediately fire tore through the Mig's tail section and the enemy pilot put the aircraft into a slight climb as if trying to get away. Instead

---

[5] In his logbook there is a star beside this incident that denotes a kill. However other sources such as the Max Hastings book *The Korean War* indicate that he had only one confirmed kill.

the burning Mig began to disintegrate and went into a quick spin, crashing into the ground. Nicholls turned and headed for Kimpo; the battle had been over in a matter of minutes. After completing 100 missions, Nicholls left Korea, his war over. He was awarded the DFC by the RAF and the US DFC and Air Medal.

Originally, 77 Squadron of the Royal Australian Air Force had arrived in Korea flying the American P51 Mustang single-seat piston-engined fighter, but by the early part of 1951 the Australians were earmarked for jets. They hoped it would be the Sabre but it wasn't to be. Instead their new mounts were British Meteors. Early in May 1950, the Meteor was tested in combat by Flight Lieutenant Daniel,[6] the first of the RAF pilots attached to the 335th at Johnson Air Base in the USA. He put the Meteor through its paces for two days against the Sabre to see how the British machine would fare. It was generally considered that the Sabre could hold its own against the Mig 15, so if the Meteor could do well against the Sabre then . . . The British jet was found wanting in a steep dive or long straight and level flight against the Sabre, although in turning, zooming and in a sustained climb the Meteor had the advantage.[7]

It was thought that the Meteor could hold its own against the Mig, depending entirely on tactics and how the aircraft was flown. Fly it in the same manner as a Sabre and the Meteor pilot would be lost, as the Mig's superior speed was a definite advantage. Australian pilots were impatient to get at the enemy jets even though some did feel the Migs would hopelessly outclass the Meteor[8].

In February 1951 fifteen Mark VIII single-seat jets along with two Mark VII Meteor trainers were shipped out to Japan, and throughout May and June 77's pilots worked up on the Meteor. The squadron leader, Richard Cresswell, had flown F80 Shooting Stars so he was already experienced in flying jet fighters.

According to Richard Jackson in *Air War Korea*, there was a very tight air of security on the arrival and conversion to the British jets because Britain did not want to appear too closely allied to the Korean War.

Some accidents occurred during the conversion process such as that of Sergeant Stoney. On 14 June he climbed his Meteor away from Iwakuni where conversion was taking place when suddenly his ejection seat went off. He was blasting through the canopy head first, still strapped into his ejection seat, then his parachute deployed and he was free of the seat. There was another danger, however. The jet from which he'd just been hurled was spiralling around him, getting closer and closer as he descended towards dry land. In the end it crashed into a hillside, and he reached the ground safely.

The new British jets had to be fitted with radio compasses and were not allowed to fly on operations until they were.[9] By the end of the month, while

---

[6] He later went to Korea as one of the RAF exchange pilots.
[7] This information is documented in *Meteor Aircraft in Action*.
[8] There is conflicting opinion over this. The Australians were generally not satisfied with the Meteor but some people believe it was bad tactics and poor training rather than the jet itself.
[9] This order was later rescinded as the enemy air activity increased.

the new compasses were still being fitted, the squadron moved to Kimpo to take up residence with the 335th.

At the same time Squadron Leader Cresswell was convinced that good tactics were the answer to the threat of the Migs. He was sure the Meteor would perform well if they operated it in conjunction with the Sabres, but the senior RAAF and USAF officers had to be convinced. Officially, 77 Squadron was part of the American Fifth Air Force, and so Cresswell had to go to the American top brass to get his message across that the Meteors could be successful aircraft if the tactics were right.

In the end, when 77 Squadron went into conflict, it was in the interceptor role. At the time the Meteor and its pilots were not checked out for ground attack and, even though they had serious combat limitations compared with the Mig, interception was the name of the game. One of the worst of its limitations was poor rearward vision due to a metal fairing at the back of the cockpit.

Throughout July, the squadron flew training and familiarization flights, and finally went operational on the 30th. Sixteen Meteors flew a fighter sweep with an equal number of Sabres, but they saw no sign of the enemy. It wasn't until 25 August that two Migs were sighted heading south near Sinuiju that the Meteors finally got close to their enemy. One Meteor wheeled away from its formation, firing a long burst at the retreating enemy jets but none of the cannon shells reached their targets.[10]

Bullets started flying on 29 August when eight Meteors were escorting B29 bombers and another eight flew a diversionary sweep north of Sunan led by Squadron Leader Wilson. Flying at 35,000 feet, he spotted several Migs over Chongju at 40,000 feet. Gradually, he managed to move his formation around up-sun of the Migs, so that they couldn't be seen coming out of the sun. As he was preparing to attack, however, he spotted two Migs below and quickly dived on the two jets. His wingman peeled off with sudden aircraft trouble, leaving Wilson to go after the two Migs alone.

Suddenly, shells shot past his wings and fuselage as a Mig jumped him from out of the sun. Wilson yanked hard on the stick, pushing the rudders as he whipped the Meteor into a tight turn. Already the Mig's cannon shells had sent pieces flying from Wilson's aircraft. Fighting to get rid of his pursuer he was saved when two Meteors drove the enemy pilot away. Wilson made it back to base escorted by the rest of his formation, but his aircraft had been badly shot up.

While Wilson was having his adventure, a fierce battle had developed between the Migs and the Meteors on escort duties. Thirty Migs and eight Meteors battled it out in the Korean skies with one of the Australian aircraft shot down. Not one Mig fell to the Meteor's cannon.

On 5 September, things weren't much better for 77 Squadron. Migs flying in pairs at 20,000 feet bounced six Meteors escorting F80 Shooting Stars. During the five-minute battle three Meteors opened fire on the Migs but saw no result. Nothing happened until several days later when Flight Lieutenant Dawson fired several bursts at a Mig and saw pieces fly off it. However, this was never confirmed.

---

[10] Documented in greater detail in *Meteor Aircraft in Action*.

24 October saw sixteen Meteors from 77 Squadron escorting some of the big B29 heavy bombers who were heading for Sonchon where they were to bomb a railway bridge. En route they ran into a huge battle between Sabres and some sixty Migs. Within minutes one Meteor had been hit and rolled into a dive as its starboard engine flamed out. The pilot managed to land safely. Again, no Migs fell to Meteor cannon.

Finally on 27 October, Meteors inflicted serious damage on Migs in a battle that saw sixteen Australian fighters and thirty-two F84 Thunderjets bounced by ninety-five Migs.[11] Over Sinanju the communist jets overwhelmed the fighters who were escorting B29 bombers. In this battle Flying Officer Reading saw his cannon shells hit a Mig so many times it began trailing smoke. Other Meteors claimed hits on enemy jets as well.

On 1 December, the Meteors shot down their first Migs, but at a high price. Led by Flight Lieutenant Geoff Thornton twelve Meteors were flying a fighter sweep at 19,000 feet when they sighted more than fifty Migs high above them. The communist jets dropped down in pairs to attack the Australians. Thornton turned tightly away from the attacking Migs. Flying Officer Bruce Gogerly manoeuvred his Meteor behind a Mig and plastered it with cannon fire, shooting it down in flames. He was then attacked head-on by several Migs in sweeping passes and fired his cannon at the marauding jets. Another Mig went down on fire during the whirling dogfight. Rather than be able to celebrate their victories, they discovered when they landed that Migs had shot down three Meteors. Two pilots survived to be taken prisoner, but one was lost.

The Meteor wasn't living up to expectations. By early 1952, with only a handful of aircraft left serviceable, it was relegated to area and airfield defence. The new CO however, Wing Commander Ron Susans, convinced the authorities the jet was ideal for ground attack. To prove his point he led a flight of four on 8 January in a cannon attack on the Changdon water tower. This proved to be such a success that 77 Squadron took on ground-attack duties as their main occupation for the remainder of their time flying Meteors.

On 27 March 1953 Meteors tangled with Migs again. On patrol over Simak Sergeants John Hale and David Irlam spotted three Migs south-east of Pyongyang. Attacking immediately, one of the Migs made away while the rest turned on their attackers. Jettisoning his central fuel tank Hale fired two rockets at the oncoming Migs, which took evasive action. One of them overshot the Meteor as he tried to get on Hale's tail. Presenting itself to Hale as a tempting target, he extended his own airbrakes and managed to rake the Mig with cannon shells.

For a few seconds only, the Mig flew parallel with Hale who could easily see the pilot. Swinging behind the Mig he thumbed the firing button, his cannon shells ripping into the communist jet and sending pieces of it flying in all directions. Suddenly, the Mig rolled onto its back; black smoke was pouring from it as it headed straight down. Hale didn't see the Mig crash because the sky was suddenly filled with enemy jets. Two came straight at Hale, their guns blazing. Turning and climbing he managed to do an S-turn to get behind the two

---

[11] Detailed in *Meteor Aircraft in Action* by Glen Ashley.

Migs, his own cannon shells ripping into the closest one. Bright flashes appeared all over the wing root of the Mig as it tried to climb away. Instead, white smoke poured from the stricken aircraft and it flipped over, dropping quickly away to its doom. His ammunition expended, Hale now needed to get out of the fight and head for home. Luckily, more Meteors arrived on the scene and Hale was able to get back safely.[12]

---

[12] This event is detailed in *Meteor Aircraft in Action*.

Chapter Fifteen

FLYING WITH THE US NAVY

Lieutenant J. Joe MacBrien

Experienced Canadian naval pilot Lieutenant J. Joe MacBrien was the first jet fighter pilot on an exchange programme between the US Navy and the Royal Canadian Navy, and flew off American aircraft carriers in the air war over Korea. The signal that had come through from Canadian Naval Headquarters in Ottawa was very sparse indeed. It had simply told MacBrien to report to the US Navy in San Diego, California on 1 April 1952. He had no idea what might lie ahead of him, but he did know he was ultimately bound for Korea. What follows are his experiences, in his own words, of flying and fighting over Korea with the American Navy, recorded in 1992:[1]

"I arrived in San Diego with no clear idea of what to expect and neither did the petty officer at the front desk. He did, however, refer this unexpected foreign arrival to the senior foreign officer, a RAF squadron leader serving on exchange as an ASW specialist. With the assistance of the RAF I eventually found the right office and was posted to VF781a Reserve Unit, one of two jet fighter squadrons of Air Group 102 at NAS Miramar."

For the first weeks of training the Air Group used the Grumman F9F-2 Panther jet aircraft but then they became the first USN squadrons to receive the brand new F9F-5 Panther; this was slightly bigger, had a thinner wing and hence a slightly higher limiting Mach number than the F9F-2. With twenty per cent more power the new version was slightly faster than the old model. The Air Group's third squadron was equipped with the F4U-5 Corsair and the fourth squadron had the AD-4s[2] for the attack role.

"There were thirty-two of us but everyone was told that the number would be reduced to twenty-eight by the time we deployed, which brought an element of competition into the proceedings and permitted some selection based on weapons qualification etc."

MacBrien had completed his jet conversion courses with the Royal Navy on Sea Vampires and Meteor jet fighters. "It was clear to me that first of all the squadron had to assess the capabilities of this unknown quantity [himself] that had been sent to them from somewhere up north. As fighter pilots depend heavily upon each other I flew on a wing with quite a few of the more experienced pilots.

---

[1] MacBrien's account is reprinted by kind permission of the Fleet Air Arm Museum.
[2] Perhaps more commonly known as the Skyraider. It was a slow piston-engined fighter-bomber that could carry a heavier load than the B17s of the Second World War with just one mighty radial engine.

"I had one interesting day when the squadron was told to send someone to attend a briefing at the NORAD HQ at Norton AFB, near San Bernadino, California. Since I was a squadron weapons officer, I was told to fly up there for the day and represent the Air Group. We were told that a seventy-hour test of NORAD readiness would start in exactly twelve hours, that the US Strategic Air Command would be the enemy and would attack various targets in southern California during the three-day period and that the fighter squadrons at Miramar would be a major component of the air defence of the Los Angeles/San Diego area. The exercise involved hours of immediate readiness (in the cockpit) and was not very exciting, but it did give us a chance to see SAC aircraft at close quarters (we had to record an aircraft's serial number to be credited with a 'kill' and this involved close formation)."

The Air Group was to deploy in the attack carrier the USS *Oriskany* and for MacBrien much of August 1952 was spent working up on the ship before she set sail for the Korean War. At the end of August and just before shipping out, the seventeen-year-old King Faisal II of Iraq came aboard for a day of carrier demonstrations. "He was very late arriving on board so the demonstration started late. We launched and recovered, attacked towed targets beside the ship and made lots of noise and low passes, etc., but because of the late start we finished in the dark. Some got an unscheduled night landing in an F9F Panther. The unfortunate King was assassinated in a bloody coup only seven years later.

"The USS *Oriskany* (CVA 34) was the attack carrier in which the Air Group would deploy. She had been completely renovated and fitted with the most recent modifications that included dedicated spaces and equipment needed for special weapons. The ship was the first USN carrier in the western Pacific with a full special weapons delivery capability. Although steam catapults, angled decks and mirror-landing systems were still in the future, the jet squadrons particularly appreciated the USS *Oriskany*'s new and more powerful hydraulic catapult.

"By the time the Air Group started operating from the ship it had been augmented by various splinter groups, each consisting of a few aircraft and aircrew with special capabilities such as ASW, AEW, ECM, photo, night attack and night fighter roles.[3] We of the fighter squadrons worked with the attack squadrons on escort tactics and with the ship's fighter direction team on air intercepts."

During the passage to Japan the flight deck was too crowded to permit flying so the pilots spent their time reading and re-reading intelligence briefings on all aspects of the air war over Korea. Specific information on how to evade capture and detailed accounts of every successful escape was drummed into them. They were heavily briefed on the methods and procedures the North Koreans used during their interrogations of POWs.

"It was vital to convince the initial interrogator that you were nothing special and could not provide them with any more information than they already had. If you attracted their attention and interest your prospects became

---

[3] ASW = anti-submarine warfare, AEW = anti-electronic warfare, ECM = electronic countermeasures, and photo = photo-reconnaissance.

increasingly dim. The USN predicted that, if I was unlucky enough to become the first RCN aircrew POW, I could expect to receive a full interrogation. They offered me false ID but I was warned that it was very difficult to create a credible false identity and maintain it during interrogation, and that failure to carry it off could have unpleasant consequences. This prediction was borne out many years later when I met Squadron Leader Andy McKenzie RCAF and learned from him some of what he had experienced as a Canadian POW; Andy was taken prisoner while flying as a RCAF exchange pilot with the USAF. He was immediately transported across the Yalu River into China where he was held incommunicado until long after the formal POW exchange in 1953."

As the ship sailed towards Japan and conflict over Korea, the pilots feverishly studied the topography of the enemy's terrain; they were expected to memorize the main roads, towns, railways, rivers and cities. "The final test was to be able to draw a map of the main features of North Korea from memory," wrote MacBrien.

By 22 October 1952, the USS *Oriskany* had docked at Yokosuka, once the main base of the Japanese Navy during the Second World War. It was now the main base for the American attack carriers of Task Force 77:

"The ship carried out training flights for two days to get everyone back in the groove and then on 2 November we joined the rest of Task Force 77 off the east coast of Korea where we commenced operations against the enemy. Responsibility for air support over North Korea was split east and west, with the USAF and others responsible for the western half and the US Navy's Task Force 77 responsible for the eastern half. This gave TF77 the largest area of responsibility – which ran right up to the far north-eastern corner of North Korea where the Tumen River is North Korea's border with the Soviet Union. The east coast supply route originating in the Soviet Union was of critical importance to the enemy forces and carried the largest volume of supplies."

For the US Navy the operating cycle for the carriers was four to six weeks conducting flight operations, then sailing to Yokosuka for ten days' rest and recreation. During operations, the carriers would replenish at sea every three or four days as they were emptied of aviation fuel and ordnance. There were normally two carrier groups on station and a further one replenishing at sea. This is much different to the Royal Navy, which had only one carrier.

"Sometimes three carriers would operate together for a day or so. The staff always took advantage of increased strength to schedule attacks against major targets and the carriers always had a full anti-submarine screen of destroyers and frigates while at sea. A typical strike mission would involve 1.6 to 1.8 hours in the air but the pilot was usually kept busy for quite a few additional hours. First there was the preliminary look at maps and photographs of the target, and initial mission planning, then came the process of getting undressed and putting on a G-suit[5] followed by an immersion suit. This suit was similar to a diving suit with watertight seals at the wrists and neck. They weren't very comfortable

---

[4] This is a flight suit that is designed to help the pilot's circulation flow during high gravity manoeuvres where the blood tends to drain away from the head and chest into the legs and feet.

but without one you would last only a few minutes in the cold water of the
Korean winter. But once in the suit the problem then was to keep cool enough
to avoid sweating because any moisture inside would destroy the thermal
insulation that was the whole reason for wearing the suit. The Navy helped by
air conditioning the ready-rooms and keeping them very cold; they also
provided an escalator up to the flight deck so that we could avoid the exertion
of climbing ladders. The jets used a high rate of fuel when operating at low
altitudes against ground targets so we quickly learned to monitor our fuel state
more closely than we ever had before."

It wasn't just a question of a couple of hours in the cockpit then straight to
the bar for a few drinks because one strike mission would keep a pilot very busy
indeed. "The formal briefing would include photography of the target and
everything that was known about the target's defences. The flight leaders would
then give their briefings about the tactics to be employed. Meanwhile the
teletype was providing the most recent ship's position, and both local and target
area weather. A few minutes before the scheduled launch time, the aircraft
assignments would be received and then came the command 'Pilots, man your
aircraft!'

"The plane captain of the aircraft assigned to you helped you to settle into
the cockpit, the ship turned into the wind, engines were started, and the launch
began. By the time you landed aboard at the end of the mission you had been
in the cockpit for approximately two hours. And then everyone gathered to be
de-briefed by the intelligence officer with emphasis on damage assessment. All
of this meant that a pilot was kept busy for the best part of five hours to
complete one strike mission."

As with the Sea Furies and Fireflies of the Fleet Air Arm operating off the
west coast, the USN F9F jets would launch their armed recce flights around
dawn so they would be in the target area as soon as there was just enough light
to see their targets:

"We often found vehicles still on the roads which had not yet pulled off to
hide during the day. The main supply routes in North Korea were divided into
segments with each one assigned a colour/number codename. A typical armed
recce mission might be to cover two or three such segments with four aircraft
in two sections of two. The height above ground was critical: too low and the
terrain went by so quickly it was difficult to detect targets, too high and it was
harder to resolve detail on the ground. An altitude of 1,200 to 1,400 feet above
ground we deemed the best compromise, with the second section trailing the
first by a mile or so. Targets were normally identified when they were almost
directly below, and this meant that time was required to climb and turn in order
to initiate the attack. In some cases, a target spotted by the lead section could
be called to the trailing section that could attack seconds later with the
advantage of surprise."

Flying a jet at low level in the mountainous terrain of North Korea meant
having good map-reading skills, among many others. The rough terrain had a
distinct lack of recognizable features while severe shadows at the bottoms of
valleys where roads, railway lines and rivers were situated made interpreting
photographs difficult. However, the F9F Panther jet, which MacBrien flew, was

capable of multiple roles aside from the strike role.

"On flak suppression missions we usually carried six or eight 260lb fragmentation bombs and, if the mission went as planned, we would start our attack just a few seconds before the Skyraiders were ready to start theirs. We would start from above 10,000 feet if the cloud base permitted and dive, aiming at the defensive gun positions. We would fire our 20mm cannon and then between 3,000 and 4,000 feet, release a pair of bombs. If our aim and timing were good the Skyraiders often received no defensive fire at all and would be able to make several unopposed runs on the primary target. We would make a series of attacks on the enemy guns until the Skyraiders were finished and clear of the target. I can't remember an instance where a Skyraider was lost when F9Fs were providing flak suppression."

The F9F-5, which MacBrien flew, usually carried a bomb load of two 500lb bombs and four or six 250lb bombs and rarely used rockets: "Snow tends to contain the blast effect of an explosion and significantly reduces the incendiary effect. To counter this we sometimes carried fragmentation bombs with daisy-cutter fuses; these were a steel rod about four feet long projecting straight out from the nose of the bomb. Detonation occurred at the instant when the end of the rod struck the ground, at which time the bomb was still four feet in the air and the fragments spread horizontally unimpeded by the snow cover."

On 18 November MacBrien flew a mission during which the task group was operating well north of the east coast of Korea, not more than 100 miles from the Soviet naval base at Vladivostok. "There had been numerous radar contacts that morning well to the north but none approached the force and my colleagues and I had an uneventful Combat Air Patrol (CAP). However, shortly after we'd been relieved and landed aboard a new radar contact was picked up: thirty-five miles and closing. One of the aircraft on CAP, also from our squadron, had experienced partial fuel pump failure and had to remain below 20,000 feet while the other three remaining aircraft climbed and were vectored out to intercept. Minutes later the flight leader visually identified seven Migs high overhead. The Migs initiated an attack and within seconds an uncoordinated mêlée developed. Our pilots gave a good account of themselves; one F9F was damaged but our pilots were credited with two Migs confirmed and one damaged. One F9F actually orbited an enemy pilot[5] descending into the water by parachute. Neither side sought any further contact although there was a great deal of enemy activity near the position of the parachute; this activity included a slow-moving radar target, which was assumed to be a rescue aircraft. We spent the afternoon at general quarters (action stations) ready to launch additional fighters, and although there were two more Mig sightings by the CAP the enemy did not close the task force and there was no further contact. By late afternoon the enemy activity had ceased and the radar screen was clear. An exciting day with gratifying results, particularly in view of the disparity in numbers and aircraft performance."

On 1 February 1953 MacBrien led one of his squadron's most successful strikes: "The strike was to be led by our squadron commander with our

---

[5] The Mig had Soviet markings. So much for the Soviet Union's assertion they were taking no active role in the war.

operations officer leading the second division. However, when we started engines, they both had mechanical problems and could not launch. The ship told me what had happened just after my wingman and I were launched, that I was now leading the strike, and that two standbys were being launched to bring the flight up to strength. The spares joined up; we had a quick reorganisation by radio and then departed for the target area on schedule.

"Bombing that day was very accurate and the damage done during our first run was such that I was able to move the aiming point for subsequent runs. The flight scored a number of direct hits and as we left the target we were able to count at least five separate fires. My luck continued – one of our photo aircraft was using the same tactical radio frequency; he heard us discussing the damage assessment and asked for the target frames as he returned to the task force. At the de-briefing our intelligence officer was somewhat sceptical of our enthusiastic damage assessment claim but a few hours later the photo interpreters settled the matter – they reported no less than seven fires and even more damage than we had claimed. This was without question the most successful mission that I led during my time in Korea.

"Another mission that I remember well took place early in the morning of 25 March when I was scheduled to lead a CAP mission. The CAP was always launched first and recovered last to maintain constant coverage. My wingman and I were already in place on the two catapults before the ship turned into wind. The weather near the ship was poor with strong winds and low cloud and, if it was the same over the beach, conditions would be marginal for effective operations. At the last moment, Rear Admiral Hickey, who was in the USS *Oriskany*, decided to put all sorties on hold and to launch only one section as a weather reconnaissance. Since my wingman and I were all set to go, our CAP mission was cancelled and we were briefed by radio on the areas that were to be checked. Maps were not a problem since we always carried maps for the whole of Korea regardless of the expected mission, but a bit of rapid map folding was required before we were launched a few minutes later.

"The weather got worse as we approached the coast; the cloud at about nine-tenths at 1,000 feet, and as we moved inland the cloud was right down on the hilltops. We had to stay on top to conserve fuel but ducked down through the odd hole to check conditions below cloud. We were quite far north having crossed the coast near Chongjin – no other aircraft were airborne and we were truly on our own, a long way from home.

"I reported the weather as we returned to the task force and when we entered the landing pattern it was apparent that the local weather had deteriorated quite markedly during the one and one half hours or so since we were launched. I concentrated on my instruments and followed the controller's vectors. Although we were let down quite rapidly and the descent took only a few minutes we were down to 500 feet before we were below cloud!

"Ensign Randy Scoggan USNR became my wingman early on during the work-up programme. Randy was a very good pilot and he was also the youngest in the squadron – he had his twenty-first birthday while we were deployed. He and I flew together on practically all our missions; the only exceptions were when one of us was on standby or scheduled for photo escort.

I never worried about him failing to do his job well.

"During the final week of operations the squadron flight assignments were modified so that each pilot would end up with exactly the same number of missions. So on our second to last day I was not on the flight schedule and Randy was put down to take part in a typical strike mission. During the last run over the target he called on the radio that he had been hit by ground fire; after that single message he did not respond to the calls from the other pilots who were nearby and had him in sight. His aircraft went into a steep full-power climb for several minutes before it rolled over quite slowly and then dived into the sea just off the coast. There was no sign of an attempt to bail out, or of a parachute, and there was no sign of an attempt by the pilot to recover from the dive into the sea. No one will ever know exactly what happened but I suspect that it was Randy himself rather than his aircraft that was hit and that he lost consciousness after his one and only radio message. The Air Group lost a total of eleven pilots during the deployment but Randy was the first from our squadron. His loss during what would have certainly been his last mission was a cruel twist of fate which made it even harder for us to accept."

On 25 April 1953 the USS *Oriskany* launched its final mission. MacBrien was on the very last one, eight aircraft on a special photo mission. This final flight brought the total number of missions flown by the Air Group to 7,000 since the previous November when their tour had started.

"During my exchange tour of duty, I accumulated 233 total hours in the F9F, ninety-two catapult launches and arrested landings aboard the USS *Oriskany*, and a total of sixty-six combat missions while the carrier was deployed on operations in Korean waters," concluded MacBrien.

THE END

At 1000hrs on 27 July 1953, the armistice was at last signed at Panmunjom by all parties, and would go into effect twelve hours later at 2200hrs. The air war was maintained throughout the day, however, as Migs and Sabres continued to battle it out, while B29 bombers dropped psychological warfare leaflets over North Korea. Marine jets bombed enemy supply dumps and elsewhere other targets in North Korea were attacked or photographed.

At 2200hrs that night the guns across the 38th Parallel fell silent. The war that had raged for three years and claimed nearly two million dead was finally over. Above the war-torn countryside, the skies were eerily empty of aircraft. Both sides were exhausted by the war and had ultimately achieved very little. Today, the two countries of North and South Korea remain as they were in 1953, still observing a ceasefire and both eyeing each other uneasily across the divide of the 38th Parallel.

Appendix I

THE PRISONER

Lieutenant Derek Graham Mather's story is unique in that he was one of the few British airmen taken prisoner by the North Koreans. For nine months he was moved from place to place and kept under permanent guard. In 2002 he talked to me about what happened and what his impressions were during his incarceration. What follows are his own words embellished by a more detailed account published in John Lansdown's *With the Carriers in Korea*.

"By night the Chinese used lights for transports. On one sortie I flew with Hugh McKenry as my wingman. He said 'Do you see all those transports over there?' He put a row of tracer through them and I then saw the camouflage that he'd already seen much further away. We started doing a few pre-dawn take-offs about an hour and half before daybreak with a couple of destroyers out in front of the ship with lights to act as artificial horizon. We could catch them on their headlights as they moved before the sun came up.

"As I came in to strafe this line of trucks we went over a platoon of infantry who pointed their rifles up to the sky. They went into rapid fire and a bullet hit my fuel line. The engine stopped. A lucky shot. All of a sudden I had no power and climbed up with the excess speed and glided towards the sea, but I couldn't get that far and landed in a rice paddy field. The drop tanks acted as a pair of skis and I skidded through a field and then through a hedge where I finally came to a standstill.

"For about an hour I sat on the wing waiting for somebody to come and get me. Eventually an American chopper came in from Kung sun-ni and it picked me up and took me back to the island. They dangled a loop on the end of a cable and I grabbed the rope and wrapped it under my arms, then I was just dangling there. Then the following morning a Dakota came and picked me up from the island. The pilot was a Greek and he landed on the beach. He picked me up and off we went to Seoul. Years later I went to Greece and ran into the same pilot as an air commodore."

The next time Mather was shot down was his last, and he was incarcerated until the end of hostilities. By this time, 5 January 1953, he was flying from HMS *Glory*:

"We'd been dive-bombing some bridges on a river. I was the No. 3, the section leader of a flight of four aircraft. The CO was Pete Stuart. The weather was pretty miserable, snow-storms, low cloud and poor visibility. We attacked the first bridge with bombs and he went in with his No. 2 and they got that bridge."

As we have seen elsewhere, the cardinal rule for virtually every mission was not to go around again for another attack. Some of the losses suffered during the conflict can be attributed directly to this practice. Mather continued:

"Staying in the area longer than necessary was a bad idea. So my wingman Ted Anson and I went off on an armed reconnaissance and came back around twenty minutes later after the area had cooled down a little. We attacked some secondary targets, one of which was another bridge up the river.

"I led the second attack in, and as we came down in our dives they were waiting for us. It was a flak trap. They had AA guns at the bridge and I released my bombs and we were pulling up to get away from this. Suddenly there was a bang at my feet from a 76mm shell that had come in under the seat. I called up to Ted that I'd been hit and he said he'd come and have a look.

"Unfortunately, the shell blew up. The debris from my Fury shot back right at him but fortunately he pulled away and got free of it. Next thing I knew I was tumbling in the air, still in my seat and most of the engine had gone. The canopy had gone as well. The remaining part of the aircraft was spinning out of control so I decided the best thing to do was to get out. I undid my harness and stood up on the seat, or what was left of it. I peered over the side and pushed the parachute over, then did a quick somersault and I was suddenly rolling around in fresh air. Ted said that I appeared over the side in the conventional ball that we are taught to do during training. I had no idea I'd actually gone over that way. We'd done it so many times during our operational flying school in RAF Lossiemouth that I just did it automatically.

"I was free falling through the air so I pulled the ring on the parachute and that deployed rather suddenly. The next thing I knew I was dangling at the end of the chute moving rather rapidly towards the ground. Instead of the standard Smith and Wesson revolver I had a 9-millimetre automatic[1] pistol that I'd got from an American in exchange for the Smith and Wesson.

"Well, the closer I got to the land I found I was being shot at. I returned fire and then I thought it would be prudent if I didn't have the gun on me when I came down so I tossed it away."

Landing hard in the snow, the North Koreans were waiting for him.

"This was winter. And I came down in the snow and was captured.

[1] Anson had referred to it as a 45 Colt automatic.

I stood up to surrender to them but there were still bullets flying around so I lay down again. They jumped me very quickly. Visibility was pretty poor and it was very cold. Although it wasn't snowing at the time, the ground was covered in very deep snow."

Mather's biggest fear on his way down to the ground was that his parachute might go up in flames from ground fire. A scene from the Hollywood film *One Minute to Zero* stood out in his mind as he floated through the air. At the end of that picture an American airman parachutes out of his aircraft to the ground. He gets shot at by ground fire, the parachute explodes into flame and he crashes to his death. Mather felt the same thing could easily have happened to him. Fortunately, it didn't.

Despite the cold, Mather's immersion suit kept him pretty warm.

"We had our goon suits on. The suit was in two halves but it was waterproofed and sealed. Both the bottom and the top half had rubber seals which helped to keep the cold out. That gave you a reasonable chance if you had to ditch or got shot down behind enemy lines. They searched me pretty thoroughly then we marched to the local Command Post where I was searched again."

At this point they took away Mather's watch and his translation sheet along with his blood chit. Without the translation sheet he would not be able to communicate but it seemed they weren't concerned about communication. Mather had a few flash burns on his face where the skin had been exposed between his goggles and his oxygen mask. Also one side of his beard was singed and he asked for treatment. The North Koreans simply applied some antiseptic liquid to the wound and left it.

"In the extreme cold it healed very quickly. After spending a night at that post they marched me off the next day north along a frozen river bed. It was about forty miles and I think it was one of their main supply routes that ran down the west coast."

While they were marching a Firefly, which was rocketing a bridge not far away, attacked them. It was an odd feeling being on the receiving end of a rocket attack, he later recalled.

Walking in the immersion suit was difficult and to make it easier, Mather took off the seals around the wrists and the neck, and separated the trousers from the boots, which made the slow progress over the snow a little easier. The suit kept the icy wind at bay and kept his feet dry. But because he'd cut the seals, the intense cold seeped in when he slept.

"We marched about ten miles up towards Sariwon which was a headquarters town. From the air you don't see much activity and the place looked deserted but down on the ground it was a different story. You see people and there was expertly camouflaged transport that perfectly blended into the background of snow and buildings. We spent the night in Sariwon and then in the middle of the night we got on top of a truck moving up north towards the capital of North Korea. Most of the local villages had been pretty well flattened. On the road you saw evidence of camouflaging where trucks were laid up during the day and they moved at night.

"The railway bridges were very flimsy-looking affairs but they knew they would be blown down again very quickly so they were probably rebuilt just to take one or two trains. In the villages the Korean civilians lived in the rubble or underground in cellars. Everything was basic. The houses in the villages were made of wood and things and they had been fairly flattened."

The snow and ice made the going towards Pyongyang slow. Although it was only fifty miles to the capital it took the convoy in which Mather was marching two days to get there. As they rumbled over the road he saw how the North Koreans were using hordes of peasant labourers to rebuild shattered bridges to the minimum standards. They had become experts at rebuilding and camouflaging their assets. In Pyongyang he was transferred from the roof of a truck to a Jeep and was covered with a blanket, not for warmth but to avoid hostile action from people in the capital.

"My main thoughts were – I'm still alive. But what was coming next? We had very little briefing about what would happen. We had various lectures where you expected something like the German POW camps from the Second World War where it was formal. But life wasn't like that."

The first place Mather stopped at for any length of time was the Korean Headquarters Interrogation Centre. It was here that he met recently captured American aircrew and Army ground crews. In one room up to ten would live together. But the rooms were so small that there was no space for all ten to lie on the floor at the same time. Naturally, they exchanged names just in case one of them managed to escape.

"There were two Americans, one who died as he had been tied up so tightly that he'd lost the circulation in his hands. He'd also been left outside a command post all night. One of the other Americans, who'd been captured after crashing with his aircraft, had his boots and gloves taken away by the North Koreans. By then his feet had got fairly advanced frostbite and gangrene and they were beginning to smell. He was in a very bad state. We had to help him to the toilets because he couldn't move. After I left that place I gather he didn't last very long.

"The human state is such that most people can push down the worst times so they disappear. You can recall them but you don't linger over them and don't keep them bubbling at the surface. Every once in a while you got the better of the North Koreans and it gave you a good feeling.

But most of the time you were on your own and there was nobody there to see if you were keeping up the norm, keeping your duty. There was nobody to talk to day after day because they didn't know any English."

It was at a camp at Pyongyang that Mather was taken out of the room with the other prisoners and placed in a solitary cell for interrogation. He had no fire and his immersion suit was taken away. For an hour every day he was made to stand outside in the freezing air. His interrogators made sure he didn't go to sleep. His boots were taken away as well, leaving him in working dress similar to long johns, pyjamas and socks.[2]

"I went through a period of weeks where they were carrying out their interrogation. We were taken out one at time and sometimes you never saw the other prisoners again. I was deprived of clothing, made to feel cold, fairly small fry as if they weren't interested. We were not physically beaten. The war had another nine months to run. It could have been like Vietnam, which went on for eight years. They realised that things were coming to a halt sooner rather than later and I think they started cleaning up their act, because people before had been beaten. Solitary is an attack on you. Once in a while they gave you some books to read, mostly Russian ones. At one point they gave me *David Copperfield*, and then when it was finished they took it away. All the time there were phases of interrogation.

"I remember one time in Pak's Palace[3] I'd had my goon suit removed and was dressed in pale blue cotton shirt, dark trousers and cotton underwear and was pretty cold. I was taken to this room with no heating and it was divided by a piece of parachute silk and I went to see what was behind it. There were a lot of *Daily Telegraph* newspapers behind it. This was all part of their intelligence gathering."

Eventually he was given a fire once a day and his boots and immersion suit were both returned to him. Mather stayed in solitary confinement for three or four weeks before he was returned to the room with the other prisoners.

"They would know which squadron you were from. You gave your name and number so that it could get back to your squadron and let them know you were alive. They tried to get you to believe they had more knowledge than they really had. But most of it was unclassified stuff."

Instead of sending them to a proper POW camp, the Chinese called Mather and his fellow prisoners war criminals, and said they were therefore not represented under the Geneva Convention. His captors did not allow them to wash or clean their teeth for up to nine weeks. They were forced to dig slit trenches in the miserable freezing weather before being given a hot bath. Then one day Mather

---

[2] See *With the Carriers in Korea.*
[3] This was the North Korean Interrogation Centre in Pyongyang.

was taken out again, and presumed it was for another round of interrogation. Instead he was put on a truck and transported some sixty miles or so south-east of Pyongyang to another camp, which was run by the Chinese. Here they took away his clothes and he was issued with a cotton uniform, boots and an overcoat. To ensure he stayed clean, the Chinese also issued Mather with soap, a toothbrush, a tin of DDT and some tobacco.

"You went into a village and if there was a small command post there you were guarded by the chap in charge of you. You had one man one guard. Apart from Pyongyang, most of the time I was in solitary confinement.

"We didn't look like the average man in the street in China or Korea which is why I didn't have any occasion to consider escaping. You were closely guarded and you never talked to the guards. The only people you did talk to were the interrogators. One of them was a graduate of the London School of Economics. Most of us in there were apolitical. Their main aim was to convert everybody to communism. We left one man behind because he was a party member and he decided to stay with it. He was a good soldier before he was captured. They glossed over the fact of how he had performed."

During that time Mather lived in a single room with his guard who spoke no English and he was given no exercise. His only chance of speaking to anyone was the interrogator who spoke fluent English. Though speaking with him was a relief after days of nothing, he had to keep his answers simple, direct and not give anything away.

One day, he was taken out to another Jeep and ordered to sit on a mudguard with another prisoner on the other mudguard. Between the two prisoners was a guard with a machine gun. Before Mather knew it they were off again.

"We stopped at a command post for the night and by chance myself and the other prisoner on the other mudguard both asked to go to the toilet at the same time so we were able to exchange our names."

This time it was a 200-mile journey north. They ended up at Pyoktong, which was a big interrogation centre in a large town. Once again he was put into solitary confinement but this time with one guard for every three or four cells. The food was two bowls of rice a day and occasional rice broth.

"We had perhaps ten weeks there before the war was over. We were up by the Yalu in the last few weeks and one night they said you've got to come out of the huts. I was taken out to the foothills behind the town and told to dig a hole. They explained to me that it should be just big enough to take me in a crouching position. I dug this hole for two hours over two or three nights and each time I heard shots and some odd screams. As you did you put two and two together and got five but there was nothing else to do. You had nothing else to think about. You imagined the worst and then you were called out the last night and you thought this is it. But that day passes and you go on looking ahead.

"The passage of time changes everything. You were on your own. You were not exactly expecting you'd get away with it because no prisoners had been exchanged. Your hopes were you'd get to a POW camp. But every day you didn't was very depressing. My great fondness at school was maths so I spent a lot of time trying to prove geometric theorems. Flights of fancy, really. But there was nothing else to do.

"I was surprised that the North Koreans weren't more aggressive to me because I'd been attacking their country. I don't remember them trying to get me or attack me. I had expected more retribution. They seemed to be pretty cowed. They lived a simple existence almost as if this was over their heads. They seemed to be kept in control by those in charge of them. I remember when I was in solitary confinement I lived in a room in a house which had about three rooms. The kitchen area had a flue that went under the floor and out the far end. They used to feed us with a vegetable that was pretty hot and they baked a form of bread. I didn't like the vegetable so I gave it to them and they gave me little rolls of bread in exchange.

"We did it very discreetly. The house I was in was filled with civilians, peasants. My room was just four walls and a hole for getting in and out. You just sat there or you lay down and that was all. Sometimes they let me walk up and down outside the room, but inside for something to do I used to measure the diagonal across the room, the longest direction I could, then I'd try to walk a mile a day."

At this point his morale was at a very low ebb and he told his interrogators to just get on and shoot him. Instead of doing so, Mather was called out the next evening and put onto another truck for the journey to the Chinese headquarters at Chang-ni. Even though they passed many POWs en route, Mather was restrained from calling out to them. He stayed at the headquarters a few days before being moved again. At one point he was able to very quickly exchange information with another POW. After spending so much time alone or in the company of his captors, it was a relief to have one minute speaking to another English-speaking person.

From the headquarters, he was moved to a hut by a river, and put in solitary confinement. But this time things were different. He was given reading material, mostly communist papers. He was also allowed to sit outside his hut, wash in the river and take exercise that enabled him to see the prisoners in some of the other huts. The food was better and during this time Mather was able to exchange names with one or two other prisoners. Although his interrogation continued it was more relaxed than it had been. "There was an air of excitement," said Mather. A low flying aircraft came over the village one night but the Koreans didn't fire at it, which Mather thought strange.

Next day he was put onto a mule cart and was off again. This time he had a companion in the cart with him – an American USN pilot, Maury Yerger. "We were able to talk to each other which was a great relief." For three hours they talked freely while the mule cart trundled along, discussing everything they could during the short journey.

"We got close to a main camp and met all the other prisoners who kept saying the war was over." Here they were told that peace had been signed ten days before. The low flying aircraft he'd heard the day before had been a Dakota equipped with loudspeakers. "They were allowed to fly over and broadcast that the war was over. Unfortunately, we never heard the loudspeakers because they went unserviceable when they flew over our village."

During this time at the main camp, groups of prisoners would move off every so often as they were slowly repatriated. Mather was now able to mingle freely with the other prisoners and to aid some of the least educated ordinary soldiers in the camp he helped to set up classes to teach these soldiers how to read and write. As the prisoners thinned out from the camp it was Mather's time to go and he was taken by truck to a railhead. Put on a cattle train with many other prisoners they were taken down to Panmunjom for final repatriation.

> "We left that camp with the last lot and they started moving people out by cattle truck down to the place at the end. I was with the last group when the war ended and was one of the last people out. I left with the last of the officers. Almost assuredly we were better fed than we had been before. I'd lost weight, but I wasn't starved as such. In retrospect the diet did us some good. I had the early stages of beriberi where you lose feelings in your toes and they weren't feeling as they normally were. Later, when I was free I bought a pair of shoes and I realised there were too short for me because my toes were starting to fall out. That was the only really serious side effect of my being a prisoner."

He stayed at Panmunjom for two weeks until it was his turn to get into a truck that would take him to a rendezvous point. Here he climbed into a US Army truck and was driven into Freedom Village, a repatriation centre. The date was 2 September 1953. After returning to the UK the Navy sent Mather on three months' repatriation leave. "I said, I don't want that, I want to go back to work. They said, 'You might be contaminated from communism', but I just wanted to get back to flying."

Posted to a training station at Lee-on-Solent he was unofficially allowed to fly, then later it became official.

> "I rejoined the squadron and flew out to Malta where I stayed for some time. After that, I taught at the Royal Naval College for two years. Then I went back to test flying at Fleetlands for a couple of years before they asked me to go to America and work with the Americans in an aircraft repair yard."

Mather did this for two years and during that time he met General Bill Burke who . . .

"had Korean ribbons. He'd been one of the clandestine Leopard troops put in behind enemy lines. On one occasion I'd taken a Fury up for a test flight and got into some trouble. I had to land on this beach on Point X-Ray where General Burke was. The Fury intrigued him and later on he was also the man who was sent in to see if I was alive after being shot down. He came back saying I'd landed by parachute, been captured and taken away."

Mather's naval career lasted a span of thirty-seven years until he retired in 1983 as a captain. What about flying the mighty Sea Fury, I asked? "I have a very high opinion of the Fury," Mather said. "When I went back to flying I was doing practice dummy deck landings on the airfield when one of the legs came off and I had to land on one wheel which I did. I'd been shot down in one, and I landed in a paddy field in one, and I got away with both landings. It had virtually no vices. It flew well and looked good."

Appendix II

MOUNTS OF THE FLEET AIR ARM

The Hawker Sea Fury
The aircraft that flew from HMS *Ocean*, HMS *Triumph*, HMS *Glory* and others was a direct descendant of the Hawker Tempest that appeared in the later stages of the Second World War. There were two main versions of the Tempest. The first Tempests to go into service were powered by the inline liquid-cooled Napier Sabre VEE engine. The huge chin radiator under the spinner on the Napier Sabre-powered Tempests made these aircraft highly distinctive. The second version of the Tempest came later, just at the very end of the war. This was the Centaurus radial air-cooled engined version. In profile, the Tempest Mark II with its Centaurus engine looks very similar to the Sea Fury. The main visual difference is the raised canopy of the Fury, which is not on the Tempest.

The Fury was originally intended to have the Napier Sabre 24-cylinder inline VEE liquid-cooled engine like its older cousin but experiments made with this engine found it had limited development potential. Other experiments were made with Furies powered by Rolls-Royce Griffon 85 engines, using contra-rotating propellers. Again, these tests did not see the light of day and were cancelled in favour of the Centaurus XII.

The Fury prototype had a few faults. Rudder control on take-off was critical to correct a pronounced swing to the left. During landing the prototype had problems with directional stability. Both these faults were corrected before the aircraft went into production. Early production Furies had the designation F.X., and were powered by the Bristol Centaurus 18 radial engine, pumping out a massive 2,560 horsepower with a five-blade Rotol propeller fitted. These aircraft were soon replaced by the definitive version found on the carriers in the Yellow Sea – the FB.11 fighter-bomber version. This aircraft was capable of carrying a wide variety of armaments from rockets and bombs to drop tanks.

Perhaps the Fury's greatest claim is that it was probably the finest and fastest piston-engined aircraft to enter service. It has the reputation of being the first piston-engined aircraft to shoot down a jet. In the hands of a good pilot it could tangle with Migs and get away. In the words of one of the men who flew the Fury, "she was a beautiful aircraft to fly."

Specifications for the Sea Fury FB.11

Powerplant:	Centaurus 18 radial 18 cylinder, two-row, air-cooled single sleeve-valve engine
Horsepower:	2,560

Wingspan:	38 feet 5 inches
Length:	34 feet 8 inches
Height:	15 feet 11 inches
Empty weight:	9,240 pounds
All-up max weight:	14,650 pounds
Maximum speed:	405 mph at 18,000 feet
Range:	700 miles at 30,000 feet
Armament:	4 x 20mm cannon, 12 x 60 pound rocket projectiles, or 2 x 1,000 pound bombs

The Fairey Firefly

The Firefly was a much older design than the Sea Fury, dating back to 1939, when the Royal Navy issued a specification for a multi-purpose fighter.

Rolls-Royce was developing the Griffon engine at the outbreak of the Second World War primarily for the Royal Navy. First marks of the aircraft had a similar chin type radiator as the Tempests and were powered by the Griffon 2b 1,750 horsepower inline liquid-cooled engine. Right from the start the Firefly had excellent low-speed handling characteristics, perfect for operating from aircraft carriers. It had Fairey Youngman flaps, which extended from the ailerons to the fuselage centre-line giving the aircraft its good low-speed handling. These flaps could be fully extended or retracted for take-off or landing.

Later versions of the aircraft had major changes. The radiators were moved from under the engine to forward extensions in the centre-section. That meant the chin radiator housing disappeared, giving the Firefly a more graceful look. The introduction of the Mark 4 had the Griffon 74 2,250 horsepower engine. This new Griffon had a two-stage, two-speed supercharger that drove a four-blade propeller. To improve the Firefly's rate of roll the wings on the Mark 4 were square-clipped.

The Mark 5 Firefly that saw action in Korea was a variation of the Mark 4 with wing folding for carrier operations.

Specifications for the Fairey Firefly 5

Powerplant:	Rolls-Royce Griffon 74 inline V liquid-cooled supercharged engine
Horsepower:	2,250
Wingspan:	41 feet 2 inches
Length:	37 feet 11 inches
Height:	14 feet 4 inches
Empty weight:	9,674 pounds
All-up maximum weight:	16,000 pounds
Maximum speed:	340 mph at 14,000 feet
Cruising Speed:	194 mph
Range:	660 mph
Armament:	4 x 20mm cannon, 16 x 60 pound rocket projectiles, or 2 x 1,000 pound bombs

MAP OF THE AREA

CHRONOLOGY

1950

25 June	The war begins when the North Korean People's Army (NKPA) pours across the 38th Parallel in an all-out offensive on the Republic of Korea (ROK). The North Koreans claim on the radio that they were launching the attack because the South Korean Army tried to invade the north.
26 June	An emergency session of the United Nations Security Council calls the attack a breach of peace and demands an immediate cessation of hostilities and the withdrawal of North Korean forces to the 38th Parallel.
27 June	Another resolution passed by the Security Council asks members of the UN to provide assistance to the ROK to repel the attack and restore peace and security to the region. At this meeting Warren Austin, the US representative, informs the Council that his Government has decided, in accordance with the resolution of 26 June, to order air and sea forces to provide cover and support to the South Korean Government troops. US president Harry S. Truman orders the US Air Force and US Navy to help South Korea.
28 June	Seoul, the capital of South Korea, falls to the invaders.
29 June	The British Government places the ships of the Royal Navy in Japanese waters at the disposal of the US authorities.
30 June	President Truman authorizes General MacArthur to use the four infantry divisions of the US Eighth Army, based in Japan, for action in Korea. Australia commits 77 Squadron RAAF to combat duties. American ground troops are sent to Korea and the Air Force is authorized to bomb targets in North Korea.
1 July	Task Force Smith, the first American ground troops, arrive in Korea under the command of General William F. Dean.
2 July	77 Squadron RAAF flies its first combat mission over Korea. The North Korean Navy is destroyed off Chumunjin.
3 July	The North Koreans capture the vital port of Inchon in the south.
5 July	Task Force Smith battles with North Korean troops at Osan, which ends with a US withdrawal.
7 July	General Douglas MacArthur is appointed Supreme Commander of United Nations Command in Korea by virtue of a Security Council recommendation that says all military assistance provided by member nations to the UN should be made available to a unified command under US authority.
8-12 July	The North Korean advance is stalled by the US 21st Infantry at Chochiwon.
13 July	All ground operations in Korea are placed under the command of Lieutenant General Walton H. Walker.
14 July	As the North Koreans continue to advance, the UN appeals for more

	ground forces to support the ROK and other UN forces in Korea.
15 July	US 19th and 34th Infantry Regiments, 24th Infantry Division, fight delaying actions against the North Koreans at the Kum River line but communist forces push across the river.
18 July	From 10 July to 18 July more US troops move into Korea. The US 25th Infantry and 1st Cavalry Divisions arrive from Japan. From Okinawa the 29th Regimental Combat Team set sail for Korea and the 2nd Infantry Division embarks from Seattle.
20 July	UN Command forces abandon Taejon and the North Koreans take prisoner Major General William Dean.
25 July	29th Regiment engages the enemy near Chinju.
29 July	Chiang Kai Shek offers to send 33,000 soldiers to Korea but the UN declines.
30 July	UN forces begin the defence of the Pusan Perimeter.
31 July	5th Regimental Combat Team arrives in Korea from Hawaii.
4 August	The UN Command sets up the Naktong River Perimeter to defend Pusan while the Soviet Union ends its boycott of the UN Security Council. UN delegate from the Soviet Union, Jacob Malik, declares the Korean War is a civil war and demands all foreign troops to leave Korea. The North Koreans establish a bridgehead across the Naktong River, threatening the collapse of Pusan.
6 August	US headquarters at Taegu are threatened by the North Korean offensive. In Tokyo, General MacArthur begins planning the Inchon landings with Generals Norstad, Almond and Ridgway to push the North Koreans out of the south.
10 August	American United Nations delegate, Warren Austin, says that the goal of the UN was the unification of Korea. Troops from the North Korean People's Army attack the Pusan Perimeter in the First Battle of the Naktong Bulge to push the UN Forces into the sea but are stopped by US 24th, 2nd and 25th Infantry Divisions as well as elements of the Marines.
15 August	The Battle of the Bowling Alley west of Taegu begins when elements of the US 23rd and 27th Infantry Regiments alongside ROK 1st Division troops successfully defend their part of the Naktong (Pusan) Perimeter.
17 August	The first victory of the UN forces is gained by the US Marines when they attack No Name Ridge.
28 August	The British 27th Brigade arrives at Pusan.
31 August	The Battle of the Pusan Perimeter reaches its climax over the next six days as the North Koreans launch their offensive against Pusan on 1 September 1950, which lasts until 6 September. During this period the second Battle of the Naktong River takes place.
12 September	US 1st and 9th Marine Corps become operational in Korea.
15 September	Operation Chromite begins with UN forces landing at Inchon. US Marines landing at Inchon outflank the North Korean forces.
16 September	At Pusan UN forces led by the US Eighth Army begin an offensive northwards against the North Koreans.
18 September	UN forces capture Kimpo airfield near Seoul.
20 September	American marines drive across the Han River.
22 September	Troops of the US Eighth Army break out of the Pusan Perimeter.
25 September	North Korean troops flee from the UN offensive, heading north for

	the 38th Parallel with UN forces in hot pursuit.
26 September	American troops of the 31st Infantry Regiment, the 7th Infantry Division, moving-east from Inchon, link up with elements of the Eighth Army driving north-east, south of Suwon.
27 September	General MacArthur wins authorization from US Joint Chiefs of Staff to conduct operations north of the 38th Parallel.
28 September	ROK and American forces retake Seoul, the capital of South Korea.
30 September	The Chinese foreign minister warns that the Chinese people will not supinely tolerate seeing their neighbours savagely invaded by imperialist troops.
1 October	South Korean troops of 1 Corps cross the 38th Parallel and race up the east coast behind retreating North Koreans. MacArthur calls upon North Korea to surrender.
2 October	Chou En-lai informs the Indian ambassador to Beijing that China will intervene in the Korean War if US forces cross the 38th Parallel.
6-7 October	In Central Korea two more ROK divisions cross the 38th Parallel and advance northwards.
7 October	UN General Assembly gives official permission for UN forces to cross the 38th Parallel and to establish the United Nations Commission for the Unification and Rehabilitation of Korea (UNCURK).
8 October	Chinese "volunteers" are ordered to cross into North Korea by Chinese premier Mao Tse Tung.
9 October	Attacking north towards Pyongyang, the US Eighth Army crosses the 38th Parallel through Kaesong towards Sariwon and Pyongyang.
10 October	The major North Korean port of Wonsan is captured by the 3rd ROK Division.
12 October	General Douglas MacArthur is advised by the Interim Committee of UNCURK to assume provisional responsibility for administering the territory occupied by the UN forces in North Korea.
14 October	Chinese troops, totalling over 300,000 men, begin crossing the Yalu River.
14-17 October	Preparations for amphibious landings by US Marine 10th Corps along the east coast above the 38th Parallel are made by the US 7th Infantry Division loading ships at Pusan.
19 October	The capital of North Korea, Pyongyang, is captured by 1st ROK Division and US 1st Cavalry Division.
25 October	North of Unsan offensive operations begin with the Communist Chinese Forces (CCF) fighting ROK forces. The first Chinese soldier is captured.
26 October	At Wonsan the 1st Marine Division, 10th Corps lands while ROK forces reach the Yalu River border between Korea and Manchuria at Chosan.
27-31 October	Chinese first phase offensive is launched.
29 October	Australian battalion reaches Chongju, the most northerly point of its advance. US 7th Division lands at Iwon.
1 November	US troops begin their first battle with the Chinese at Unsan.
3 November	The communists' offensive stiffens as they mount attacks against the US Eighth Army.
5 November	General MacArthur orders a heavy air offensive on the bridges at

Sinuiju over the Yalu River to stop supplies streaming into North Korea from the Chinese.

8 November	The first ever air to air jet victory occurs when Lieutenant Russell J. Brown of the US 16th Fighter Interceptor Squadron shoots down a communist Mig 15 jet fighter while flying a F80C Shooting Star.
11 November	US Marines of the 10th Corps continue to advance north.
16 November	US President Harry S. Truman declares the United States has no intention of invading China.
24 November	The US Eighth Army launches its drive towards the Yalu River from its position from Chongchon River.
25 November	The second phase of the Chinese offensive is launched. The US Eighth Army centre and right flanks are attacked by Chinese forces while ROK troops of 2nd Corps are smashed by Chinese attack in the central sector near Tokchon.
26 November	Over 200,000 Chinese attack the US Eighth Army north of the Chongchon River and inflict heavy casualties.
27 November	The Marines of 1st Marine Division come to the aid of the Eighth Army but are encircled and attacked by Chinese forces at the Chosin Reservoir.
29 November	General withdrawal against the Chinese offensive begins with the Eighth Army pulling out from Chongchon River line to hold a defensive line near Pyongyang.
29 November-1 December	The US 2nd Infantry Division takes heavy casualties as it guards the Eighth Army withdrawal.
30 November	US Marines of the 10th Corps fall back to port of Hungnam. President Truman publicly refers to the possible use of the atomic bomb in Korea.
5 December	Unable to hold Pyongyang the Eighth Army falls back from the city.
7 December	It is reported by UNCURK that UN forces were engaged with between 231,000 and 400,000 Chinese troops.
11 December	US troops from the 1st Marine Division and the 7th Division form a defensive perimeter at Hungnam.
11-24 December	US Marines begin loading troops and material onto ships for evacuation to Pusan. General Almond sails on Christmas Eve.
12 December	A draft resolution is submitted to the UN by thirteen Arab and Asian nations proposing a committee be set up to look at the basis for a ceasefire in Korea.
15 December	UN forces withdraw against Chinese attacks south of the 38th Parallel.
23 December	North of Seoul, Eighth Army field commander General Walker is killed in a road accident. General Matthew B. Ridgway is appointed as his successor.
24 December	The evacuation of the 10th US Marine Corps is completed at Hungnam beachhead and North Korea returns to communist control.
26 December	The new commander of the Eighth Army, Lieutenant General Ridgway, arrives in Korea.

1951

1 January	The Chinese reject the efforts of the UN Ceasefire Group and start a new winter offensive.
3-4 January	UN forces evacuate Seoul and withdraw to a defensive line forty miles back to regroup.
5 January	UN forces withdraw from the port of Inchon.
7-15 January	The Chinese offensive begins to subside and the situation stabilizes while intelligence reports show that the communists have pulled many units back to refit. The Chinese attempt to enter Wonju but are stopped just south by the US 2nd Division.
11 January	Five principles are proposed by the Ceasefire Group for an armistice in Korea.
13 January	The Ceasefire Group's proposals are approved by the UN in a dramatic vote of 50-7 with only one abstention.
15 January	General J. Lawton Collins US Army Chief of Staff visits Korea where he declares, "We are going to stay and fight."
17 January	The Five Principles are rejected by the Chinese Government who want a seven-nation conference on Far Eastern issues. The Eighth army moves into Suwon.
25 January	Operation Thunderbolt, a UN counter-offensive, is launched, which sees the 1st and 9th US Marine Corps pushing towards the Han River.
1 February	In New York, the UN labels China as an aggressor nation and the resolution is accepted by the General Assembly.
10 February	Inchon and Kimpo airfield are taken for the UN by the US Eighth Army.
13 February	The US 10th Marine Corps is attacked by Chinese forces and the advancing ROK units fall back to Wonju.
15 February	At the Battle of Chipyong-ni the communists are defeated.
18 February	UN Command receives intelligence reports confirming the communist forces are withdrawing along the entire central front.
21 February	Operation Killer is launched by the Eighth Army.
28 February	Resistance from communist forces collapses south of the Han River.
7 March	UN forces launch the Ripper Offensive, an advance across the Han River by US Marines.
15 March	Still moving, the UN forces recapture Seoul.
22 March	The UN forces reach the 38th Parallel.
3 April	The 38th Parallel is crossed by Eighth Army divisions.
5 April	The UN launches Operation Rugged, a general advance to an offensive position, the Kansas Line, north of the 38th Parallel. MacArthur's letter criticizing President Truman's administration is made public.
11 April	President Truman relieves General MacArthur of his position as Supreme Commander and hands over the post to General Ridgway.
15 April	The command of the US Eighth Army is assumed by General James Van Fleet as UN forces reach the Kansas Line.
19 April	The US Marines reach the Utah Line as they continue their advance. In Washington, MacArthur denounces before Congress Truman's policy of containing the war to Korea rather than widening it to China.
22-28 April	The Chinese launch the first stage of a new spring offensive with the

strongest attacks in the west towards Seoul. During this time the Battle of the Imjin River begins and elements of the US Eighth Army get pushed back up to twenty miles.

1 May	The Chinese offensive pushes the UN forces back but they stand firm at a new defensive line north of Seoul and the Han River.
8 May	The UN forces are charged with using germ warfare by the North Koreans.
16-23 May	The Chinese begin the second stage of their spring offensive focusing on the eastern and central regions of Korea while General Van Fleet begins a counter-attack.
17 May	The communist advance is stopped by the US 2nd Division.
18 May	A UN resolution is passed that calls for an embargo on strategic goods to China and the North Koreans. The vote is won by 47-0 with eight abstentions.
23 May	The Eighth Army counter-attacks.
28 May	Hwachon and Inje are recaptured by UN forces.
30 May	The Kansas Line just north of the 38th Parallel is regained by the US Eighth Army.
1 June	UN forces launch Operation Piledriver as General Van Fleet consolidates the Kansas Line and sends elements of the US Marines further north some thirty kilometres to the Wyoming Line.
13 June	Pushing the communists north UN forces retake Chorwon and Kumhwa.
25 June	A desire for a ceasefire is voiced by Chinese Radio.
29 June	The communists are offered talks on a ceasefire by General Ridgway.
1 July	Kim Il Sung, the North Korean leader and Peng Teh-hui, commander of the Chinese forces, agree to discuss a ceasefire.
3 July	At the UN Security Council the US delegation denies any use of germ warfare and introduces a resolution refuting the North Korean claim.
10 July	The UN delegation, led by Vice-Admiral Charles Turner Joy of the US Navy, begins talks with the North Korean delegation, led by Lieutenant General Nam Il at Kaesong.
28 July	The 1st Commonwealth Division is formed.
17 August	The communists claim the UN violated the neutral zone and demand an apology, which is refused.
23 August	The North Korean delegation, led by Nam Il, claims the UN tried to bomb them from the air and walk out on the truce talks.
31 August	In the eastern sector the 1st US Marine Division opens an assault against Communist forces.
5 September	The North Koreans are outflanked at Bloody Ridge by UN forces led by US 2nd Infantry Division's 9th Infantry and abandon their positions.
18 September	US Marines advance on the Soyang River.
3-19 October	UN forces, including five divisions, advance four miles in support of the Seoul-Chorwon railway.
5 October	Lieutenant General Bridgeford becomes the new Commander-in-Chief of British Commonwealth Overseas Forces replacing Lieutenant General Sir Horace Robertson.
12 October	US Marines advance north of the Imjin River.
13 October	After heavy fighting the US 2nd Infantry Division, with the help of

	the 72nd Tank Battalion, seizes Heartbreak Ridge.
25 October	The peace talks start up again but in a different place, this time at Panmunjom.
12 November	General Ridgway, fearing a collapse of the talks, orders all offensive operations to cease. At the same time the first demarcation line is proposed if all other outstanding issues can be resolved within thirty days.
17 December	The thirty-day deadline expires making the demarcation line invalid. The lists of prisoners of war are exchanged by both sides.

1952

1 January	The UN forces begin a month long artillery and air bombardment of communist positions.
2 January	The UN Command proposes a non-forcible repatriation scheme for prisoners of war.
3 January	China rejects the UN's non-forcible repatriation scheme.
11-15 January	Representatives from Britain, France and the US meet in Washington to discuss South-East Asian security.
19 April	The Chinese delegation at Panmunjom is told by UN delegates that only 70,000 prisoners of war out of 132,000 want to be repatriated to the communists.
28 April	The name of the British Commonwealth Overseas Forces is changed to British Commonwealth Forces Korea. (BCFK).
7 May	North Korean and Chinese prisoners of war riot on Koje Island as screening of prisoners begins. The peace talks at Panmunjom are deadlocked over the issue of prisoner repatriation.
12 May	General Ridgway leaves Korea for Europe. Ridgway is succeeded by General Mark W. Clark as overall commander of UN forces in the Far East.
22 May	Vice-Admiral Joy, leader of the UN delegation, is replaced by Major General William Harrison.
25 May	In South Korea President Rhee arrests a number of people of the Korean National Assembly and declares martial law in Pusan.
10 June	UN troops put down a riot of communist prisoners of war at Kojet Island and the Soviet newspaper *Pravda* calls the American troops worse than Hitler.
22 June	The US government agrees to a British Deputy Chief of Staff for General Clark's headquarters.
23-27 June	Major hydroelectric plants at Suiho, Fusen, Chosin and Kyosen are bombed by UN air forces to get more cooperation from the communists at the talks.
29 August	Pyongyang is bombed by UN air forces in the heaviest air strike of the war.
6 October	Chinese and North Korean forces launch a heavy offensive.
7 October	The US Eighth Army takes heavy bombardment from Chinese forces.
8 October	The communists reject the UN's final offer of repatriation of prisoners of war and the peace talks are suspended.
16 October	The ten-day communist offensive ends.
20 October	Claims of the use of germ warfare are refuted in the General Assembly by US delegates who cite the evidence provided by Sir MacFarlane Burnet.

4 November	Dwight D. Eisenhower is elected President of the United States.
2 December	Before taking office President-elect Eisenhower goes on a three-day fact-finding mission to Korea.
14 December	After his Korean trip Eisenhower announces he will have a new policy of firmness when dealing with the communists.

1953

20 January	Eisenhower is inaugurated President.
2 February	President Eisenhower orders the US Seventh Fleet to stop preventing Chiang Kai-Shek's forces from attacking the Communist Chinese mainland.
11 February	General Van Fleet retires and is succeeded by Lieutenant General Maxwell Taylor as the new commander of the Eighth Army.
22 February	The UN Command proposes an exchange of sick and wounded prisoners of war as a run up to a full exchange of prisoners.
5 March	Soviet Premier Josef Stalin dies.
30 March	The communists agree to the UN's proposal of exchanging the sick and wounded prisoners of war.
20 April- 3 May	The exchange of the sick and wounded takes place at Panmunjom.
26 April	The armistice negotiations resume.
7 May	The communists present an eight-point proposal on the repatriation of prisoners that includes creating a Neutral Nations Repatriation Commission.
13 May	General Clark is given the go ahead to establish four more South Korean divisions for the conflict.
20 May	A decision is taken by the National Security Council to widen the war with air attacks into China itself and to escalate the ground war in Korea should the need arise.
28 May	The UN delegation at Panmunjom make their final proposals to the communists. Elements of the US 25th Division are attacked by the communists.
8 June	Most of the proposals are accepted by the communists.
10 June	Chinese and North Korean forces launch a six-day offensive against ROK troops at Kumsong. From there until the end of the month Chinese forces continue to attack US forces.
17 June	A revised line of demarcation is settled at the negotiations.
18 June	South Korean President Rhee orders his forces to release the 25,000 prisoners of war that do not want to be repatriated back to China or North Korea.
13 July	The communists launch their final offensive to gain more ground before the fighting ends.
16 July	UN forces manage to stop the communist offensive from gaining much ground.
19 July	Both sides reach agreement on all aspects of the armistice at Panmunjom.
27 July	At 1000hrs the armistice is signed and comes into effect at 2200hrs the same day.
5 August- 6 September	Prisoners of war are exchanged.
8 August	The ROK and the US initial a Mutual Defence Treaty in Seoul.

GLOSSARY

38th Parallel: The boundary between North and South Korea.

Amphibious force: These are land-related forces such as armour and infantry landing from the sea.

Anti-submarine patrols: These were flights carried out by Fireflies and Sea Furies to detect submarines either on the surface or just below the surface. Radar at the time was rudimentary so these flights were difficult indeed. Anti-submarine patrols would normally be carried out by ships.

Armed reconnaissance: This is a flight whose primary goal is to reconnoitre specific areas to collect information on more targets for future missions. Aircraft on these missions are fully armed and were usually tasked to hit other targets with bombs, rockets or cannon fire.

Bailing out: The act of jumping out of a stricken aircraft as it spins towards earth. Usually, this meant pulling the canopy back, undoing the strap harnesses that held the pilot to the seat, and then standing on the seat and jumping out curled up in a ball to avoid hitting the tail plane of the aircraft. Now with the advent of the ejection seat the same emergency leaving of the aircraft is often referred to as ejecting.

Barrier: The British light fleet carriers had two barriers on the deck. Each one was made of wire and designed to stop aircraft from crashing into the parked aircraft on the forward deck.

Biplane: An aircraft with an upper wing and a lower wing usually held together by wing struts connecting both wings, and struts from the upper wing to the body of the fuselage. The biplane era lasted until the beginning of the Second World War when monoplanes such as the Spitfire came into service.

Blockade: This is the act of sealing off a place or region by aircraft and ships to prevent the enemy from leaving or entering, in this case to prevent the North Koreans from receiving supplies from western ports such as Chinnampo. The main reason for Royal Navy aircraft carriers to be on station on the west coast was to keep up the blockade, forcing the communists to be supplied out of Manchuria.

Bombardment spotting: Aircraft would fly high above a target and direct naval gunfire via radio to bombard the target which was usually close to the coast.

Boxcars: Boxcars is a term used for railway freight cars that look like rectangular boxes on wheels. They are designed to hold boxes. This term is well used in North America but in Britain the term railway wagons could apply to the same thing.

Break: Verbal command by a flight leader for his flight (usually of three aircraft behind him) to break formation and roll into their dives either onto other formations of enemy aircraft or ground targets.

Cannon fire: British aircraft in the Korean War were all fitted with 20mm cannon, and this term relates to the fire from these wing guns in the case of the Firefly or Sea Fury. In the case of the Meteor jet fighter the cannon were in the nose. Cannon are heavy automatic guns, which have a much longer range and use bigger shells, making them more effective than machine guns.

Canopy: The clear hood over the cockpit of an aircraft.

CAP: Combat Air Patrol. This is a defensive patrol usually flown by fully armed aircraft ahead of or near an aircraft carrier to protect it from incoming enemy aircraft or surface vessels.

Catapulting: This is a device used to launch an aircraft into the sky from an aircraft carrier. The light fleet carriers of the Royal Navy used hydraulic driven catapults that could send off one aircraft at a time.

Close Army Support: This term relates to the flights in direct support of the Army. Aircraft could strike enemy positions immediately in front of an advancing army to clear the way or behind to ease a retreat. If the Army was bogged down by enemy fire air strikes would be called in by the Army.

CO: Abbreviation for commanding officer.

Coaster: A ship carrying cargo close to the coast from port to port.

Cockpit hood: Another term for the canopy.

Delayed fuses: Fuses used on bombs designed to go off several hours or minutes after landing on or near the target.

Detail: Another word for flight. Usually comprised four aircraft.

Ditch: A forced landing by an aircraft in the sea, lake or river. This term is often used no matter where the aircraft came down – dry land or on water.

Drop tanks: Fuel tanks slung to the underside of an aircraft. Usually carried under the wings and can be jettisoned when they are empty to cut down the drag and release excess weight.

Dummy dives: Practice dives by pilots on friendly targets without ammunition for training purposes.

Elevator control: A British term relating to the controls for lifting or dropping the aircraft by the use of flaps on the wings.

Flak: Anti-aircraft fire directed towards aircraft, usually from the ground. Can be anything from small arms fire such as rifles, pistols and light machine guns to much larger calibre big guns designed specifically for the task.

Flight: A section of four aircraft.

Fighter: Fighters are usually single-seat aircraft designed for attacking other aircraft.

Fighter-bomber: In the case of the Firefly this was a two-seat aircraft designed for attacking ground and sea targets. One exception to this is the Douglas Skyraider. It was a single-seat aircraft but could carry a massive payload and was designed as a dive-bomber/fighter-bomber to hit ground targets.

Flaps: A hinged or sliding section of the aircraft's wing that provides lift.

Guerrillas: Small, independent groups of soldiers fighting against an enemy or a government. They are usually well organised and often supported by organisations or other countries opposed to the same government they are.

Island: Huge superstructure sticking up from the side of the flight deck of an aircraft carrier.

Incendiary: A bomb designed to specifically cause fires.

Interdiction: Air strikes deep into enemy territory against railway lines, bridges, tunnels, ports and communication centres designed to prohibit the enemy from mounting an effective defence and ultimately forcing the enemy to surrender.

Junk: A flat-bottomed sailing boat with a prominent stern (rear).

Lee of the ship's island: This is the shelter the huge superstructure of the aircraft carrier's island provides against the wind.

Line astern: One behind the other in a line.

Mêlée: A confused or disorderly fight.

Milk run: In terms of flying, this refers to a route Royal Navy pilots would fly to targets they regularly attacked.

Nacelle fuel tanks: Refers to the Firefly whose streamlined wing fuel tanks were permanent parts of the wings and could not be released.

Napalm: This is a jelly-like form of petrol that is highly flammable.

NKAF: North Korean Air Force.

Patrol: For the Royal Navy aircraft carriers the patrols were ten days on station off the coast of Korea when the fighting would take place, then between patrols they would have ten days off back in Japan for repairs, training and rest.

Peel off: Leaving a formation of aircraft by veering away. Often by bringing up one wing then dropping into a dive with other aircraft following the leader down.

Pitching: Swaying or oscillation of the aircraft when the weight distribution is uneven or when the controls are no longer balanced. The swaying motion is perpendicular to the horizontal axis of the aircraft.

R/T: Radio in an aircraft.

Railway wagons: The same as boxcars but could also be used to describe open railway wagons such as coal cars or tank cars.

RATOG: Rocket Assisted Take-Off Gear. This was a method for aircraft to take off from the aircraft carrier when the catapult was down or not in use. It meant strapping rockets to either side of the aircraft under the wings and fuselage and firing them simultaneously to give the aircraft enough lift to get into the air.

Replenishment at sea: In every patrol during the Korean War Royal Navy aircraft carriers would move further out to sea and rendezvous with a supply vessel where they would take on stores such as ammunition, fuel, aircraft parts, food etc. This would normally take a day and a half.

Rocketing: A term describing the method of hitting targets with underwing rockets carried by Fireflies.

Round: The amount of ammunition needed to fire a single shot. Each shell or bullet carried in the guns of an aircraft is known as a round.

Scramble: In terms of aircraft this term refers to emergency or immediate take-off of a section of aircraft for action.

Shrapnel: Metal fragments thrown out by the explosion of a bomb or a shell. Low flying aircraft would often get hit with shrapnel from explosions of their own bombs or rockets on the targets. Also, the rocket motors of the projectiles used by the Royal Navy Fleet Air Arm pilots in Korea would often explode just after release, peppering the wing with bits of metal.

Span or spar: A section of a bridge that supports it.

Strafing: Usually this refers to an attack by low flying aircraft with machine guns or bombs. In the case of Sea Furies and Fireflies their strafing runs meant attacking targets at low level with cannon fire.

Sortie: This is an operational flight by a single aircraft.

Tail fin: The housing at the end of an aircraft where the rudder is.

Tail plane: These are the horizontal aerofoils (or little wings) at the tail of an aircraft.

The stick: Control column inside the cockpit of an aircraft. This controls the direction, lift, height etc of the aircraft.

Tour: For the Royal Navy aircraft carriers during the Korean War the term tour stood for the duration of all the patrols (usually eight) that each aircraft carrier did. This would often last six months or so.

Tracers: Shells or rounds fired that trace a path by using smoke or flame to help in accurately aiming for the target. Ammunition loaded into the aircraft would have a certain amount of tracer shells in them so pilots could accurately direct their fire onto the targets.

Vectored: Given a specific course or coordinates by ground or air controllers of a direct route to the target.

Wingman: Aircraft flew in pairs within a flight. The second aircraft would be positioned behind and to the side of the leading aircraft in a loose formation, enabling him to cover his leader and also see any approaching enemy aircraft.

BIBLIOGRAPHY

Air War Korea, 1950-1953, Robert Jackson, published in the UK in 1998 by Airlife Publishing Ltd.

Air War over Korea, Jerry Scutts, published in 1982 by Arms and Armour Press.

Meteor Aircraft in Action, Aircraft Number 152, Glen Ashley, illustrated by Robert Harrison, colour by Don Greer and Tom Tullis, published in 1995 by Squadron Signals Publications.

The British Aircraft Carrier, Paul Beaver, published in 1982 by Patrick Stephens Ltd.

The Korean War, Max Hastings, published in 1987 by Michael Joseph Ltd.

With the Carriers in Korea, The Fleet Air Arm Story 1950-1953, John R.P. Lansdown, published in 1992 by Square One Publications.

With the Yanks in Korea, Volume One, Brian Cull and Dennis Newton, published in 2000 by Grub Street.

Squadron histories from the Fleet Air Arm Museum.

INDEX

NB: The names of the pilots who have chapters devoted to them, and the ships on which they served, are not listed in the index.